Study Guide

Volume 1, Chapters 1-12

for use with

Intermediate Accounting

Fifth Edition

J. David Spiceland
University of Memphis

James F. Sepe
Santa Clara University

Mark W. Nelson
Cornell University

Lawrence A. Tomassini
The Ohio State University

 **McGraw-Hill Irwin**

Boston   Burr Ridge, IL   Dubuque, IA   New York   San Francisco   St. Louis
Bangkok   Bogotá   Caracas   Kuala Lumpur   Lisbon   London   Madrid   Mexico City
Milan   Montreal   New Delhi   Santiago   Seoul   Singapore   Sydney   Taipei   Toronto

The *McGraw-Hill* Companies

Study Guide, Volume 1, Chapters 1-12, for use with
INTERMEDIATE ACCOUNTING
J. David Spiceland, James F. Sepe, Mark W. Nelson, and Lawrence A. Tomassini

Published by McGraw-Hill/Irwin, an imprint of The McGraw-Hill Companies, Inc., 1221 Avenue of the
Americas, New York, NY 10020. Copyright © 2009, 2007, 2004, 2001, 1998 by The McGraw-Hill Companies, Inc. All rights
reserved.

2 3 4 5 6 7 8 9 0 QPD/QPD 0 9 8

ISBN: 978-0-07-332459-3
MHID: 0-07-332459-0

www.mhhe.com

Contents

Environment and Theoretical Structure
of Financial Accounting

LEARNING OBJECTIVES

After studying this chapter, you should be able to:

1. Describe the function and primary focus of financial accounting.
2. Explain the difference between cash and accrual accounting.
3. Define generally accepted accounting principles (GAAP) and discuss the historical development of accounting standards.
4. Explain why the establishment of accounting standards is characterized as a political process.
5. Explain the purpose of the FASB's conceptual framework.
6. Identify the objectives of financial reporting, the qualitative characteristics of accounting information, and the elements of financial statements.
7. Describe the four basic assumptions underlying GAAP.
8. Describe the four broad accounting principles that guide accounting practice.

CHAPTER HIGHLIGHTS

PART A: FINANCIAL ACCOUNTING ENVIRONMENT

Financial accounting is concerned with providing relevant and reliable financial information to various external decision makers that do not have direct access to a company's internal records. The primary focus of financial accounting is on the information needs of investors and creditors. The process of providing information to a company's internal decision makers, that is, its managers, is called **managerial accounting**. In this course, you study financial accounting. The primary means of conveying financial information to investors, creditors, and other external users is through financial statements and related disclosure notes. The financial statements most frequently provided are:

(1) The balance sheet or statement of financial position
(2) The income statement or statement of operations
(3) The statement of cash flows
(4) The statement of shareholders' equity

The Investment-Credit Decision

In the United States, we have a highly developed free-enterprise economy with the majority of productive resources privately owned rather than government owned. It's important in this type of system that a mechanism exists to allocate the scarce resources of our society, both natural resources and labor, in an efficient manner. The mechanisms that foster this efficient allocation of resources are the **capital markets**. We can think of the capital markets simply as a composite of all investors and creditors. Investors and creditors are both interested in earning a fair return on the resources they provide to a company. A company will be able to provide a fair return only if it can generate a profit from selling its products or services. That is, it must be able to use the resources provided by investors and creditors to generate cash receipts from selling a product or service that exceeds the cash disbursements necessary to provide that product or service.

Cash Versus Accrual Accounting

Even though predicting future cash flows is the primary objective, the model best able to achieve that objective is the **accrual accounting** model. A competing model is **cash basis accounting**. Each model produces a periodic measure of performance that could be used by investors and creditors for predicting future cash flows. With cash basis accounting, the measure of performance, called **net operating cash flow**, is the difference between cash receipts and cash disbursements from providing goods and services. The accrual accounting model provides a measure of periodic performance called **net income**, the difference between **revenues** and **expenses**. Net income is considered a better indicator of future operating cash flows than is current net operating cash flow.

ILLUSTRATION

Cash Versus Accrual Accounting

Listed below are several transactions that took place during the first year of operations for the consulting firm of Robertson and Son.

Amounts billed to customers for services rendered	$385,000
Cash collected from customers	332,000
Cash disbursements:	
Salaries paid to employees for services rendered during the year	220,000
Utilities	40,000
Purchase of insurance	30,000
Advertising	10,000

In addition, you learn that the company incurred advertising costs of $25,000 in year one, that there were no liabilities at the end of year one other than the amount owed for advertising, no anticipated bad debts on receivables, and that the insurance policy purchased covers a three-year period.

Net operating cash flow for year one is determined as follows:

Cash receipts from customers		$332,000
Cash disbursements:		
Salaries	$220,000	
Utilities	40,000	
Purchase of insurance	30,000	
Advertising	10,000	300,000
Net operating cash flow		$ 32,000

Net income is determined as follows:

Revenues		$385,000
Expenses:		
Salaries	$220,000	
Utilities	40,000	
Insurance (one-third)	10,000	
Advertising (amount incurred)	25,000	295,000
Net income		$ 90,000

The Development of Financial Accounting and Reporting Standards

Investors and creditors use financial information to make their resource allocation decisions. It's critical that they be able to *compare* financial information among companies. To facilitate these comparisons, financial accounting employs a body of standards known as **Generally Accepted Accounting Principles**, often abbreviated as **GAAP** (and pronounced "gap"). GAAP are a dynamic set of both broad and specific guidelines that companies should follow when measuring and reporting financial information.

The U.S. Congress created the **Securities and Exchange Commission (SEC)** with the 1934 Securities Exchange Act. The SEC has both the power and responsibility for setting accounting and reporting standards (principles) for companies whose securities are publicly traded, but has delegated the responsibility, not the power, for setting accounting standards to the private sector. The SEC has influenced FASB decisions on a number of occasions. The present private sector standard-setting body is the **Financial Accounting Standards Board (FASB)**. The Board has issued over 150 specific standards, called **Statements of Financial Accounting Standards (SFASs)**, as well as numerous interpretations, technical bulletins, and seven concept statements. These pronouncements, along with those of the FASB's predecessors, various SEC pronouncements, and publications of the American Institute of Certified Public Accountants, constitute generally accepted accounting principles in the United States.

The Establishment of Accounting Standards—A Political Process

Accounting standards affect our society in many ways. The FASB must consider potential economic consequences of a change in an accounting standard or the introduction of a new standard. For this reason, the FASB undertakes a series of information gathering steps before issuing a substantive accounting standard. These steps include open hearings, deliberations, and requests for written comments. These steps are the FASB's attempt to acquire consensus as to the preferred method of accounting, as well as to anticipate adverse economic consequences. The board's process is similar to that of an elected political representative, a U.S. congresswoman for example, trying to determine consensus among her constituency before voting on a bill on the floor of the House of Representatives. For this reason, accounting standard setting is a political process.

Global Accounting Standards

Many U.S. and foreign companies operate and raise capital in more than one country. Accounting standards can differ significantly from country to country, making it difficult for multinational companies to comply with more than one set of standards. In response to this problem, the **International Accounting Standards Committee (IASC)** was formed in 1973 to develop global accounting standards. The IASC reorganized itself and created a new standard-setting body called the **International Accounting Standards Board (IASB)**. The IASC now acts as an umbrella organization similar to the Financial Accounting Foundation (FAF) in the United States. The IASB's objectives are (1) to develop a single set of high quality, understandable and enforceable global accounting standards that require transparent and comparable information in general purpose financial statements, and (2) to cooperate with national accounting standard-setters to achieve convergence in accounting standards around the world.

The Role of the Auditor

Auditors provide credibility to financial statements and disclosure notes by verifying that they are presented fairly in conformity with generally accepted accounting principles. The auditor's opinion as to the fairness of the financial statements is expressed in the audit report. The audit report also contains the auditors' opinion on the effectiveness of the company's internal control over financial reporting.

Financial Reporting Reform

Public outrage over accounting scandals at high-profile companies like Enron and WorldCom prompted Congress to pass the *Public Company Accounting Reform Act of 2002*, commonly referred to as the Sarbanes-Oxley Act for the two congressmen who sponsored the bill. The law provides for the regulation of auditors and the types of services they furnish to clients, increases accountability of corporate executives, addresses conflicts of interest for securities analysts, and provides for stiff criminal penalties for violators.

Ethics in Accounting

Ethics deals with the ability to distinguish right from wrong. Accountants are faced with ethical dilemmas, just like others operating in the business world. Many accountants belong to professional organizations that have articulated expected standards of behavior in codes of ethics. These codes provide guidance and rules to organization members in the performance of their professional responsibilities.

PART B: THE CONCEPTUAL FRAMEWORK

The increasing complexity of business transactions adds to the already difficult task of the FASB of balancing the information needs of external decision-makers and economic consequences. To make the task easier, the FASB has formulated a **conceptual framework** to provide an underlying theoretical and conceptual structure for accounting standards. The framework, comprised of seven **Statements of Financial Accounting Concepts (SFACs)**, is not intended to prescribe GAAP, but to provide structure and direction to financial accounting and reporting. SFAC 4 deals with the objectives of financial reporting for nonprofit organizations and SFAC 3 was superseded by SFAC 6. The remaining five statements are summarized as follows:

SFAC 1 - Objectives of Financial Reporting by Business Enterprises
SFAC 2 - Qualitative Characteristics of Accounting Information
SFAC 5 - Recognition and Measurement in Financial Statements of Business Enterprises
SFAC 6 - Elements of Financial Statements
SFAC 7 - Using Cash Flow Information and Present Value in Accounting Measurements

Objectives of Financial Reporting

The purpose of financial reporting is to provide useful information for decision making. The following three specific reporting objectives of SFAC 1 affirm that investors and creditors are the primary external decision makers and that they are interested in predicting cash flows:

1. Financial reporting should provide information that is useful to present and potential investors and creditors and other users in making rational investment, credit, and similar decisions.

2. Financial reporting should provide information to help present and potential investors and creditors and other users to assess the amounts, timing, and uncertainty of prospective cash receipts.

3. Financial reporting should provide information about the economic resources of an enterprise; the claims to those resources (obligations); and the effects of transactions, events, and circumstances that cause changes in resources and claims to those resources.

Qualitative Characteristics of Accounting Information

To satisfy the stated objectives, information should possess certain characteristics. The key characteristic is **decision usefulness**, the ability to have an impact on a decision. The *primary* decision-specific qualities that make accounting information useful are **relevance** and **reliability**.

Relevance - The information should be relevant to the decision. The ingredients of relevance are:
- **Predictive value** and/or **feedback value** - Information helps predict future events and confirms prior expectations.
- **Timeliness** - The information must be available before the decision is made.

Reliability - The information can be relied upon. The ingredients of reliability are:
- **Verifiability** - Implies a consensus among different measurers.
- **Representational faithfulness** - Exists when there is agreement between a measure and a real-world phenomenon that the measure is supposed to represent.
- **Neutrality** - Assumes the information being relied on does not favor any particular group of companies nor influence behavior in any specific way.

Secondary qualitative characteristics are **comparability**, the ability to help users see similarities and differences among events and conditions, and **consistency**, the consistent application of accounting principles from period to period. The ability of investors to compare financial information across companies is critical to their resource allocation decisions. Consistency enhances the ability of investors and creditors to *compare* financial information across time.

There are some practical boundaries (constraints) to achieving the desired qualitative characteristics. Information is cost effective only if the perceived benefit of increased *decision usefulness* exceeds the anticipated costs of providing that information. This is referred to as the **cost effectiveness** constraint. **Materiality** is another pervasive constraint. Information is material if it can have an effect on a decision made by users. One consequence of considering materiality is that GAAP need not be followed if an item is immaterial. **Conservatism** is a frequently cited characteristic of accounting information. It is not, however, a desired qualitative characteristic but a practical justification for some accounting choices.

Elements of Financial Statements

The 10 elements of financial statements defined in SFAC 6 describe financial position and periodic performance. They are the building blocks with which financial statements are constructed. The elements and their definitions are as follows:

Elements of Financial Statements	
Assets	Probable future economic benefits obtained or controlled by a particular entity as a result of past transactions or events.
Liabilities	Probable future sacrifices of economic benefits arising from present obligations of a particular entity to transfer assets or provide services to other entities in the future as a result of past transactions or events.
Equity(or net assets)	Called shareholders' equity or stockholders' equity for a corporation is the residual interest in the assets of an entity that remains after deducting its liabilities.
Investments by owners	Increases in equity of a particular business enterprise resulting from transfers to it from other entities of something of value to obtain or increase ownership interests in it.
Distributions to owners	Decreases in equity of a particular enterprise resulting from transfers to owners.
Comprehensive income	The change in equity of a business enterprise during a period from transactions and other events and circumstances from nonowner sources. It includes all changes in equity during a period except those resulting from investments by owners and distributions to owners.
Revenues	Inflows or other enhancements of assets of an entity or settlements of its liabilities during a period from delivering or producing goods, rendering services, or other activities that constitute the entity's ongoing major or central operations.
Expenses	Outflows or other using up of assets or incurrences of liabilities during a period from delivering or producing goods, rendering services, or other activities that constitute the entity's ongoing major or central operations.
Gains	Increases in equity from peripheral or incidental transactions of an entity.
Losses	Represent decreases in equity arising from peripheral or incidental transactions of an entity.

Comprehensive income often does not equal net income.

Recognition and Measurement Concepts

Recognition refers to the process of admitting information into the basic financial statements, while **measurement** is the process of associating numerical amounts to the financial statement elements. SFAC 5 provides general recognition criteria and essentially confirms existing practice in the area of measurement. SFAC 5 also confirms some of the more important generally accepted accounting principles used in practice. These principles are predicated on some important underlying assumptions.

SFAC No. 7 provides a framework for using future cash flows in accounting measurements. Present value measurements have long been associated with accounting valuation. SFAC No. 7 provides a framework for using future cash flows as the basis for accounting measurement and also asserts that the objective in valuing an asset or liability using present value is to approximate the fair value of that asset or liability.

Underlying Assumptions

The four basic assumptions underlying GAAP are as follows:

Economic Entity Assumption	- Economic events can be identified with a particular economic entity.
Going Concern Assumption	- It is anticipated that the business entity will continue to operate indefinitely.
Periodicity Assumption	- The life of a company can be divided into artificial time periods to provide timely information.
Monetary Unit Assumption	- In the United States, financial statement elements should be measured in terms of the United States dollar.

Accounting Principles

The following four key broad accounting principles guide accounting practice:

Historical Cost Principle	- Asset and liability measurements should be based on the amount given or received in the exchange transaction that occurred when the asset or liability was initially acquired.
Realization Principle	- Revenue should be recognized only after the earnings process is virtually complete and collection is reasonably assured.
Matching Principle	- Expenses should be recognized in the same reporting period as the related revenues.
Full-Disclosure Principle	- Any information useful to decision makers should be provided in the financial statements, subject to the cost effectiveness constraint.

In addition to information provided in the basic financial statements, supplemental information is disclosed in a number of ways, including **parenthetical comments** or **modifying comments**, **disclosure notes**, and **supplemental financial statements**.

The Asset/Liability Approach

The realization and matching principles sometimes are described as "income-statement focused," because they focus on determining when we recognize revenues and expenses in the income statement. From this perspective, sometimes referred to as the **revenue/expense approach**, principles for recognizing revenues and expenses are emphasized, with assets and liabilities recognized as necessary to make the balance sheet reconcile with the income statement.

Under the alternative **asset/liability approach** we first measure the assets and liabilities that exist at a balance-sheet date and then recognize the revenues, expenses, gains and losses needed to account for the changes in these assets and liabilities from the previous measurement date. Under this approach, principles for asset and liability measurement are emphasized, and revenues, expenses, gains and losses are recognized as necessary to make the balance sheet reconcile with the income statement. The asset/liability approach encourages standard-setters to focus on accurately measuring assets and liabilities. It perhaps is not surprising, then, that a focus on assets and liabilities has led standard-setters to lean more and more toward fair value measurement

The Move Toward Fair value

The FASB recently issued two Standards related to using fair value in financial statements. The first of these, *SFAS No. 157*, establishes a framework for measuring fair value whenever fair value is called for in applying generally accepted accounting principles. The second, *SFAS No. 159*, gives a company the option to report some or all of its *financial* assets and liabilities at fair value.

SFAS No. 157 provides a hierarchy that prioritizes the inputs companies should use when determining fair value. The priority is based on three broad preference levels. The higher the level (Level 1 is the highest), the more preferable the input. The Standard encourages companies to strive to obtain the highest level input available for each situation.

SFAS No. 159 doesn't require a company to change the way it currently values any of its assets or liabilities. It does, however, give them the *option* to value some or all of its financial assets and liabilities at fair value. If a company chooses to value a financial asset or financial liability at fair value, then future changes in fair value are reported as gains and losses in the income statement.

Environment and Theoretical Structure of Financial Accounting

Concept Review

1. The primary focus of financial accounting is on the financial information provided by _____ companies to their present and potential _____ and _____ .

2. The primary means of conveying financial information to investors, creditors, and other external users is through _____ and related _____ .

3. The _____ and _____ or _____ of that return are key variables in the investment decision.

4. Information should help investors and creditors evaluate the _____ , _____ , and _____ of the enterprise's future cash receipts and disbursements.

5. Even though predicting future cash flows is the primary objective, the model best able to achieve that objective is the _____ model.

6. The difference between revenues and expenses is _____ .

7. _____ are a dynamic set of both broad and specific guidelines that companies should follow when measuring and reporting the information in their financial statements and related notes.

8. In the 1934 act, Congress gave the _____ both the power and responsibility for setting accounting and reporting standards for companies whose securities are publicly traded.

9. The _____ is the current private sector standard-setting body.

10. The FASB's dilemma is to balance _____ considerations and _____ considerations resulting from perceived possible adverse economic consequences.

11. One objective of the International Accounting Standards Board is to bring about convergence of _____ standards and _____ standards.

12. _____ serve as independent intermediaries to help insure that management has appropriately applied GAAP in preparing the company's financial statements.

13. The conceptual framework is a _____ , a coherent system of interrelated _____ and fundamentals that can lead to consistent standards and that prescribes the nature, function, and limits of financial accounting and reporting.

14. The primary decision-specific qualities that make accounting information useful are _____ and _____ .

15. To be relevant, information must possess _____ and/or _____ and must be provided on a _____ basis.

16. Reliability is the extent to which information is _____ , _____ , and _____ .

17. _____ exists when there is agreement between a measure or description and the phenomenon it purports to represent.

18. _____ and _____ impart practical constraints on each of the qualitative characteristics of accounting information.

19. Assets are _____ obtained or controlled by a particular entity as a result of past transactions or events.

20. Liabilities are _____ of economic benefits arising from present obligations of a particular entity to transfer assets or provide services to other entities in the future as a result of past transactions or events.

21. Revenues are _____ or other enhancements of _____ or settlements of liabilities from delivering or producing goods, rendering services, or other activities that constitute the entity's ongoing major or central operations.

22. Expenses are _____ or other using up of _____ or incurrences of _____ during a period from delivering or producing goods, rendering services, or other activities that constitute the entity's ongoing major or central operations.

23. _____ is the change in equity of an entity during a period from nonowner transactions.

24. The _____ assumption presumes that economic events can be identified specifically with an economic entity.

25. Another necessary assumption is that, in the absence of information to the contrary, it is anticipated that a business entity will continue to operate _____ .

26. The realization principle states that revenue should be recognized when the earnings process is _____ and collection is _____ .

27. The _____ means that the financial reports should include any information that could affect the decisions made by external users.

Answers:

1. profit-oriented, investors, creditors **2.** financial statements, disclosure notes **3.** expected rate of return, uncertainty, risk **4.** amounts, timing, uncertainty **5.** accrual accounting **6.** net income **7.** GAAP **8.** SEC **9.** Financial Accounting Standards Board **10.** accounting, political **11.** national accounting, international accounting **12.** Auditors **13.** constitution, objectives **14.** relevance, reliability **15.** predictive value, feedback value, timely **16.** verifiable, representationally faithful, neutral **17.** Representational faithfulness **18.** Cost effectiveness, materiality **19.** probable future economic benefits **20.** probable future sacrifices **21.** inflows, assets **22.** outflows, assets, liabilities **23.** Comprehensive income **24.** economic entity **25.** indefinitely **26.** virtually complete, reasonably assured **27.** full-disclosure principle

REVIEW EXERCISES

Exercise 1

The Craigmile Advertising Agency began business in 2009. The following transactions took place during the year:

Amounts billed to customers for services rendered	$655,000
Cash collected from customers	580,000
Cash disbursements:	
Salaries paid to employees for services rendered during the year	420,000
Utilities	55,000
Payment of rent	20,000
Purchase of supplies	3,000

The rent on the company offices is $10,000 per year. The $20,000 in payments made in 2009 applies to 2009 and 2010. At the end of the year, $1,000 in supplies were still on hand and available for future use. Also, in addition to the $55,000 paid for utilities, the company owed $5,000 for utility cost incurred during 2009 that will not be paid until 2010.

Required:

Calculate the difference between **net operating cash flow** and **net income** for 2009.

Solution:

Net operating cash flow for 2009 is determined as follows:

Cash receipts from customers		$580,000
Cash disbursements:		
Salaries	$420,000	
Utilities	55,000	
Payment of rent	20,000	
Purchase of supplies	3,000	498,000
Net operating cash flow		$ 82,000

Net income for 2009 is determined as follows:

Revenues		$655,000
Expenses:		
Salaries	$420,000	
Utilities ($55,000 + 5,000)	60,000	
Rent (one-half)	10,000	
Supplies ($3,000 - 1,000)	2,000	492,000
Net income		163,000
Difference — Net income higher by		$ 81,000

Exercise 2

Match each of the following characteristics with the phrase most related to that characteristic.

Characteristic	**Related Phrase**
_____ 1. Cost effectiveness	A. Predictive/feedback value, timely.
_____ 2. Materiality	B. Two accountants independently measure an asset at the same value.
_____ 3. Relevance	C. Agreement between measure and phenomenon.
_____ 4. Representational faithfulness	D. Verifiability, neutrality, and representational faithfulness.
_____ 5. Consistency	E. Benefits of increased decision usefulness exceed costs.
_____ 6. Neutrality	F. Facilitates comparisons over time.
_____ 7. Reliability	G. Charging the cost of a stapler to expense.
_____ 8. Verifiability	H. Lack of favoritism.

Answers:

1.	E.		5.	F.
2.	G.		6.	H.
3.	A.		7.	D.
4.	C.		8.	B.

Environment and Theoretical Structure of Financial Accounting

Exercise 3

Match the following concepts with the statement or phrase most closely related to the concept.

Concept	Related Phrase
_____ 1. Going concern assumption	A. Preparation of annual and quarterly financial statements.
_____ 2. Matching principle	B. Disclosure notes.
_____ 3. Realization principle	C. Depreciating the cost of a building over its useful life.
_____ 4. Full-disclosure principle	D. Not valuing assets at their current replacement costs.
_____ 5. Comparability	E. Valuing inventory at the lower of cost or market.
_____ 6. Periodicity assumption	F. Not listing the owner's home as a company asset.
_____ 7. Economic entity assumption	G. Not valuing land at its liquidation value.
_____ 8. Historical cost principle	H. Recognition of revenue when it is earned.
_____ 9. Conservatism	I. Consistency in accounting principles.

Answers:

1.	G.	6.	A.
2.	C.	7.	F.
3.	H.	8.	D.
4.	B.	9.	E.
5.	I.		

MULTIPLE CHOICE

Enter the letter corresponding to the response that **best** completes each of the following statements or questions.

_____ 1. The process of providing financial information to *external decision makers* is referred to as:
   a.   Public accounting.
   b.   Government accounting.
   c.   Financial accounting.
   d.   Managerial accounting.

_____ 2. Financial statements generally include all of the following except:
   a.   Income statement.
   b.   Federal income tax return.
   c.   Balance sheet.
   d.   Statement of cash flows.

_____ 3. One of the primary objectives of financial reporting is to provide information:
   a.   About a firm's financing and investing activities.
   b.   About a firm's management team.
   c.   About a firm's product lines.
   d.   Useful in predicting cash flows.

_____ 4. GAAP include which of the following pronouncements:
   a.   Statements of Financial Accounting Standards.
   b.   Accounting Research Bulletins.
   c.   Accounting Principles Board Opinions.
   d.   All of the above.

_____ 5. The SEC exerts a continuing influence on the establishment of accounting standards. It does so primarily by:
   a.   Monitoring the development of GAAP within the accounting profession and using its stature to influence that development.
   b.   Exercising its statutory authority to prescribe external financial reporting requirements.
   c.   Allying with the AICPA to lobby the efforts of the FASB.
   d.   Providing auxiliary funding to the FASB.

_____ 6. The documents that set forth *fundamental concepts* on which financial accounting and reporting standards will be based are:
   a.   Statements of Financial Accounting Standards.
   b.   Statements of Financial Accounting Concepts.
   c.   Accounting Principles Board Opinions.
   d.   All of the above.

_____ 7. The two primary decision-specific qualities that make accounting information useful are:
   a. Verifiability and representational faithfulness.
   b. Predictive value and feedback value.
   c. Cost effectiveness and materiality.
   d. Relevance and reliability.

_____ 8. Relevance requires that information possess predictive and/or feedback value and be:
   a. Neutral.
   b. Comparable.
   c. Timely.
   d. Reliable.

_____ 9. The qualitative characteristic that means there is agreement between a measure and a real-world phenomenon is:
   a. Verifiability.
   b. Representational faithfulness.
   c. Neutrality.
   d. Materiality.

_____10. Which of the following is considered a practical constraint on the qualitative characteristics:
   a. Verifiability.
   b. Conservatism.
   c. Cost effectiveness.
   d. Timeliness.

_____11. Which of the following characteristics **does not** describe an asset:
   a. Probable future economic benefits.
   b. Controlled by an entity.
   c. Requires the receipt of cash.
   d. Result of a past transaction.

_____12. Which of the following characteristics **does not** describe a liability:
   a. Result of a past transaction.
   b. Probable future sacrifices.
   c. Present obligation.
   d. Must be legally enforceable.

_____13. The underlying assumption that presumes a company will continue indefinitely is:
   a. Periodicity.
   b. Going concern.
   c. Economic entity.
   d. Monetary unit.

_____14. The underlying assumption that assumes that the life of a company can be divided into artificial time periods is:
   a.   Periodicity.
   b.   Going concern.
   c.   Economic entity.
   d.   Monetary unit.

_____15. In general, revenue is recognized when the earnings process is virtually complete and:
   a.   Collection of the sales price is reasonably assured.
   b.   A purchase order is received.
   c.   Cash is collected.
   d.   Production is completed.

_____16. The primary objective of the matching principle is to:
   a.   Provide timely information to external decision-makers.
   b.   Provide full disclosure.
   c.   Recognize expenses in the same period as the related revenue.
   d.   All of the above.

Answers:

1.	c.	5.	a.	9.	b.	13.	b.
2.	b.	6.	b.	10.	c.	14.	a.
3.	d.	7.	d.	11.	c.	15.	a.
4.	d.	8.	c.	12.	d.	16.	c.

Review of the Accounting Process

LEARNING OBJECTIVES

After studying this chapter, you should be able to:
1. Analyze routine economic events — transactions — and record their effects on a company's financial position using the accounting equation format.
2. Record transactions using the general journal format.
3. Post the effects of journal entries to T-accounts and prepare an unadjusted trial balance.
4. Identify and describe the different types of adjusting journal entries.
5. Determine the required adjustments, record adjusting journal entries in general journal format, and prepare an adjusted trial balance.
6. Describe the four basic financial statements.
7. Explain the closing process.
8. Convert from cash basis net income to accrual basis net income.

CHAPTER HIGHLIGHTS

The Accounting Equation

Financial position is portrayed in the **accounting equation**.

Assets = Liabilities + Owners' Equity (Shareholders' Equity for a corporation)

This equation shows the equality between the total economic resources of an entity (its assets) — shown on the left side — and the total claims to those resources (liabilities and equity) — shown on the right side. The equation also underlies the process used to capture the effect of economic events — transactions. Each transaction has a dual effect on the equation because resources will always equal claims to those resources.

Review of the Accounting Process

ILLUSTRATION

Transaction Analysis

The Ajax Janitorial Service Corporation began business early in 2009. The following transactions took place during January:

1. Jan. 2 Owners invested $10,000 in exchange for common stock.
2. 2 An additional $10,000 was borrowed from a local bank and a note payable was signed. The note requires interest at 12% plus principal to be repaid in six months.
3. 4 Supplies costing $2,000 were purchased on account.
4. 5 Paid $1,500 in office rent for the month.
5. 5 Purchased furniture and fixtures for $6,000 cash.
6. 20 Received $2,200 from a customer for services to be performed in February.
7. 1-31 Janitorial services performed during the month on account totaled $12,000.
8. 31 Salaries of $7,000 were paid to employees.
9. 31 $1,200 was paid on account to the supplies vendor.

The accounting equation can be used to process the dual effect of these transactions as follows:

Assets	=	Liabilities	+	Shareholders' Equity
1. + $10,000 (cash)				+ $10,000 (common stock)
2. + $10,000 (cash)		+ $10,000 (note payable)		
3. + $2,000 (supplies)		+ $2,000 (accounts payable)		
4. − $1,500 (cash)				− $1,500 (rent expense)
5. + $6,000 (furniture and fixtures)				
− $6,000 (cash)				
6. + $2,200 (cash)		+ $2,200 (unearned revenue)		
7. + $12,000 (accounts receivable)				+ $12,000 (service revenue)
8. − $7,000 (cash)				− $7,000 (salaries expense)
9. − $1,200 (cash)		− $1,200 (accounts payable)		

Account Relationships

Elements of the accounting equation are represented by accounts that are contained in a general ledger. Each general ledger account can be classified as either *permanent* or *temporary*. **Permanent accounts** represent assets, liabilities, and shareholders' equity at a point in time. For a corporation, shareholders' equity is classified by source as either **paid-in capital** (common stock) or **retained earnings**. **Temporary accounts** represent changes (the retained earn`ings component of shareholders' equity for a corporation) caused by revenue, expense, gain, and loss transactions. The balances in these temporary accounts are periodically, usually once a year, closed or zeroed out and the net effect is recorded in the permanent retained earnings account. T-accounts often are used for instructional purposes instead of formal ledger accounts. A debit (left side) or a credit (right side) reflects an increase or decrease to a specific account, depending on the type of account as follows:

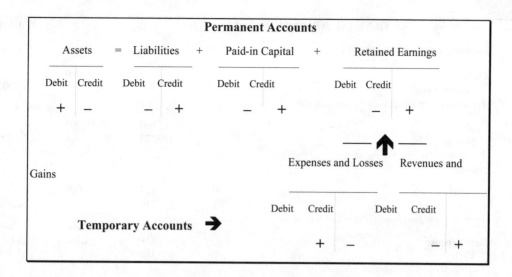

The Accounting Processing Cycle

There are 10 steps in the accounting processing cycle.

STEP 1: Obtain information about external transactions from **source documents**.

The first objective of an accounting system is to identify the economic events that directly affect the financial position of the company. Events, or transactions, can be classified as either **external events** or **internal events**. External events are those that involve an exchange between the company and another entity, and **internal events** are those that do not involve an exchange transaction. External transactions are triggered by source documents. For example, a sales invoice provides the information necessary to process a sale transaction and a bill from a supplier initiates the recording of a purchase on credit. Each of the transactions listed in the above illustration is an external transaction. Internal transactions are addressed in Step 6.

STEP 2: **Transaction analysis**.

Transaction analysis is the process of reviewing the source documents to determine the dual effect on the accounting equation and the specific elements involved. The nine transactions analyzed on the previous page are examples.

STEP 3: Record the transaction in a **journal**.

Using the accounting equation to process transactions is cumbersome even for small companies. The **double-entry system** is used instead. **Journals** provide a chronological record of all economic events affecting a firm. Each journal entry is expressed in terms of equal debits and credits to accounts affected by the transaction being recorded. Debits and credits represent increases or decreases to specific accounts, depending on the type of account, as explained earlier. For example, the transactions listed in the illustration above are recorded in general journal format as follows:

	GENERAL JOURNAL			PAGE 1
Date 2009	**Account Title and Explanation**	**Post Ref.**	**Debit**	**Credit**
Jan. 2	Cash	100	10,000	
	Common stock	300		10,000
	To record the issuance of common stock.			
2	Cash	100	10,000	
	Note payable	220		10,000
	To record the borrowing of cash and the signing of a note payable.			
4	Supplies	125	2,000	
	Accounts payable	210		2,000
	To record the purchase of supplies on account.			
5	Rent expense	510	1,500	
	Cash	100		1,500
	To record the payment of rent.			
5	Furniture and fixtures	130	6,000	
	Cash	100		6,000
	To record the purchase of furniture and fixtures.			
20	Cash	100	2,200	
	Unearned revenue	230		2,200
	To record revenue received in advance.			
1-31	Accounts receivable	110	12,000	
	Service revenue	400		12,000
	To record credit sale.			
31	Salaries expense	520	7,000	
	Cash	100		7,000
	To record the payment of salaries for the first half of the month.			
31	Accounts payable	210	1,200	
	Cash	100		1,200
	To record the payment of accounts payable.			

STEP 4: Posting from the journal to the general ledger accounts.

The debits and credits from the journal entries recorded in the general journal are *posted* to the general ledger accounts. The reference GJ1 refers to page 1 of the general journal. Since this is the first month of operations, the retained earnings account has a zero balance.

GENERAL LEDGER
BALANCE SHEET ACCOUNTS

Cash 100

Jan. 2 GJ1	10,000	1,500	Jan. 5 GJ1
Jan. 2 GJ1	10,000	6,000	Jan. 5 GJ1
Jan. 20 GJ1	2,200	7,000	Jan. 31 GJ1
		1,200	Jan. 31 GJ1
Jan. 31 Bal.	6,500		

Supplies 125

Jan. 4 GJ1	2,000	
Jan. 31 Bal.	2,000	

Accounts receivable 110

Jan. 1-31 GJ1	12,000	
Jan. 31 Bal.	12,000	

Furniture and fixtures 130

Jan. 5 GJ 1	6,000	
Jan. 31 Bal.	6,000	

Accounts payable 210

Jan. 31 GJ1	1,200	2,000	Jan. 4 GJ1
		800	Jan. 31 Bal.

Note payable 220

	10,000	Jan. 2 GJ1
	10,000	Jan. 31 Bal.

Unearned revenues 230

	2,200	Jan. 20 GJ1
	2,200	Jan. 31 Bal.

Common stock 300

	10,000	Jan. 2 GJ1
	10,000	Jan. 31 Bal.

Retained earnings 310

	0	
	0	Jan. 31 Bal.

INCOME STATEMENT ACCOUNTS

Service revenue 400

	12,000	Jan. 1-31 GJ1
	12,000	Jan. 31 Bal.

Salaries expense 520

Jan. 31 GJ1	7,000	
Jan. 31 Bal.	7,000	

Rent expense 510

Jan. 5 GJ1	1,500	
Jan. 31 Bal.	1,500	

STEP 5: Preparation of an **unadjusted trial balance**.

The general ledger accounts provide the information for preparation of the trial balance. A trial balance is simply a list of general ledger accounts and their balances at a particular date. The unadjusted trial balance at the end of January for our illustration is as follows:

AJAX JANITORIAL SERVICE CORPORATION
Unadjusted Trial Balance
January 31, 2009

Account Title	Debits	Credits
Cash..	6,500	
Accounts receivable....................................	12,000	
Supplies..	2,000	
Furniture and fixtures.................................	6,000	
Accounts payable..		800
Note payable		10,000
Unearned revenue		2,200
Common stock		10,000
Retained earnings..		- 0 -
Service revenue...		12,000
Rent expense	1,500	
Salaries expense..	7,000	
Totals	35,000	35,000

STEP 6: Record **adjusting entries** and post to the general ledger accounts.

Adjusting entries record the effect of *internal events* (transactions) on the accounting equation. They are recorded at the end of any period when financial statements must be prepared. Adjusting entries are necessary for three situations:

1. **Prepayments**, sometimes referred to as deferrals.
2. **Accruals**.
3. **Estimates**.

Prepayments

Prepayments are transactions in which the cash flow *precedes* expense or revenue recognition.

Prepaid Expenses

Prepaid expenses represent assets recorded when a cash disbursement creates benefits beyond the current period. The adjusting entry recognizes the amount of the asset that has expired. In our illustration, we have two prepaid expenses, supplies and furniture and fixtures. Supplies costing $2,000 were purchased on January 4th. Let's assume it is determined that $1,300 in supplies remains on hand at the end of January. The following adjusting journal entry is required:

January 31		
Supplies expense ($2,000 - 1,300)..	700	
Supplies..		700

Assume that the furniture and fixtures have a useful life of five years or sixty months, will be worthless at the end of the period, and that we choose to allocate the cost equally over the period of use. The amount of monthly expense, called depreciation expense, is $100 ($6,000 ÷ 60 months = $100), and the following adjusting entry is recorded:

January 31		
Depreciation expense ($6,000 ÷ 60 months).................................	100	
Accumulated depreciation		100

Unearned Revenues

Unearned revenues represent liabilities recorded when cash is received from customers in advance of providing a good or service. The adjusting entry required when unearned revenues are earned is a *debit to a liability* and a *credit to revenue*. In our illustration, on January 20th, $2,200 was received from a customer for revenue to be performed in the following month and unearned revenue, a liability, was recorded. The following adjusting entry is required *when the services are performed*:

When the services are performed:		
Unearned revenue..	2,200	
Service revenue..		2,200

Accruals

Accruals involve transactions where the cash outflow or inflow takes place in a period subsequent to expense or revenue recognition.

Accrued Liabilities

Accrued liabilities represent liabilities recorded when an expense has been incurred prior to cash payment. In our illustration, on January 2, the company borrowed $10,000 and signed a note payable requiring interest at 12% and principal to be repaid in six months. At the end of January, one-month's interest ($1/12$) is accrued as follows:

January 31		
Interest expense ($10,000 × 12% × $1/12$)...	100	
Interest payable		100

Another example of an accrued liability is income taxes. As a corporation, AJAX JANITORIAL SERVICE would accrue the amount of estimated taxes payable that are applicable to the month of January. Accounting for income taxes is introduced in subsequent chapters and we ignore the required accrual in this illustration.

Accrued Receivables

Accrued receivables involve situations when the revenue is earned in a period prior to cash receipt. There are no adjusting entries required in our illustration to reflect accrued receivables. If, for example, the company had lent a customer $3,000 on January 2, requiring the customer to repay the loan plus 8% interest in two months, an adjusting entry would record a debit to interest receivable and a credit to interest revenue for $20 ($3,000 x 8% x $1/12$).

Estimates

Accountants often make estimates in order to comply with the accrual accounting model. A number of these estimates, such as the calculation of depreciation expense, involve prepayments or accruals. One situation involving an estimate that does not involve a prepayment or accrual is the estimation of bad debt expense. The January 31, 2009, unadjusted trial balance in our illustration shows a balance in accounts receivable of $12,000. Assume company management estimates that of this amount only $11,000 will ultimately be collected. The following adjusting journal entry reflects the anticipated uncollectible amount of $1,000:

January 31		
Bad debt expense...	1,000	
Allowance for uncollectible accounts..		1,000

STEP 7: Preparation of an **adjusted trial balance**.

After posting the adjusting journal entries to the general ledger accounts, an adjusted trial balance is prepared.

AJAX JANITORIAL SERVICE CORPORATION
Adjusted Trial Balance
January 31, 2009

Account Title	Debits	Credits
Cash..	6,500	
Accounts receivable..................................	12,000	
Allowance for uncollectible accounts		1,000
Supplies...	1,300	
Furniture and fixtures...............................	6,000	
Accumulated depreciation		100
Accounts payable.....................................		800
Interest payable		100
Note payable		10,000
Unearned revenue		2,200
Common stock..		10,000
Retained earnings.....................................		- 0 -
Service revenue..		12,000
Rent expense	1,500	
Salaries expense.......................................	7,000	
Supplies expense......................................	700	
Depreciation expense................................	100	
Interest expense.......................................	100	
Bad debt expense	1,000	
Totals	36,200	36,200

STEP 8: Preparation of **financial statements**.

The adjusted trial balance provides the necessary information for preparation of the financial statements.

The Income Statement

The **income statement** is a change statement that summarizes the operating transactions that caused shareholders' equity (retained earnings) to change during the period. The January income statement for AJAX JANITORIAL SERVICE CORPORATION reveals a profit (net income) of $1,600.

AJAX JANITORIAL SERVICE CORPORATION
Income Statement
For the Month of January 2009

Service revenue		$12,000
Operating expenses:		
Rent	$1,500	
Salaries	7,000	
Supplies	700	
Depreciation	100	
Bad debt	1,000	
Total operating expenses		10,300
Operating income		1,700
Other expense:		
Interest expense		100
Net income		$ 1,600

The Balance Sheet

The **balance sheet** is a position statement that presents an organized list of assets, liabilities, and equity at a particular point in time. The January 31, 2009, balance sheet for **AJAX JANITORIAL SERVICE CORPORATION** is as follows:

```
┌─────────────────────────────────────────────────────────────────────┐
│              AJAX JANITORIAL SERVICE CORPORATION                      │
│                         Balance Sheet                                 │
│                      At January 31, 2009                              │
│                                                                       │
│                            Assets                                     │
│  Current assets:                                                      │
│    Cash                                                    $ 6,500    │
│    Accounts receivable                         $12,000                │
│    Less: Allowance for uncollectible accounts   (1,000)    11,000     │
│    Supplies                                                 1,300     │
│        Total current assets                                18,800     │
│  Property and equipment:                                              │
│    Furniture and fixtures                        6,000                │
│    Less: Accumulated depreciation                (100)     5,900      │
│        Total assets                                       $24,700     │
│                                                                       │
│            Liabilities and Shareholders' Equity                       │
│  Current liabilities:                                                 │
│    Accounts payable                                       $   800     │
│    Interest payable                                           100     │
│    Unearned rent revenue                                   2,200      │
│    Note payable                                           10,000      │
│        Total current liabilities                          13,100      │
│  Shareholders' equity:                                                │
│    Common stock                                $10,000                │
│    Retained earnings                            1,600 (1)             │
│        Total shareholders' equity                         11,600      │
│        Total liabilities and shareholders' equity         $24,700     │
│                                                                       │
│  (1) Beginning retained earnings    + net income  – dividends         │
│                 0                   +   $1,600    –    0   = $1,600    │
└─────────────────────────────────────────────────────────────────────┘
```

The Statement of Cash Flows

The purpose of the **statement of cash flows** is to summarize the transactions that caused cash to change during the period. **AJAX JANITORIAL SERVICE CORPORATION**'s statement of cash flows for January follows:

AJAX JANITORIAL SERVICE CORPORATION
Statement of Cash Flows
For the Month of January 2009

Cash flows from operating activities:
Cash inflows:

From customers	$ 2,200	
Cash outflows:		
For rent	(1,500)	
To employees	(7,000)	
For supplies	(1,200)	
Net cash flows from operating activities		$(7,500)
Cash flows from investing activities:		
Purchase of furniture and fixtures		(6,000)
Cash flows from financing activities:		
Issue of common stock	$10,000	
Increase in notes payable	10,000	
Net cash flows from financing activities		20,000
Net increase in cash		$ 6,500

The Statement Shareholders' Equity

The **statement of shareholders' equity** discloses the sources of changes in the permanent shareholders' equity accounts. The January statement of shareholders' equity for AJAX JANITORIAL SERVICE CORPORATION appears below:

AJAX JANITORIAL SERVICE CORPORATION
Statement of Shareholders' Equity
For the Month of January 2009

	Common Stock	Retained Earnings	Total Shareholders' Equity
Balance at January 1, 2009	- 0 -	- 0 -	- 0 -
Issue of common stock	$10,000		$10,000
Net income for January, 2009		$1,600	1,600
Balance at January 31, 2009	$10,000	$1,600	$11,600

STEP 9: **Closing** the temporary accounts to retained earnings (at year-end only).

STEP 10: Preparation of a **post-closing trial balance** (at year-end only).

At the end of the fiscal year, the temporary accounts (revenues, expenses, gains, and losses) are closed (zeroed out) and the balances are transferred to retained earnings. After the closing entries are posted to the ledger accounts, a **post-closing trial balance** is prepared to verify that the closing entries were prepared and posted correctly.

Conversion from Cash Basis to Accrual Basis

When converting from cash to accrual income, we add increases and deduct decreases in assets. For example, a decreases in accounts receivable means that the company earned less revenue than cash collected, requiring the deduction to cash basis income. Conversely, we add decreases and deduct increases in accrued liabilities. For example, an increase in interest payable means that the company incurred more interest expense than the cash interest it paid, requiring the deduction to cash basis income.

SELF-STUDY QUESTIONS AND EXERCISES

Concept Review

1. The first objective of any accounting system is to identify the _____ events that can be expressed in financial terms by the system.

2. _____ events involve an exchange between the company and a separate economic entity.

3. The _____ underlies the process used to capture the effect of economic events.

4. Owners' equity for a corporation, called shareholders' equity, is classified by source as either

   _____ or _____ .

5. A _____ is a collection of storage areas, called accounts, used to keep track of increases and decreases in financial position elements.

6. In the double-entry system, debit means _____ side of an account and credit means _____ side of an account.

7. Asset increases are entered on the _____ side of accounts and decreases are entered on the _____ side. Liability and equity account increases are _____ and decreases are _____ .

8. _____ is the process of reviewing the source documents to determine the dual effect on the accounting equation and the specific elements involved.

9. A _____ provides a chronological record of all economic events affecting a firm.

10. Step 4 of the accounting process is to periodically transfer or post the debit and credit information from the _____ to individual _____ accounts.

11. A _____ is simply a list of the general ledger accounts and their balances at a particular date.

12. Adjusting entries are necessary for three situations:
    a. _____ .
    b. _____ .
    c. _____ .

13. _____ are the costs of assets acquired in one period and expensed in a future period.

14. The adjusting entry required for a prepaid expense is a debit to an *expense* and a credit to an _____.

15. Unearned revenues represent _____ recorded when cash is received from customers in advance of providing a good or service.

16. The adjusting entry required to record an accrued liability is a debit to an _____ and a credit to a _____ .

17. _____ involve the recognition of revenue earned before cash is received.

18. The purpose of the _____ is to summarize the operating activities of the company during a particular period of time.

19. The _____ is a statement that presents an organized list of assets, liabilities and shareholders' equity at a point in time.

20. The purpose of the _____ is to summarize the transactions which caused cash to change during the period.

21. The statement of cash flows classifies all transactions affecting cash into one of three categories: (a) _____ , (b) _____ , and (c) _____ .

22. The statement of shareholders' equity discloses the sources of _____ in the permanent shareholders' equity accounts.

23. The purpose of the _____ is to verify that the closing entries were prepared and posted correctly and that the accounts are now ready for next year's transactions.

Answers:
1. economic 2. External 3. accounting equation 4. paid-in capital, retained earnings
5. general ledger 6. left, right 7. debit, credit, credits, debits 8. Transaction analysis
9. journal 10. journal, ledger 11. trial balance 12. a. Prepayments, b. Accruals,
c. Estimates 13. Prepaid expenses 14. expense, asset 15. liabilities 16. expense, liability
17. Accrued receivables 18. income statement 19. balance sheet
20. statement of cash flows 21. a. operating activities, b. investing activities, c. financing activities 22. change 23. post-closing trial balance

REVIEW EXERCISES

Exercise 1

Indicate by letter whether a debit (**D**) or a credit (**C**) will *increase* the following accounts:

Debit (D) or Credit (C)	Account
_____	Accounts receivable
_____	Accounts payable
_____	Prepaid rent
_____	Sales revenue
_____	Common stock
_____	Wages payable
_____	Cost of goods sold
_____	Utility expense
_____	Equipment
_____	Depreciation expense
_____	Accumulated depreciation
_____	Supplies
_____	Bad debt expense
_____	Interest expense
_____	Interest revenue

Solution:

D	Accounts receivable
C	Accounts payable
D	Prepaid rent
C	Sales revenue
C	Common stock
C	Wages payable
D	Cost of goods sold
D	Utility expense
D	Equipment
D	Depreciation expense
C	Accumulated depreciation
D	Supplies
D	Bad debt expense
D	Interest expense
C	Interest revenue

Exercise 2

Prepare December 31, 2009, **adjusting entries** for the Canton Trading Company for each of the following items:

a. Canton borrowed $20,000 from its bank on May 1, 2009. The entry recorded at that time included a credit to notes payable for $20,000. No payments are due until 2010. The annual interest rate is 12%.

b. On December 1, 2009, Canton collected rent of $3,600 (for December and January rent) from a tenant renting some space in its warehouse and credited *unearned rent revenue* for that amount.

c. An inventory of office supplies on hand reveals a count of $900. The ledger reflects a balance in the *office supplies* account of $1,850.

d. A one-year insurance policy insuring the company's truck was purchased on October 1, 2009. The entry at that time included a debit to *prepaid insurance* of $2,400.

e. Depreciation expense for 2009 was $7,000.

Solution:

a.	Interest expense ($20,000 x 12% x $8/12$)	1,600	
	Interest payable...		1,600
b.	Unearned rent revenue ($3,600 x $1/2$)	1,800	
	Rent revenue...		1,800
c.	Supplies expense ($1,850 - 900)..	950	
	Supplies		950
d.	Insurance expense ($2,400 x $3/12$)	600	
	Prepaid insurance...		600
e.	Depreciation expense..	7,000	
	Accumulated depreciation		7,000

Exercise 3

During the course of your examination of the financial statements of the Haley Sporting Goods Corporation for the year ended December 31, 2009, you discover the following:
a. Net income reported in the 2009 income statement is $42,000 before reflecting any of the following items.
b. On November 1, 2009, $6,000 was paid for rent on the company's office building. The payment covered the three-month period ending January 31, 2010. The entire amount was debited to rent expense and no adjusting entry was made for this item.
c. During 2009, the company received a $5,000 cash advance from a customer for merchandise to be manufactured and shipped in 2010. The $5,000 was credited to sales revenue. No entry was made for the cost of the merchandise.
d. Haley borrowed $30,000 from a local bank on September 1, 2009. Principal and interest at 10% will be paid on August 31, 2010. No accrual was made for interest.
e. There were no supplies listed in the balance sheet under assets. However, you discover that supplies costing $1,200 were on hand at December 31.

Required:
Determine the proper amount of net income for 2009.

Solution:	
Net income as reported	$42,000
Adjustments:	
Only $4,000 of rent should be expensed	+ 2,000
Sales revenue overstated	- 5,000
Interest expense understated ($30,000 x 10% x $4/12$)	- 1,000
Supplies expense overstated	+ 1,200
Adjusted net income	$39,200

Review of the Accounting Process

MULTIPLE CHOICE

Enter the letter corresponding to the response that **best** completes each of the following statements or questions.

_____ 1. The journal entry to record the borrowing of cash and the signing of a note payable involves:
   a. A debit to note payable and a credit to cash.
   b. Debits to cash and interest expense and a credit to note payable.
   c. A debit to cash and a credit to note payable.
   d. None of the above.

_____ 2. Which of the following is most likely an accrued liability?
   a. Depreciation.
   b. Interest.
   c. Cost of goods sold.
   d. Office supplies.

_____ 3. A prepaid expense is an expense:
   a. Incurred before the cash is paid.
   b. Incurred and paid.
   c. Paid but not yet incurred.
   d. None of the above.

_____ 4. The Esquire Clothing Company borrowed a sum of cash on October 1, 2009, and signed a note payable. The annual interest rate was 12% and the company's year 2009 income statement reported interest expense of $1,260 related to this note. What was the amount borrowed?
   a. $22,000
   b. $31,500
   c. $10,500
   d. $42,000

_____ 5. Which of the following adjusting entries creates a **decrease** in assets?
   a. Recording the earned portion of revenue collected in advance.
   b. Recording depreciation expense.
   c. Accruing unrecorded salaries expense.
   d. Accruing unrecorded interest revenue.

_____ 6. Which of the following adjusting entries creates an **increase** in liabilities?
   a. Accruing unrecorded interest expense.
   b. Recording the amount of expired prepaid insurance.
   c. Accruing unrecorded interest revenue.
   d. Recording depreciation expense.

_____ 7. If the required adjusting entry for depreciation expense is omitted:
   a. Assets will be overstated and income understated.
   b. Assets will be overstated and income overstated.
   c. Assets will be understated and income overstated.
   d. Assets will be understated and income understated.

_____ 8. The *accumulated depreciation* account is a contra (valuation) account to:
   a. Owner's equity account.
   b. Expense account.
   c. Asset account.
   d. Liability account.

_____ 9. The correct amount of prepaid insurance shown on a company's December 31, 2009, balance sheet was $900. On July 1, 2010, the company paid an additional insurance premium of $600. In the December 31, 2010, balance sheet, the amount of prepaid insurance was correctly shown as $500. The amount of *insurance expense* that should appear in the company's 2010 income statement is:
   a. $1,500
   b. $1,400
   c. $1,000
   d. $ 600

_____ 10. The Wazoo Times Newspaper Company showed an $11,200 liability in its 2009 balance sheet for subscription revenue received in advance. During 2010, $62,000 was received from customers for subscriptions and the 2010 income statement reported subscription revenue of $63,700. What is the liability amount for unearned subscription revenue that will appear in the 2010 balance sheet?
   a. $0
   b. $11,200
   c. $12,900
   d. $9,500

_____ 11. In a classified balance sheet, *allowance for uncollectible accounts* would be classified among:
   a. Noncurrent assets.
   b. Current liabilities.
   c. Current assets.
   d. Noncurrent liabilities.

_____ 12. In a statement of cash flows, cash received from the issuance of common stock would be classified as a:
   a. Financing activity.
   b. Investing activity.
   c. Operating activity.
   d. Non-cash activity.

_____13. The closing process involves:
    a.   Recording year-end adjusting entries.
    b.   Transferring revenue and expense balances to retained earnings.
    c.   Closing out the permanent account balances.
    d.   None of the above.

_____14. If revenues exceed expenses for the accounting period, the income summary account:
    a.   Will have a debit balance after closing.
    b.   Will have a debit balance prior to closing.
    c.   Will have a credit balance prior to closing.
    d.   None of the above.

Answers:

1.	c.	6.	a.	11.	c.
2.	b.	7.	b.	12.	a.
3.	c.	8.	c.	13.	b.
4.	d.	9.	c.	14.	c.
5.	b.	10.	d.		

The Balance Sheet and Financial Disclosures

LEARNING OBJECTIVES

After studying this chapter, you should be able to:
1. Describe the purpose of the balance sheet and understand its usefulness and limitations.
2. Distinguish among current and noncurrent assets and liabilities.
3. Identify and describe the various balance sheet asset classifications.
4. Identify and describe the two balance sheet liability classifications.
5. Explain the purpose of financial statement disclosures.
6. Explain the purpose of the management discussion and analysis disclosure.
7. Explain the purpose of an audit and describe the content of the audit report.
8. Describe the techniques used by financial analysts to transform financial information into forms more useful for analysis.
9. Identify and calculate the common liquidity and financing ratios used to assess risk.

CHAPTER HIGHLIGHTS

PART A: THE BALANCE SHEET

The purpose of the **balance sheet** is to report a company's financial position (assets, liabilities, and shareholders' equity) on a particular date. The balance sheet *does not* portray the market value of the entity (number of common stock shares outstanding multiplied by price per share) because many assets and liabilities are measured at their historical cost rather than their fair value and many valuable company resources such as its experienced management team are not recorded as assets at all. The balance sheet does, however, provide information useful for assessing future cash flows, liquidity, and long-term solvency.

Classifying assets and liabilities into categories based on common characteristics enhances the usefulness of the balance sheet. The usual types of classifications are listed next and discussed below.

Assets:
    Current assets
    Investments
    Property, plant, and equipment
    Intangible assets
    Other assets

Liabilities:
    Current liabilities
    Long-term liabilities

Shareholders' equity:
    Paid-in capital
    Retained earnings

Current Assets

In addition to cash, **current assets** include all other assets that are expected to become cash or be consumed during one year or the **operating cycle** of the business, whichever is longer. The **operating cycle** for a typical manufacturing company refers to the period of time necessary to convert cash to raw materials, raw materials to a finished product, the finished product to receivables, and then finally receivables back to cash. Classifying assets as current or noncurrent assists investors and creditors in assessing liquidity.

Individual current assets are listed in order of their liquidity (nearness to cash). The typical types of current assets, described below, include **cash and cash equivalents**, **short-term investments**, **accounts receivable**, **inventories**, and **prepaid expenses**.

Cash includes cash on hand and in banks that is available for use in the operations of the business and such items as bank drafts, cashier's checks, and money orders. **Cash equivalents** frequently include certain negotiable items such as commercial paper, money market funds, and U.S. treasury bills. These are highly liquid investments that can be quickly converted into cash.

Liquid investments not classified as cash equivalents that are expected to be liquidated in the next twelve months or operating cycle, whichever is longer, are reported as **short-term investments**.

Accounts receivable represents the amounts due from customers from the sale of goods or services on credit. They are reported net of allowances, that is, net of the amount not expected to be collected.

Inventories consist of assets that a retail or wholesale company acquires for resale or goods that manufacturers produce for sale.

A **prepaid expense** represents an asset recorded when an expense is paid in advance, creating future benefits. If the benefits purchased in advance will be consumed in the next year or operating cycle, whichever is longer, the prepaid expense is classified as a current asset.

Investments

Investments are assets not used directly in operations. They include investments in equity and debt securities of other corporations not classified as current, land held for speculation, noncurrent receivables, and cash set aside for special purposes. These assets are classified as noncurrent because management intends not to convert the assets into cash in the next year or operating cycle if that's longer.

Property, Plant, and Equipment

Tangible, long-lived assets used in the operations of the business are classified as **property, plant, and equipment**. This classification includes land, buildings, equipment, machinery, and furniture, as well as natural resources such as mineral mines, timber tracts, and oil wells. They are reported at original cost less accumulated depreciation (or depletion for natural resources) to date. Property, plant, and equipment, along with intangible assets, often are referred to as **operational assets**.

Intangible Assets

Intangible assets generally represent exclusive rights that the company can use to generate future revenues. They include such items as patents, copyrights, and franchise rights and are reported in the balance sheet net of accumulated amortization. Some companies include intangible assets as part of property, plant, and equipment, while others report them in a separate intangible asset classification in the balance sheet.

Other Assets

Balance sheets often include a catch-all classification of noncurrent assets called **other assets**. This classification includes long-term prepaid expenses, called deferred charges, and any noncurrent asset not falling in one of the other classifications.

Current Liabilities

Current liabilities are those obligations that are expected to be satisfied within one year or the operating cycle, whichever is longer. Current liabilities usually include **accounts payable** (obligations to suppliers of merchandise or of services purchased on open account), **notes payable** (written promises to pay cash at some future date), **unearned revenues** (cash received from a customer for goods or services to be provided in the future), **accrued liabilities** (obligations created when an expense has been incurred but won't be paid until a subsequent reporting period), and the **current maturities of long-term debt**.

Long-term Liabilities

Long-term liabilities are obligations that will *not* be satisfied in the next year or operating cycle, whichever is longer. Examples are long-term notes, bonds, pension obligations, and lease obligations. Interest rates, payments terms, and other details about long-term liabilities are reported in a disclosure note.

Shareholders' Equity

Shareholders' equity, or stockholders' equity, arises primarily from two sources: (1) amounts *invested* by shareholders in the corporation, and (2) amounts *earned* by the corporation (on behalf of its shareholders). These are reported as (1) **paid-in capital** and (2) **retained earnings**. Retained earnings represents the net income earned from the inception of the corporation and not (yet) paid to shareholders as dividends.

ILLUSTRATION

The following is a post-closing trial balance for the Masters & Sons Carpet Company at December 31, 2009:

Account Title	Debits	Credits
Cash	25,000	
Accounts receivable	120,000	
Allowance for uncollectible accounts		6,000
Inventories	180,000	
Prepaid expenses	10,000	
Note receivable (due in four months)	50,000	
Investments	30,000	
Machinery and equipment	420,000	
Accumulated depreciation - machinery and equipment		170,000
Patent (net of amortization)	30,000	
Accounts payable		135,000
Salaries payable		17,000
Interest payable		4,000
Note payable (due in ten years)		80,000
Common stock		300,000
Retained earnings		153,000
Totals	865,000	865,000

The $30,000 balance in the investment account consists of marketable equity securities of other corporations. The company's intention is to hold the securities for at least four years. The December 31, 2009, balance sheet is as follows:

Masters & Sons Carpet Company
Balance Sheet
At December 31, 2009

Assets

Current assets

Cash		$ 25,000
Accounts receivable	$120,000	
Less: Allowance for uncollectible accounts	(6,000)	114,000
Note receivable		50,000
Inventories		180,000
Prepaid expenses		10,000
Total current assets		379,000
Investments		30,000

Property, plant, and equipment

Machinery and equipment	420,000	
Less: Accumulated depreciation	(170,000)	
Net property, plant, and equipment		250,000

Intangibles

Patent		30,000
Total assets		$689,000

Liabilities and Shareholders' Equity

Current liabilities

Accounts payable		$135,000
Salaries payable		17,000
Interest payable		4,000
Total current liabilities		156,000

Long-term liabilities

Note payable		80,000

Shareholders' equity

Common stock	$300,000	
Retained earnings	153,000	
Total shareholders' equity		453,000
Total liabilities and shareholders' equity		$689,000

PART B: FINANCIAL DISCLOSURES

Critical to understanding the financial statements and to evaluating the firm's performance and financial health are disclosure notes and other information included in the annual report. Some of the more important of these disclosures are discussed below. Others are discussed and illustrated in later chapters in the context of related financial statement elements.

Disclosure Notes

Typically, the first disclosure note consists of a **summary of significant accounting policies**. This disclosure conveys valuable information about the company's choices from among various alternative accounting methods (for example, inventory valuation methods and depreciation methods).

A **subsequent event** is a significant development that takes place after the company's fiscal year-end but before the financial statements are issued. These events are described in a disclosure note.

Disclosure notes are required for certain transactions and events that occur infrequently, but are potentially important to investors and creditors and other financial statement users. Examples include **irregularities** (intentional distortion of financial statements), **illegal acts** (for example, bribes or kickbacks), and **related-party transactions** (transactions with owners, management, families of owners or management, affiliated companies, and other parties that can significantly influence or be influenced by the company).

Management Discussion and Analysis

Each annual report includes a fairly lengthy discussion and analysis provided by the company's management. The **management discussion and analysis (MDA)** provides a biased but informed perspective of a company's (a) operations, (b) liquidity, and (c) capital resources.

Management's Responsibilities

Auditors *examine* financial statements and the internal control procedures designed to support the content of those statements. However, management *prepares* the financial statements and all other information in the annual report. The **management's responsibilities** section of the annual report discusses the relative roles of the auditor and management and asserts the responsibility of management for the company's financial statements as well as its internal control system. The Sarbanes-Oxley Act of 2002 requires corporate executives to personally certify the financial statements.

Auditors' Report

The **auditors' report** provides the analyst with an independent and professional opinion about the fairness of the representations in the financial statements. Most reports are unqualified. That is, the report states that the auditor is satisfied that the financial statements present fairly the financial position, results of operations and cash flows and are in conformity with generally accepted accounting principles. The audit report also provides the auditors' opinion on the effectiveness of the company's internal control over financial reporting.

Compensation of Directors and Top Executives

The **proxy statement**, which is sent each year to all shareholders, contains disclosures on compensation to directors and executives. These disclosures include a summary compensation table, a table of stock options granted, and a table of stock option holdings.

PART C: RISK ANALYSIS

Investors, creditors, and others must be able to *compare* financial information among firms and over time. **Comparative financial statements** enable users to compare year-to-year financial position, results of operations, and cash flows. This comparison is enhanced by expressing each item as a percentage of that same item in the financial statements of another year (base amount). This is referred to as **horizontal analysis**. **Vertical analysis** involves expressing each financial statement item as a percentage of an appropriate corresponding total or base amount within the same year. For example, net income and each expense can be restated as a percent of revenues.

The most common way of comparing accounting numbers is **ratio analysis**. Evaluating information in ratio form facilitates comparisons by controlling for size differences over time and among firms and by highlighting important relationships.

Investors and creditors use financial information to assess the future risk and return of their investments in a business enterprise. Financial ratios often are used in risk analysis to investigate a company's liquidity and long-term solvency.

Liquidity Ratios

Liquidity refers to the readiness of assets to be converted to cash. By comparing a company's liquid assets (current assets or a subset of current assets) with its short-term obligations (current liabilities), we can obtain a general idea of the firm's ability to pay its short-term debts as they come due. Two common measures of liquidity (1) the **current ratio**, and (2) the **acid-test ratio** (or **quick ratio**) are calculated as follows:

Current ratio	=	$\dfrac{\text{Current assets}}{\text{Current liabilities}}$
Acid-test ratio (or **quick ratio**)	=	$\dfrac{\text{Quick assets}}{\text{Current liabilities}}$

The acid test ratio provides a more stringent indication of a company's ability to pay its current obligations by eliminating inventories and prepaid items from current assets (current assets minus inventories and prepaid items equals quick assets).

Financing Ratios

Financing ratios provide some indication or the riskiness of a company with regard to its ability to pay its long-term debts (long-term solvency). Two common financing ratios are (1) the **debt to equity ratio**, and (2) the **times interest earned ratio**. These ratios are calculated as follows:

Debt to equity ratio	=	$\dfrac{\text{Total liabilities}}{\text{Shareholders' equity}}$
Times interest earned ratio	=	$\dfrac{\text{Net income} + \text{interest expense} + \text{taxes}}{\text{Interest expense}}$

The **debt to equity ratio** indicates the extent of reliance on creditors, rather than owners, in providing resources. Other things being equal, the higher the ratio, the higher the risk. The **times interest earned ratio** indicates the margin of safety provided to creditors. For this ratio, the higher the ratio the lower the risk.

APPENDIX 3: REPORTING SEGMENT INFORMATION

Many companies operate in several business segments as a strategy to achieve growth and to reduce operating risk through diversification. To address this problem, the accounting profession requires companies engaged in more than one significant line of business to provide *supplementary* information concerning individual operating segments.

Reporting by Operating Segment

Reportable segments are determined based on the way that management organizes the segments within the enterprise for making operating decisions and assessing performance. The segments are, therefore, evident from the structure of the enterprise's internal organization. The following characteristics define an operating segment:

An **operating segment** is a component of an enterprise:

- That engages in business activities from which it may earn revenues and incur expenses (including revenues and expenses relating to transactions with other components of the same enterprise).

- Whose operating results are regularly reviewed by the enterprise's chief operating decision maker to make decisions about resources to be allocated to the segment and assess its performance.

- For which discrete financial information is available.

Only segments of a certain size (10% or more of total company revenues, assets, or net income) must be disclosed. However, a company must account for at least 75% of consolidated revenue through segment disclosures.

For areas determined to be reportable segments, the following disclosures are required:

    a. General information about the operating segment.
    b. Information about reported segment profit or loss, including certain revenues and expenses included in reported segment profit or loss, segments assets, and the basis of measurement.
    c. Reconciliations of the totals of segment revenues, reported profit or loss, assets, and other significant items to corresponding enterprise amounts.
    d. Interim period information.

Reporting by Geographic Area

GAAP require an enterprise to report certain geographic information unless it is impracticable to do so.

Information about Major Customers

If 10% or more of the revenues of an enterprise is derived from transactions with a single customer, the enterprise must disclose that fact, the total amount of revenues from each such customer, and the identity of the operating segment or segments earning the revenues. The identity of the major customer need not be disclosed.

SELF-STUDY QUESTIONS AND EXERCISES

Concept Review

1. The information contained in the balance sheet is useful not only in predicting future cash flows, but also in the related assessments of _____ and _____ .

2. The purpose of the balance sheet is to report a company's _____ as of a particular date.

3. The assets of a company minus its liabilities as shown in the balance sheet usually will not directly measure the company's _____ .

4. _____ refers to the period of time before an asset is converted to cash or until a liability is paid. _____ refers to the riskiness of a company with regard to the amount of liabilities in its capital structure.

5. The key classification of assets and liabilities in the balance sheet is the _____ versus _____ distinction.

6. _____ include cash and several other assets that are reasonably expected to be converted to cash or consumed during the coming year, or within the normal operating cycle of the business if that's longer than one year.

7. The _____ for a typical manufacturing company refers to the period of time necessary to convert cash to raw materials, raw materials to a finished product, the finished product to receivables, and then finally receivables back to cash.

8. _____ are highly liquid investments that can be quickly converted into cash.

9. Accounts receivable are valued net of _____ that is, net of the amount not expected to be collected.

10. Inventories for a manufacturer include _____ , _____ , and _____ .

11. Tangible, long-lived assets used in the operations of the business are classified as _____ .

12. Property, plant, and equipment, along with intangible assets, often are referred to as _____ . They usually are the primary revenue-generating assets of the business.

13. Intangible assets generally represent exclusive _____ that the company can use to generate future revenues.

14. _____ are those obligations that are expected to be satisfied through the use of current assets or the creation of other current liabilities.

15. _____ are obligations to suppliers of merchandise or of services purchased on open account, with payment usually due in 30 to 60 days.

16. _____ represent obligations created when an expense has been incurred but won't be paid until a subsequent reporting period.

17. Shareholders' equity is comprised of two primary classifications: _____ and _____ .

18. Typically, the first disclosure note consists of a _____ that discloses the choices the company makes.

19. A _____ is a significant development that takes place after the company's fiscal year-end but before the financial statements are issued.

20. The Management Discussion and Analysis provides a biased but informed perspective of a company's (a) _____ , (b) _____ , and (c) _____ .

21. If the auditors are satisfied that the financial statements "present fairly" the financial position, results of operations, and cash flows and are "in conformity with generally accepted accounting principles," an _____ is issued.

22. The _____ , which is sent each year to all shareholders, contains disclosures on compensation to directors and executives.

23. _____ expresses each item as a percentage of that same item in the financial statements of another year (base amount) in order to more easily see year-to-year changes.

24. The most common way of comparing accounting numbers to evaluate the performance and risk of a firm is _____ .

25. The difference between current assets and current liabilities is called _____

26. The current ratio is computed by dividing _____ by _____ .

27. The acid-test ratio excludes _____ and _____ from current assets before dividing by current liabilities.

28. The _____ compares resources provided by creditors with resources provided by owners.

29. Favorable _____ means earning a return on borrowed funds that exceeds the cost of borrowing the funds.

30. The times interest earned ratio is calculated by dividing _____ before subtracting either interest expense or taxes by _____ .

Question 31 is based on Appendix 3.

31. If _____ of the revenues of an enterprise are derived from transactions with a single customer, the enterprise must disclose that fact.

Answers:
1. liquidity, long-term solvency **2.** financial position **3.** market value **4.** Liquidity, Long-term solvency **5.** current, noncurrent **6.** Current assets **7.** operating cycle **8.** Cash equivalents **9.** allowance for uncollectible accounts **10.** finished goods, work-in-process, raw materials **11.** property, plant, and equipment **12.** operational assets **13.** rights **14.** Current liabilities **15.** Accounts payable **16.** Accrued liabilities **17.** paid-in capital, retained earnings **18.** summary of significant accounting policies **19.** subsequent event **20.** a. operations, b. liquidity, c. capital resources **21.** unqualified opinion **22.** proxy statement **23.** Horizontal analysis **24.** ratio analysis **25.** working capital **26.** current assets, current liabilities **27.** inventories, prepaid items **28.** debt to equity ratio **29.** financial leverage **30.** income, interest expense **31.** 10% or more

The Balance Sheet and Financial Disclosures

REVIEW EXERCISES

Exercise 1

The following are the typical classifications used in a balance sheet:

a. Current assets
b. Investments
c. Property, plant, and equipment
d. Intangible assets
e. Other assets

f. Current liabilities
g. Long-term liabilities
h. Paid-in-capital
i. Retained earnings
j. Not reported in the balance sheet

Required:

For each of the following balance sheet items, use the letters above to indicate the appropriate classification category. If the item is a contra account (valuation account), place a minus sign before the chosen letter.

_____ 1. Cost of goods sold
_____ 2. Accrued interest payable
_____ 3. Allowance for uncollectible accounts
_____ 4. Investment in stock, long-term
_____ 5. Note payable, due in 3 years
_____ 6. Rent revenue collected in advance
_____ 7. Note payable, due in 6 months
_____ 8. Income less dividends, accumulated
_____ 9. Prepaid insurance

_____ 10. Inventories
_____ 11. Copyright
_____ 12. Land, in use
_____ 13. Sales revenue
_____ 14. Accumulated dep.
_____ 15. Common stock
_____ 16. Building, in use
_____ 17. Cash equivalents
_____ 18. Salaries payable

Solution:							
1.	j.	7.	f.	13.	j.		
2.	f.	8.	i.	14.	−c.		
3.	−a.	9.	a.	15.	h.		
4.	b.	10.	a.	16.	c.		
5.	g.	11.	d.	17.	a.		
6.	f.	12.	c.	18.	f.		

Exercise 2

The following is a post-closing trial balance for the Shennendoah Milling Company:

Account Title	Debits	Credits
Cash	16,000	
Accounts receivable	48,000	
Inventories	80,000	
Prepaid insurance	3,000	
Short-term investments	7,000	
Equipment	265,000	
Accumulated depreciation - equipment		145,000
Patent (net of amortization)	30,000	
Accounts payable		70,000
Interest payable		5,000
Allowance for uncollectible accounts		4,000
Note payable (due in five years)		100,000
Common stock		100,000
Retained earnings		25,000
Totals	449,000	449,000

Required:

Prepare a classified balance sheet for the Shennendoah Milling Company at December 31, 2009.

Shennendoah Milling Company
Balance Sheet
At December 31, 2009

Assets

Liabilities and Shareholders' Equity

Solution:

Shennendoah Milling Company
Balance Sheet
At December 31, 2009

Assets

Current assets

Cash...		$ 16,000
Short-term investments		7,000
Accounts receivable	$48,000	
Less: Allowance for uncollectible accounts	(4,000)	44,000
Inventories...		80,000
Prepaid expenses		3,000
Total current assets		150,000
Property, plant, and equipment...		
Equipment	265,000	
Less: Accumulated depreciation	(145,000)	
Net property, plant, and equipment.....................................		120,000
Intangibles		
Patent..		30,000
Total assets		$300,000

Liabilities and Shareholders' Equity

Current liabilities		
Accounts payable		$ 70,000
Interest payable		5,000
Total current liabilities		75,000
Long-term liabilities		
Note payable		100,000
Shareholders' equity		
Common stock	$100,000	
Retained earnings..	25,000	
Total shareholders' equity..		125,000
Total liabilities and shareholders' equity............................		$300,000

Exercise 3
The 2009 balance sheet for the Variant Corporation is shown below.

Variant Corporation
Balance Sheet
At December 31, 2009

Assets:	($ in 000s)
Cash..	$ 60,000
Accounts receivable (net)	140,000
Inventories	160,000
Property, plant, and equipment (net)	350,000
Total assets	$710,000
Liabilities and Shareholders' Equity:	
Current liabilities	$ 180,000
Long-term liabilities	200,000
Common stock	200,000
Retained earnings..	130,000
Total liabilities and shareholders' equity.................	$710,000

The company's 2009 income statement reported the following amounts ($ in thousands):

Net sales	$1,300,000
Interest expense	20,000
Income tax expense	50,000
Net income	80,000

Required:
Calculate the following ratios for 2009:

1. Current ratio

2. Acid-test ratio

3. Debt to equity ratio

4. Times interest earned ratio

Solution:

1. Current ratio	[$60,000 + 140,000 + 160,000] ÷ $180,000 = 2.0
2. Acid-test ratio	[$60,000 + 140,000] ÷ $180,000 = 1.11
3. Debt to equity ratio	[$180,000 + 200,000] ÷ [$200,000 + 130,000] = 1.15
4. Times interest earned ratio	[$80,000 + 20,000 + 50,000] ÷ $20,000 = 7.5 times

MULTIPLE CHOICE

Enter the letter corresponding to the response that **best** completes each of the following statements or questions.

_____ 1. Which of the following is **not** a characteristic of the balance sheet?
   a. The major classifications of the balance sheet are assets, liabilities, and owners' equity.
   b. The balance sheet reports the change in financial position.
   c. Assets generally are listed in order of their liquidity.
   d. The balance sheet provides information useful in assessing liquidity.

_____ 2. The basis used to classify assets as *current* or *noncurrent* is:
   a. Whether an asset is monetary or nonmonetary.
   b. The operating cycle or one year, whichever is shorter.
   c. Usually one year, because the operating cycle typically is less than oneyear.
   d. Whether the asset is currently used in the company's operations.

_____ 3. An item **not** generally classified as a *current asset* is:
   a. Patent.
   b. Trade receivables.
   c. Prepaid rent.
   d. Inventories.

_____ 4. Included in the category of *current liabilities* would be:
   a. Pension obligations.
   b. Lease obligations.
   c. Obligations expected to require the creation of other current liabilities.
   d. Mortgages payable.

_____ 5. An item **not** generally classified as a *current liability* is:
   a. Revenue received in advance.
   b. Accrued interest payable.
   c. Accounts payable.
   d. Bonds payable.

_____ 6. Current assets minus current liabilities equals:
   a. Net assets.
   b. Working capital.
   c. The current ratio.
   d. Cash equivalents.

_____ 7. Operational assets refer to property, plant, and equipment, and:
   a. Receivables.
   b. Inventories.
   c. Investments.
   d. Intangibles.

_____ 8. Information **not** generally disclosed in the *summary of significant accounting policies* is:
    a.   The company's depreciation method.
    b.   The fact that the company uses the FIFO inventory method.
    c.   A related party transaction.
    d.   The company's revenue recognition policy.

_____ 9. The compensation of directors and top executives is disclosed in:
    a.   The proxy statement.
    b.   The annual report.
    c.   A disclosure note.
    d.   Interim financial statements.

_____10. Which ratio most directly indicates the extent of the company's reliance on *financial leverage*?
    a.   Times interest earned.
    b.   Debt to equity.
    c.   Return on shareholders' equity.
    d.   Current ratio.

_____11. The acid-test ratio excludes which of the following elements from the numerator?
    a.   Short-term investments.
    b.   Receivables.
    c.   Cash equivalents.
    d.   Inventories.

_____12. For a firm with a current ratio of 2.0, which of the following transactions would most likely cause the ratio to *decrease*?
    a.   The collection of cash from customers on account.
    b.   The sale of a building for cash.
    c.   The purchase of inventory on account.
    d.   The issuance of capital stock for cash.

The following information pertains to questions 13 through 15:

Sanchez Corporation
Selected Financial Information

	12/31/09	**12/31/08**
Cash	$ 20,000	$ 25,000
Accounts receivable (net)	100,000	110,000
Inventories	190,000	155,000
Total current assets	310,000	290,000
Noncurrent assets	230,000	210,000
Current liabilities	200,000	190,000
Long-term liabilities	40,000	50,000
Shareholders' equity	300,000	260,000
Net income	$40,000	
Interest expense	10,000	
Income tax expense	20,000	

_____13. The acid-test ratio for 2009 is:
   a. 0.8
   b. 1.6
   c. 0.6
   d. 0.34

_____14. The debt to equity ratio for 2009 is:
   a. .80
   b. .44
   c. .67
   d. .13

_____15. The times interest earned ratio is:
   a. 4.0 times
   b. 5.0 times
   c. 6.0 times
   d. 7.0 times

Answers:

1.	b.	6.	b.	11.	d.
2.	c.	7.	d.	12.	c.
3.	a.	8.	c.	13.	c.
4.	c.	9.	a.	14.	a.
5.	d.	10.	b.	15.	d.

The Income Statement and Statement of Cash Flows

LEARNING OBJECTIVES

After studying this chapter, you should be able to:
1. Discuss the importance of income from continuing operations and describe its components.
2. Describe earnings quality and how it is impacted by management practices to manipulate earnings.
3. Discuss the components of operating and nonoperating income and their relationship to earnings quality.
4. Define what constitutes discontinued operations and describe the appropriate income statement presentation for these transactions.
5. Define extraordinary items and describe the appropriate income statement presentation for these transactions.
6. Describe the measurement and reporting requirements for a change in accounting principle.
7. Explain the accounting treatments of changes in estimates and correction of errors.
8. Define earnings per share (EPS) and explain required disclosures of EPS for certain income statement components.
9. Explain the difference between net income and comprehensive income and how we report components of the difference.
10. Describe the purpose of the statement of cash flows.
11. Identify and describe the various classifications of cash flows presented in a statement of cash flows.

CHAPTER HIGHLIGHTS

PART A: THE INCOME STATEMENT AND COMPREHENSIVE INCOME

The purpose of the **income statement**, sometimes called the statement of operations or statement of earnings, is to summarize the profit-generating activities that occurred during a particular reporting period. In addition to net income, the bottom line of the income statement, the components of the income statement and their presentation also are important to financial statement users.

Income From Continuing Operations

The need to provide information to help predict future cash flows places considerable importance on GAAP for describing the amount of income from the entity's continuing operations. **Income from continuing operations** includes the revenues, expenses (including income tax expense), gains, and losses excluding those related to discontinued operations and extraordinary items.

Within continuing operations, a distinction often is made between **operating** and **nonoperating** income. Operating income includes revenues and expenses directly related to the principal revenue-generating activities of the company. Nonoperating income includes gains and losses and revenues and expenses related to peripheral or incidental activities of the company. For example, income from investments, gains and losses from the sale of operating assets and from investments, interest and dividend revenue, and interest expense are included in nonoperating income.

Income Statement Formats

No specific standards dictate how income from continuing operations must be presented. However, the two general approaches might be considered the two extremes, with income statements of most companies falling somewhere in between. The **single-step** format groups all revenues and gains together and all expenses and losses together. An advantage of this format is its simplicity. The **multiple-step** format includes a number of intermediate subtotals before arriving at income from continuing operations. An advantage of this format is that it separately reports operating and nonoperating transactions and also classifies expenses by function.

Earnings Quality

The term **earnings quality** refers to the ability of reported earnings (income) to predict a company's future earnings. To enhance predictive value, analysts try to separate a company's *transitory earnings* effects from its *permanent earnings*. Transitory earnings effects result from transactions or events that are not likely to occur again in the foreseeable future, or that are likely to have a different impact on earnings in the future. Later in this study guide we address two items that, because of their transitory nature, are required to be reported separately in the bottom of the income statement. Analysts begin their assessment of permanent earnings with income before these three items, that is, income from continuing operations.

It would be a mistake, though, to assume income from continuing operations reflects permanent earnings entirely. In other words, there may be transitory earnings effects included in income from continuing operations. In a sense, the phrase *continuing* may be misleading.

Operating Income and Earnings Quality

Should all items of revenue and expense included in operating income be considered indicative of a company's permanent earnings? No, not necessarily. Sometimes, for example, operating expenses may include some unusual items that may or may not continue in the future. A possibility is **restructuring costs** that include costs associated with shutdown or relocation of facilities or downsizing of operations. Other possibilities include the write-down of inventory and operational asset impairment losses. These items are discussed in subsequent chapters.

Revenue issues affect earnings quality as well. For example, the pressure on companies to meet their earnings numbers often has led to premature revenue recognition, reducing the quality of the current period's earnings. Accelerating revenue recognition has caused problems for many companies.

Nonoperating Income and Earnings Quality

Some nonoperating items have generated considerable discussion with respect to earnings quality; notably gains and losses generated either from the sale of operational assets or from the sale of investments. For example, as the stock market boom reached its height late in the year 2000, many companies recorded large gains from sale of investments that had appreciated significantly in value. An analyst must decide whether to consider those gains as transitory or part of a company's permanent earnings.

Separately Reported Items

The information in the income statement is useful if it can help users predict the future. Toward this end, users should be made aware of events reported in the income statement that are not likely to occur again in the foreseeable future. There are two types of events that, if they have a material effect on the income statement, require separate reporting and disclosure: (1) **discontinued operations**, and (2) **extraordinary items**. The objective is to separately report all of the income effects, *including income tax effects*, of these items *below* income from continuing operations. The order of presentation is as follows:

Income from continuing operations before taxes and extraordinary item	$xxx
Income tax expense	xx
Income from continuing operations before extraordinary item	xxx
Discontinued operations (net of $xx in taxes)	xx
Extraordinary items (net of $xx in taxes)	xx
Net income	$xxx

A third separately reported item, the *cumulative effect of a change in accounting principle*, might be included for certain mandated changes in accounting principles.

The process of associating income tax effects with the income statement components that create those effects is referred to as **intraperiod tax allocation**. For example, if a company reported income from continuing operations before income tax expense of $10 million and an extraordinary gain of $2 million, a partial income statement beginning with income from continuing operations before income tax would appear as follows (assuming a 30% income tax rate):

Income before income taxes and extraordinary gain	$10,000,000
Income tax expense	3,000,000
Income before extraordinary gain	7,000,000
Extraordinary gain (net of $600,000 tax expense)	1,400,000
Net income	$ 8,400,000

Discontinued Operations

A discontinued operation results when a company either disposes or classifies as held for sale a *component of an entity*. A component of an entity comprises operations and cash flows that can be clearly distinguished, operationally and for financial reporting purposes, from the rest of the entity. By definition, the income or loss stream from an identifiable component no longer will continue and must be separately reported.

When the Component Has Been Sold

When the discontinued component is sold before the end of the reporting period, the reported income effects of a discontinued operation will include two elements:

1. Operating income or loss (revenues, expenses, gains and losses) of the component from the beginning of the reporting period to the disposal date.

2. Gain or loss on disposal.

These two elements can be combined or reported separately, net of their tax effects. If combined, the gain or loss on disposal must be disclosed.

When the Component Is Considered Held for Sale

When the component to be discontinued has not been sold by the end of a reporting period, the income effects of the discontinued operation still are reported, but the two components of the reported amount are modified as follows:

1. Operating income or loss (revenues, expenses, gains and losses) of the component from the beginning of the reporting period *to the end of the reporting period.*

2. An "impairment loss" if the carrying value (book value) of the assets of the component is more than fair value minus cost to sell.

The balance sheet is affected, too. The assets of the component considered held for sale are reported at the lower of their carrying amount (book value) or fair value minus cost to sell. And, because it's not in use, an operational asset classified as held for sale is not depreciated or amortized.

The two income elements can be combined or reported separately, net of their tax effects. In addition, if the amounts are combined and there is an impairment loss, the loss must be disclosed, either parenthetically on the face of the statement or in a disclosure note.

ILLUSTRATION

In addition to manufacturing furniture, the Broadmoor Furniture Company also manufactures and sells mobile homes. Both the furniture and mobile home businesses are considered components of the entity. In October 2009, the company sold the mobile home business for $2.8 million. The assets of the component had a book value of $2.2 million. For the period January 1 through disposal, the mobile home business reported a pre-tax operating loss of $1.4 million. The company's income tax rate is 40% on all items of income or loss. The furniture business generated an after-tax income of $3.2 million.

The company's year 2009 income statement, beginning with income from continuing operations is as follows:

Income from continuing operations		$3,200,000
Discontinued operations:		
Loss from operations of discontinued component (including gain on disposal of $600,000*)	$(800,000) †	
Income tax benefit	320,000 ‡	
Loss on discontinued operations		(480,000)
Net income		$2,720,000

* Selling price of $2.8 million less book value of $2.2 million
† Operating loss of $1.4 million less gain on disposal of .6 million
‡ $800,000 × 40%

Extraordinary Items

Extraordinary items are material gains and losses that are both *unusual in nature* and *infrequent in occurrence*. The concepts of unusual and infrequent require judgment. The critical concern is the likelihood of the event causing the gain or loss occurring again in the foreseeable future. If the event is not likely to occur again, these gains and losses must be reported, net-of-tax, below discontinued operations.

A material gain or loss that is either unusual or infrequent, but not both, should be reported as a separate component of *continuing operations*. A common example is restructuring costs. The events may be unusual or infrequent, but, by their nature, they could occur again in the foreseeable future.

Accounting Changes

Accounting changes fall into one of three categories: (1) a change in an accounting principle, (2) a change in estimate, or (3) a change in reporting entity. The correction of an error is another adjustment that is accounted for in the same way as certain accounting changes.

Voluntary Changes in Accounting Principles

A voluntary **change in accounting principle** refers to a change from one acceptable accounting method to another. An example is a change in the method used to value inventory. The general accounting treatment for voluntary changes in accounting principles is to retrospectively recast prior years' financial statements when we report those statements again (in comparative statements, for example). For each year in the comparative statements reported, the balance of each account affected is revised. In other words, we make those statements appear as if the newly adopted accounting method had been applied all along. Then, a journal entry is created to adjust all account balances affected to what those amounts would have been. In addition, if retained earnings if one of the accounts whose balance requires adjustment, that adjustment is made to the beginning balance of retained earnings for the earliest period reported on the comparative statements of shareholders' equity.

Mandated Changes in Accounting Principles

When a new FASB standard mandates a change in accounting principle, it often allows companies to choose among multiple ways of accounting for the changes. One approach often allowed is to accounting for the change retrospectively, exactly as we account for voluntary changes in principle. A second way often allowed is to include the cumulative effect on the income of previous years from having used the old method rather than the new method in the income statement of the year of change as a separately reported item. If the later approach is chosen, the net-of-tax cumulative income effect of the changes is shown in the income statement the year the change is made as a separately reported item.

A *change in depreciation, amortization, or depletion method* is considered to be a change in accounting estimate that is achieved by a change in accounting principle. We account for these changes exactly as we would any other change in estimate (discussed in the next section).

Another type of change, a **change in accounting estimate**, is reported prospectively. Some common accounting estimates are the estimation of the amount of future bad debts on existing receivables, the estimation of useful life of a depreciable asset, and the estimation of future warranty expenses. When an estimate is revised as new information comes to light, we merely incorporate the new estimate in any accounting determinations from there on. For example, if, in 2010, a company realizes that warranty expenses in 2009 were underestimated, 2009's financial statements are not restated. Instead, the change in estimate causes warranty expenses in 2010 to be higher than they would have been if the company had correctly estimated 2009 warranty expenses. If the after-tax income effect of the change in estimate is material, the effect on net income and earnings per share must be disclosed in a note, along with the justification for the change.

A third type of accounting change, the **change in reporting entity**, involves the preparation of financial statements for an accounting entity other than the entity that existed in the previous period.

Correction of Accounting Errors

If an error is discovered in the same year as it occurs, or if an immaterial error is discovered in a year subsequent to the year the error occurs, the errors are corrected by a journal entry. A *material* error discovered in a subsequent year is considered a **prior period adjustment**. Prior years' financial statements are restated and the beginning balance in retained earnings is adjusted as needed.

Earnings Per Share Disclosures

Earnings per share (EPS) is the amount of income achieved during a period for each share of common stock outstanding. All corporations whose common stock is publicly traded must disclose basic EPS and, if there are certain potentially dilutive securities, diluted EPS. The EPS for income from continuing operations, and for each item below continuing operations, must be disclosed.

ILLUSTRATION

The following is a partial trial balance for Homer Lighting Company, a publicly traded corporation, as of December 31, 2009:

Account Title	Debits	Credits
Sales revenue		1,430,000
Gain on sale of equipment		7,000
Loss from hurricane damage (unusual and infrequent event)	220,000	
Cost of goods sold	610,000	
Restructuring costs	150,000	
Selling expenses	120,000	
Administrative expenses	130,000	
Interest expense	40,000	

Income tax expense has not yet been accrued. The income tax rate is 30%. The company had 500,000 shares of common stock outstanding during the whole year and had no potentially dilutive securities outstanding. The year 2009 income statement, using the multiple-step format, is as follows:

HOMER LIGHTING COMPANY
Income Statement
For the Year Ended December 31, 2009

Sales revenue		$1,430,000
Cost of goods sold		610,000
Gross profit		820,000
Operating expenses:		
Selling expenses	$120,000	
Administrative expenses	130,000	
Restructuring costs	150,000	
Total operating expenses		400,000
Operating income		420,000
Other income (expense):		
Gain on sale of equipment	7,000	
Interest expense	(40,000)	
Total other income (expense), net		(33,000)
Income before income taxes and extraordinary item		387,000
Income tax expense *		116,100
Income before extraordinary item		270,900
Loss from hurricane damage (net of $66,000 tax benefit)		(154,000)
Net income		$ 116,900
Basic earnings per share:		
Income before extraordinary item		$ .54
Extraordinary loss		(.31)
Net income		$ .23

* 30% × $387,000

Comprehensive Income

Comprehensive income is the total change in equity for a reporting period other than from transactions from owners. In many cases, comprehensive income will not equal net income due to certain transactions that are excluded from the calculation of net income. A FASB standard requires companies to report both net income and comprehensive income. The presentation of comprehensive income can be included as an extension to the income statement, reported (exactly the same way) as a separate statement of comprehensive income, or included in a statement of changes in shareholders' equity. The separate statement approach begins with net income followed by other comprehensive income items to arrive at comprehensive income.

The cumulative total of other comprehensive income (or comprehensive loss) is reported as accumulated other comprehensive income (or loss) an additional component of shareholders' equity that is displayed separately.

PART B: THE STATEMENT OF CASH FLOWS

The purpose of the **statement of cash flows (SCF)** is to provide information about cash receipts and cash disbursements of an enterprise that occurred during a period. Similar to the income statement, the SCF is a *change* statement. It summarizes the transactions that caused cash (and cash equivalents) to change during a reporting period.

Classifying Cash Flows

The SCF classifies all cash flows into one of three categories:

Operating Activities

Operating activities are inflows and outflows of cash related to the transactions entering into the determination of net operating income. Cash inflows include cash received from (1) customers from the sale of goods and services, and (2) interest and dividends on investments. Cash outflows include cash paid for (1) the purchase of inventory, (2) salaries, wages, and other operating expenses, (3) interest on debt, and (4) income taxes.

Two generally accepted formats can be used to report operating activities. The **direct method** reports the cash effect of each operating activity directly in the statement. By the **indirect method**, cash flows from operating activities is derived indirectly by starting with reported net income and adding and subtracting items to convert that amount to a cash basis. The indirect method is used much more frequently.

Investing Activities

Investing activities involve the acquisition and sale of (1) long-term assets used in the business, and (2) nonoperating investment assets. Cash outflows from investing activities include cash paid for (1) the purchase of long-term assets used in the business, (2) the purchase of investment securities, and (3) loans to other entities. Cash inflows from investing activities include cash received from (1) the sale of long-term assets used in the business, (2) the sale of investment securities, and (3) the collection of nontrade receivables (excluding the collection of interest, which is an operating activity).

Financing Activities

Financing activities involve cash inflows and outflows from transactions with creditors (excluding trade creditors) and owners. Cash inflows include cash received from (1) owners when shares are sold, and (2) creditors when cash is borrowed. Cash outflows include cash paid to (1) owners in the form of dividends or other distributions, (2) owners for the reacquisition of share, and (3) creditors as repayment of the *principal* amounts of debt.

Significant investing and financing transactions not involving cash also are reported.

ILLUSTRATION

The following summary transactions occurred during 2009 (fiscal year ends December 31) for the Cifelli Cheese Company:

Cash receipts from:

• Customers	$3,300,000
• Issuance of common stock	3,000,000
• Proceeds from mortgage payable	500,000
• Sale of building	425,000
• Note receivable repayment (includes $5,000 in interest)	105,000
• Dividends from investment securities	8,000

Cash disbursements for:

• Purchase of inventory	1,100,000
• Operating expenses	1,600,000
• Income taxes	200,000
• Payment of dividends to shareholders	50,000
• Interest on note payable	10,000
• Purchase of building	3,500,000
• Purchase of machinery and equipment	300,000

The company began the year 2009 with a balance of $145,000 in cash and cash equivalents and ended the year with a balance of $723,000.

The year 2009 statement of cash flows, applying the direct method for reporting operating activities, is as follows:

Cifelli Cheese Company
Statement of Cash Flows
For the Year Ended December 31, 2009

Cash Flows From Operating Activities:

Collections from customers	$3,300,000	
Interest on note receivable	5,000	
Dividends from investment securities	8,000	
Purchase of inventory	(1,100,000)	
Payment of operating expenses	(1,600,000)	
Payment of income taxes	(200,000)	
Interest on note payable	(10,000)	
Net cash inflows from operating activities		$ 403,000

Cash Flows From Investing Activities:

Purchase of building	(3,500,000)	
Purchase of machinery and equipment	(300,000)	
Sale of building	425,000	
Collection of note receivable	100,000	
Net cash outflows from investing activities		(3,275,000)

Cash Flows From Financing Activities:

Issuance of common stock	3,000,000	
Proceeds from mortgage payable	500,000	
Payment of dividends	(50,000)	
Net cash inflows from financing activities		3,450,000
Net increase in cash		578,000
Cash and cash equivalents, January 1		145,000
Cash and cash equivalents, December 31		$ 723,000

The Income Statement and Statement of Cash Flows

Concept Review

1. The purpose of the income statement is to summarize the _____ activities that occurred during a particular reporting period.

2. _____ is the total nonowner change in equity for a reporting period.

3. A distinction in the income statement often is made between _____ and _____ income.

4. A _____ income statement format groups all revenues and gains together and all expenses and losses together.

5. A _____ income statement format includes a number of intermediate subtotals before arriving at income from continuing operations.

6. The term _____ refers to the ability of reported earnings (income) to predict a company's future earnings.

7. _____ include costs associated with shutdown or relocation of facilities or downsizing of operations.

8. _____ associates tax expense or tax benefit with continuing operations and any item reported below continuing operations.

9. A_____ comprises operations and cash flows that can be clearly distinguished, operationally and for financial reporting purposes, from the rest of the entity.

10. The income effect of a discontinued operation that has been sold before the end of a reporting period includes two components: _____ and _____ .

11. The income effect of a discontinued operation that is considered held for sale at the end of a reporting period includes two components: _____ and _____ .

12. Extraordinary items are material gains and losses that are both _____ and _____ .

13. The general accounting treatment for a change in _____ is to retrospectively revise prior years' financial statements.

14. A change in _____ is reflected in the financial statements of the current period and future periods.

15. The correction of a material error discovered after the year the error is made is considered to be a _____ .

16. All corporations whose common stock is _____ must disclose earnings per share.

17. The purpose of the _____ is to provide information about cash receipts and disbursements that occurred during a period.

18. _____ activities are inflows and outflows of cash related to the transactions entering into the determination of net operating income.

19. _____ activities are inflows and outflows of cash related to the acquisition and disposition of long-term assets and investments.

20. _____ activities are inflows and outflows of cash from transactions with creditors and owners.

Answers:
1. profit-generating **2.** Comprehensive income **3.** operating, nonoperating **4.** single-step
5. multiple-step **6.** earnings quality **7.** Restructuring costs **8.** Intraperiod tax allocation
9. component of an entity **10.** Operating income or loss, gain or loss on disposal
11. operating income or loss, impairment loss **12.** unusual in nature, infrequent in occurrence
13. accounting principle **14.** accounting estimate **15.** prior period adjustment **16.** publicly
traded **17.** statement of cash flows **18.** Operating **19.** Investing **20.** Financing

REVIEW EXERCISES

Exercise 1
On October 31, 2009, the Carcione Fruit and Vegetable Company adopted a formal plan to discontinue its trucking division, a component of the entity. The company's fiscal year ends on December 31. By the end of December, the division had not been sold and was considered held for sale. The assets of the division had a book value of $6 million and a fair value, minus anticipated costs to sell of $4.2 million. For the year, the division reported a pre-tax operating income of $800,000. The company's income tax rate is 40% on all items of income. After-tax income of $3 million was generated by the company's other components.

Required:
Prepare Carcione's income statement for 2009 beginning with income from continuing operations. Ignore earnings per share disclosures.

Carcione Fruit and Vegetable Company
Income Statement (in part)
For the Year Ended December 31, 2009

Income from continuing operations

Solution:

Income from continuing operations		$3,000,000
Discontinued operations:		
Loss from operations of discontinued component		
(including impairment loss of $1,800,000*)	$(1,000,000) †	
Income tax benefit	400,000 ‡	
Loss on discontinued operations		(600,000)
Net income		$2,400,000

* Book value of $6 million less net fair value of $4.2 million
† Impairment loss of $1.8 million less operating income of $800,000
‡ $1,000,000 × 40%

Exercise 2
The Falletti Pasta Company experienced each of the following situations during 2009:
1. Restructuring costs were incurred.
2. Incurred a loss from an earthquake that was considered an unusual and infrequent event.
3. Discovered an error made in 2007 in the calculation of warranty expenses.
4. Discontinued its retail banking component.
5. Experienced losses from a strike by union employees.
6. Sold equipment and realized a gain.
7. Changed the estimate of the useful life of its warehouse building.

Required:
1. For each situation, identify the appropriate reporting treatment from the list below (consider each event to be material):

       a.   As an extraordinary item
       b.   As an unusual or infrequent gain or loss
       c.   As a prior period adjustment
       d.   As a change in accounting principle
       e.   As a discontinued operation
       f.   As a change in accounting estimate

2. Indicate whether each situation would be included in the income statement in continuing operations (CO) or below continuing operations (BC), or as an adjustment to retained earnings (RE). Use the format below to answer the requirements.

Situation	Treatment (a-f)	Financial Statement Presentation (CO, BC, or RE)
1.		
2.		
3.		
4.		
5.		
6.		
7.		

Solution:

Situation	Treatment (a-f)	Financial Statement Presentation (CO, BC, or RE)
1.	b.	CO
2.	a.	BC
3.	c.	RE
4.	e.	BC
5.	b.	CO
6.	b.	CO
7.	f.	CO

Exercise 3

The statement of cash flows classifies all cash inflows and outflows into one of three categories shown below and lettered a-c.

a.	Operating activities
b.	Investing activities
c.	Financing activities

Required:

For each of the following transactions, use the letters above, to indicate the appropriate classification category.

No.		Transaction
1.	_____	Purchase of a building for cash.
2.	_____	Payment of cash dividends to shareholders.
3.	_____	Collection of cash from customers.
4.	_____	Collection of interest on a note receivable.
5.	_____	Collection of principal on a note receivable.
6.	_____	Purchase of common stock of another corporation.
7.	_____	Reacquisition of company's own shares.
8.	_____	Payment of interest on a note payable.
9.	_____	Payment of principal on a note payable.
10.	_____	Sale of equipment for cash.

Solution:

No.		Transaction
1.	b.	Purchase of a building for cash.
2.	c.	Payment of cash dividends to shareholders.
3.	a.	Collection of cash from customers.
4.	a.	Collection of interest on a note receivable.
5.	b.	Collection of principal on a note receivable.
6.	b.	Purchase of common stock of another corporation.
7.	c.	Reacquisition of company's own shares.
8.	a.	Payment of interest on a note payable.
9.	c.	Payment of principal on a note payable.
10.	b.	Sale of equipment for cash.

MULTIPLE CHOICE

Enter the letter corresponding to the response that **best** completes each of the following statements or questions.

_____ 1. Which of the following captions would *more likely* be found in a multiple-step income statement?
    a.   Total expenses.
    b.   Total revenues and gains.
    c.   Gross profit.
    d.   None of the above.

_____ 2. An item typically included in the income from continuing operations section of the income statement is:
    a.   Discontinued operations.
    b.   Extraordinary gain.
    c.   Prior period adjustment.
    d.   Restructuring costs.

_____ 3. The application of intraperiod income taxes requires that income taxes be apportioned to each of the following items *except*:
    a.   Income from continuing operations.
    b.   Operating income.
    c.   Discontinued operations.
    d.   Extraordinary gains and losses.

_____ 4. For a manufacturing company, all of the following items would be considered nonoperating income for income statement purposes *except*:
    a.   Income from investments.
    b.   Cost of goods sold.
    c.   Interest expense.
    d.   Gain on sale of operating assets.

_____ 5. On May 31, 2009, the Arlene Corporation adopted a plan to sell its cosmetics line of business, considered a component of the entity. The assets of the component were sold on October 13, 2009, for $1,120,000. The component generated operating income from January 1, 2009, through disposal of $300,000. In its income statement for the year ended December 31, 2009, the company reported before-tax income from operations of a discontinued component of $620,000. What was the book value of the assets of the cosmetics component?
    a. $800,000
    b. $1,420,000
    c. $300,000
    d.   None of the above.

_____ 6. The Compton Press Company reported income before taxes of $250,000. This amount included a $50,000 extraordinary loss. The amount reported as income before extraordinary items, assuming a tax rate of 40%, is:
   a. $250,000
   b. $180,000
   c. $120,000
   d. $150,000

_____ 7. Which of the following material items would *not* be reported as an extraordinary item?
   a. A loss caused by an unusual and infrequent hurricane.
   b. A loss caused by an unusual and infrequent volcano.
   c. A loss caused by obsolescence of inventory.
   d. All of the above would be reported as extraordinary items.

_____ 8. The Stibbe Construction Company switched from the completed contract method to the percentage-of-completion method of accounting for its long-term construction contracts. This is an example of:
   a. A change in accounting principle.
   b. A change in accounting estimate.
   c. An infrequent but not unusual item.
   d. An extraordinary item.

_____ 9. In 2009, the Perasso Meat Packing Company revised the useful life of its equipment from eight years to six years. Depreciation recorded in prior years on existing equipment was $126,000 applying the eight-year useful life. Depreciation in prior years would have been $186,000 if the six-year useful life had been used. Assuming an income tax rate of 40%, Perasso's increase in 2009's beginning retained earnings would be:
   a. $60,000
   b. $36,000
   c. $24,000
   d. Zero.

_____ 10. Earnings per share should be reported for each of the following income statement captions *except:*
   a. Income from continuing operations.
   b. Extraordinary gains and losses.
   c. Operating income.
   d. Discontinued operations.

_____11. The following items appeared in the 2009 year-end trial balance for the Brown Coffee Company:

	Debits	Credits
Revenues		$600,000
Operating expenses	$420,000	
Gain from the early retirement of debt*		200,000
Restructuring costs	100,000	
Interest expense	20,000	
Gain on sale of operating assets		30,000

*Considered unusual and infrequent in this instance.

Income tax expense has not yet been accrued. The company's income tax rate is 40%. What amount should be reported in the company's year 2009 income statement as income before extraordinary items?
a. $90,000
b. $66,000
c. $34,800
d. $54,000

_____12. Selected information from the 2009 accounting records of Dunn's Auto Dealers is as follows:

Cost of furniture purchased for cash	$ 8,000
Proceeds from bank loan	100,000
Repayment of bank loan (includes interest of $4,000)	44,000
Proceeds from sale of equipment	5,000
Cash collected from customers	320,000
Purchase of stock of another corporation as an investment	20,000
Common stock issued for cash	200,000

In its 2009 statement of cash flows, Dunn's should report net cash inflows from *financing activities* of:
a. $260,000
b. $265,000
c. $ 60,000
d. $256,000

_____13. Using the information in question 12, Dunn's should report net cash outflows from *investing activities* of:
a. $27,000
b. $32,000
c. $28,000
d. $23,000

_____14. Which of the following items would *not* be included as a cash flow from *operating activities* in a statement of cash flows?
   a.   Collections from customers.
   b.   Interest on note payable.
   c.   Purchase of equipment.
   d.   Purchase of inventory.

Answers:

1.	c.	6.	b.	11.	d.
2.	d.	7.	c.	12.	a.
3.	b.	8.	a.	13.	d.
4.	b.	9.	d.	14.	c.
5.	a.	10.	c.		

Income Measurement and Profitability Analysis

LEARNING OBJECTIVES

After studying this chapter, you should be able to:

1. Discuss the general objective of the timing of revenue recognition, list the two general criteria that must be satisfied before revenue can be recognized, and explain why these criteria usually are satisfied at a specific point in time.
2. Describe the installment sales and cost recovery methods of recognizing revenue for some types of installment sales and explain the unusual conditions under which these methods might be used.
3. Discuss the implications for revenue recognition of allowing customers the right of return.
4. Identify situations that call for the recognition of revenue over time and distinguish between the percentage-of-completion and completed contract methods of recognizing revenue for long-term contracts.
5. Discuss the revenue recognition issues involving multiple deliverable contracts, software and franchise sales.
6. Identify and calculate the common ratios used to assess profitability.

CHAPTER HIGHLIGHTS

PART A: REVENUE RECOGNITION

Our objective is to recognize revenue in the period or periods that the revenue-generating activities of the company are performed. But we also must consider that recognizing revenue presumes that an asset (usually cash) has been received or will be received in exchange for the goods or services sold. Our judgment as to the collectibility of the cash from the sale of a product or service will, therefore, impact the timing of revenue recognition. These two concepts of performance and collectibility are captured by the general guidelines for revenue recognition in the realization principle.

The **realization principle** requires that two criteria be satisfied before revenue can be recognized:

1. The earnings process is judged to be complete or virtually complete, (*the earnings process refers to the activity or activities performed by the company to generate revenue*).
2. There is reasonable certainty as to the collectibility of the asset to be received (usually cash).

Revenue often is recognized at a point in time at or near the end of the earnings process. In other situations, revenue is recognized over time.

Premature revenue recognition reduces the quality of reported earnings, particularly if those revenues never materialize. As part of its crackdown on earnings management, the SEC issued *Staff Accounting Bulletin No. 101* summarizing the SEC's views on revenue recognition. The Bulletin provides additional criteria for judging whether or not the realization principle is satisfied:

1. Persuasive evidence of an arrangement exists.
2. Delivery has occurred or services have been rendered.
3. The seller's price to the buyer is fixed or determinable.
4. Collectibility is reasonably assured.

Soon after SAB No. 101 was issued, many companies changed their revenue recognition methods. In most cases, the changes resulted in a deferral of revenue recognition.

Completion of the Earnings Process Within a Single Reporting Period

When Collectibility is Reasonably Certain

For product sales, the product delivery date refers to the date legal title to the product passes from seller to buyer. In most cases, the realization principle criteria are satisfied at this point. The earnings process is virtually complete and the only remaining uncertainty involves the ultimate cash collection. This remaining uncertainty can be accounted for by estimating and recording allowances for possible product returns and for potential bad debts.

Service revenue, too, often is recognized at a point in time if there is one final activity that is deemed critical to the earnings process. In this case, all revenue and costs are deferred until this final activity has been performed. For example, a moving company will pack, load, transport, and deliver household goods for a fixed fee. Although packing, loading, and transporting all are important to the earning process, delivery is the culminating event of the earnings process. So, the entire service fee is recognized as revenue after the goods have been delivered.

Significant Uncertainty of Collectibility

Recognizing revenue at a specific point in time assumes we are able to make reasonable estimates of amounts due from customers that potentially might be uncollectible. For product sales, this also includes amounts not collectible due to customers returning the products they purchased. Otherwise, we would violate one of the requirements of the revenue realization principle we discussed earlier that there must be reasonable certainty as to the collectibility of cash from the customer. There are a few situations when uncertainties could cause a delay in recognizing revenue from a sale of a product or service. One such situation occasionally occurs when products (or services) are sold on an installment basis.

Installment Sales

Revenue recognition for most installment sales takes place at point of delivery, because accurate estimates can be made of potential uncollectible amounts. Two accounting methods, the **installment sales method** and the **cost recovery method** are available for situations where there is significant uncertainty concerning cash collection making it impossible to reasonably estimate bad debts. The installment sales method recognizes revenue and costs only when cash payments are made. The amount of gross profit recognized is determined by multiplying the gross profit percentage (gross profit ÷ by sales price) by the cash collected. The cost recovery method defers all gross profit until cash equal to the cost of the item sold has been received. These methods are sometimes used for **real estate sales**.

ILLUSTRATION

On April 16, 2009, the Aspen Real Estate Company sold land to a developer for $2,000,000. The buyer will make five annual payments of $400,000 plus interest on each April 16, beginning in 2010. Aspen's cost of the land is $800,000. Let's ignore interest charges and concentrate on the recognition of the $1,200,000 gross profit on the sale of land ($2,000,000 – 800,000).

Using **point of delivery** revenue recognition, all of the $1,200,000 in gross profit is recognized in 2009.

Using the **installment sales method**, the gross profit of $1,200,000 represents 60% of the sales price ($1,200,000 ÷ $2,000,000). Therefore, as $400,000 of cash is collected each year beginning in 2010, $240,000 of gross profit is recognized.

Using the **cost recovery method,** no gross profit is recognized until the $800,000 in cost is collected. Therefore, no gross profit is recognized in 2009, 2010 and 2011. Beginning in 2012, 100% of the cash collected is recognized as income.

The following table summarizes gross profit recognition for the three alternatives:

	Point of delivery	Installment Sales Method (60% × cash collection)	Cost Recovery Method
2009	$1,200,000	$ - 0 -	$ - 0 -
2010	- 0 -	240,000	- 0 -
2011	- 0 -	240,000	- 0 -
2012	- 0 -	240,000	400,000
2013	- 0 -	240,000	400,000
2014	- 0 -	240,000	400,000
Totals	$1,200,000	$1,200,000	$1,200,000

Right of Return

When the **right of return** exists, revenue cannot be recognized at the point of delivery unless the seller is able to make reliable estimates of future returns. In most retail situations, even though the right to return merchandise exists, reliable estimates can be made and revenue and costs are recognized at point of delivery. Otherwise, revenue and cost recognition is delayed until such time the uncertainty is resolved. For example, many semiconductor companies delay recognition of revenue until the product is sold by their customer (the distributor) to an end-user.

Consignment Sales

Sometimes a company arranges for another company to sell its product under **consignment.** The "consignor" physically transfers the goods to the other company (the consignee), but the consignor retains legal title. If the consignee can't find a buyer within an agreed-upon time, the consignee returns the goods to the consignor. However, if a buyer is found, the consignee remits the selling price (less commission and approved expenses) to the consignor. Because the consignor retains the risks and rewards of ownership of the product and title does not pass to the consignee, the consignor does not record a sale (revenue and related costs) until the consignee sells the goods and title passes to the eventual customer.

Completion of the Earnings Process Over Multiple Reporting Periods

Service Revenue Earned Over Time

Many service activities encompass some final activity that is deemed critical to the earnings process. In these cases, we recognize revenue when that activity occurs. However, in many instances, service revenue activities occur over extended periods and recognizing revenue at any single date within that period would be inappropriate. Instead, it's more meaningful to recognize revenue over time in proportion to the performance of the activity. Rent revenue is an example.

Long-Term Contracts

Another activity in which it is desirable to recognize revenue over time is one involving a long-term contract. In these cases, it usually is not appropriate to recognize revenue at the delivery point (that is, when the project is completed). This is known as the **completed contract method** of revenue recognition. The problem with this method is that all revenues, expenses, and resulting income from the project are recognized in the period in which the project is completed; no revenues or expenses are reported in the income statements of earlier reporting periods in which much of the work may have been performed.

A more appropriate method of recognizing revenue is the **percentage-of-completion method** which allocates a share of a project's revenue and expenses (revenues less project expenses = gross profit) to each reporting period during the contract period. The allocation is based on progress to date which can be estimated as the proportion of the project's cost incurred to date divided by total estimated costs (cost-to-cost), or by relying on an engineer's or architect's estimate.

For long-term construction contracts, under both methods, the costs of construction are debited to an inventory account, construction in progress. Using the percentage-of-completion method, this account also includes gross profit recognized to date. Also under both methods, progress billings are recorded with a debit to accounts receivable and a credit to **billings on construction contract**. This account is a contra account to construction in progress, and serves to reduce the carrying value of construction in progress by amounts billed to the customer to avoid simultaneously including both the receivable and the inventory on the balance sheet. At the end of each period, the balances in these two accounts are compared. If the net amount is a debit, it is reported in the balance sheet as an asset. Conversely, if the net amount is a credit, it is reported as a liability.

By waiting until the contract is complete, the completed contract method does not properly portray a company's performance over the construction period. The percentage-of-completion method is preferable, and the completed contract method should be used in unusual situations when forecasts of future costs are not dependable.

ILLUSTRATION

In 2009, the Calahan Construction Company contracted to build an office building for $3,000,000. Construction was completed in 2011. Data relating to the contract are as follows ($ in thousands):

	2009	2010	2011
Costs incurred during the year..............................	$ 500	$1,000	$1,050
Estimated costs to complete as of year-end...........	2,000	1,000	-
Billings during the year	400	1,500	1,100
Cash collections during the year...........................	350	1,050	1,600

Calculation of estimated gross profit:

		2009		2010		2011
Contract price		$3,000		$3,000		$3,000
Actual costs to date	$ 500		$1,500		$2,550	
Estimated costs to complete	2,000		1,000		- 0 -	
Total estimated costs		(2,500)		(2,500)		
Estimated gross profit		$ 500		$ 500		
Total actual costs						(2,550)
Actual gross profit						$ 450

Gross profit recognition:

Completed contract method:
  2009: $ - 0 -
  2010: $ - 0 -
  2011:   **$ 450**

Percentage-of-completion method (using cost-to-cost to estimate progress):

2009: $\dfrac{\$500}{\$2,500} = 20\% \times \$500 =$ **$100 gross profit to be recognized in 2009.**

2010: $\dfrac{\$1,500}{\$2,500} = 60\% \times \$500 = \$300 - 100$ (2009 gross profit already recognized) $=$ **$200 gross profit to be recognized in 2010.**

2011: $\$450 - 300$ (2009 and 2010 gross profit) $=$ **$150 gross profit to be recognized in 2011.**

The journal entries to record Calahan's construction project are as follows ($ in thousands):

2009:	Percentage-of-Completion Method		Completed Contract Method	
Construction in progress	500		500	
Cash, materials, etc.		500		500
To record construction costs.				
Accounts receivable	400		400	
Billings on construction contract		400		400
To record progress billings.				
Cash	350		350	
Accounts receivable		350		350
To record cash collection.				
Construction in progress (gross profit)	100		No income recognition	
Cost of construction (expense)	500		until project completion	
Revenue from long-term contracts		600		
To record gross profit.				
(revenue = 20% × $3 million; expense = cost incurred)				
2010:				
Construction in progress	1,000		1,000	
Cash, materials, etc.		1,000		1,000
To record construction costs.				
Accounts receivable	1,500		1,500	
Billings on construction contract		1,500		1,500
To record progress billings.				
Cash	1,050		1,050	
Accounts receivable		1,050		1,050
To record cash collection.				
(note: journal entries continued on next page)				

2010 (continued):	Percentage-of-Completion Method		Completed Contract Method	
Construction in progress (gross profit)	200		No income recognition	
Cost of construction (expense)	1,000		until project completion	
Revenue from long-term contracts		1,200		
To record gross profit.				
(revenue = 60% × $3 million less 2009 revenue;				
expense = cost incurred)				
2011:				
Construction in progress	1,050		1,050	
Cash, materials, etc.		1,050		1,050
To record construction costs.				
Accounts receivable	1,100		1,100	
Billings on construction contract		1,100		1,100
To record progress billings.				
Cash	1,600		1,600	
Accounts receivable		1,600		1,600
To record cash collection.				
Construction in progress (gross profit)	150		450	
Cost of construction (expense)	1,050		2,550	
Revenue from long-term contracts		1,200		3,000
To record gross profit.				
(revenue = $3 million less 2009 and 2010 revenue;			*(All revenue and*	
expense = cost incurred)			*cost recognized)*	
Billings on construction contract	3,000		3,000	
Construction in progress		3,000		3,000
To close accounts once title transfers to the customer.				

The balance sheet presentation for the construction-related accounts for 2009 and 2010 by both methods is as follows:

	2009	2010
Completed contract method:		
Current assets:		
Accounts receivable	$ 50	$ 500
Costs ($500) in excess of billings ($400)	100	
Current liabilities:		
Billings ($1,900) in excess of costs ($1,500)		400
	2009	**2010**
Percentage-of-completion:		
Current assets:		
Accounts receivable	$ 50	$ 500
Costs and profit ($600) in excess of billings ($400)	200	
Current liabilities:		
Billings ($1,900) in excess of costs and profit ($1,800)		100

An estimated **loss** on a long-term contract is fully recognized in the first period the loss is anticipated *regardless of the revenue recognition method used*. In addition, under the percentage-of-completion method, a loss is recognized for profitable contracts whenever previously recognized gross profit exceeds the cumulative gross profit to date.

Industry-Specific Revenue Issues

Software Revenue Recognition and Multiple-Deliverable Contracts

It is not unusual for software companies to sell multiple software deliverables in a bundle for a lump-sum contract price. The bundle often includes product, upgrades, postcontract customer support and other services. The critical accounting question concerns the timing of revenue recognition. The American Institute of Certified Public Accountants (AICPA) has issued Statement of Position (SOP) 97-2 to provide guidance in this area. These statements indicate that if an arrangement includes multiple elements, the revenue from the arrangement should be allocated to the various elements based on the relative fair values of the individual elements, regardless of any separate prices stated within the contract for each element.

More recently, the FASB's Emerging Issues Task Force (EITF) issued EITF 00-21 to broaden the application of this basic perspective to other arrangements that involve "multiple deliverables." In such arrangements, sellers must separately record revenue for a part of an arrangement if, for example, the part has value to the customer on a stand-alone basis and there is objective and reliable evidence of the fair value of the undelivered parts. However, if part of an arrangement does not qualify for separate accounting, recognition of the revenue from that part is delayed until revenue associated with the other parts is recognized. This results in deferring revenue recognition unless parts of an arrangement clearly qualify for separate revenue recognition.

Franchise Sales

The fees to be paid by the franchisee to the franchisor usually comprise: (1) the **initial franchise fee** and (2) **continuing franchise fees.** The services to be performed by the franchisor in exchange for the initial franchise fee include the right to use its name and sell its products. The continuing franchise fees are paid to the franchisor for continuing rights as well as for advertising and promotion and other services provided over the life of the franchise agreement.

The *continuing franchise fees* usually do not present any accounting difficulty and are recognized by the franchisor as revenue in the periods they are received, which correspond to the periods the services are performed by the franchisor.

The *initial franchise fee* is recognized as revenue when the franchisor has *substantially performed* the services promised in the franchise agreement and the collectibility of the fee is *reasonably assured.* This could occur in increments or at one point in time.

PART B: PROFITABILITY ANALYSIS

Chapter 3 provided an overview of financial statement analysis and introduced some of the common ratios used in risk analysis to investigate a company's liquidity and long-term solvency. We now introduce ratios related to profitability analysis.

Activity Ratios

Activity ratios measure a company's efficiency in managing assets. Key activity ratios include (1) **receivables turnover**, (2) **inventory turnover**, and (3) **asset turnover**. These ratios are calculated as follows:

$$\text{Asset turnover ratio} = \frac{\text{Net sales}}{\text{Average total assets}}$$

$$\text{Receivables turnover ratio} = \frac{\text{Net sales}}{\text{Average accounts receivable (net)}}$$

$$\text{Inventory turnover ratio} = \frac{\text{Cost of goods sold}}{\text{Average inventory}}$$

The **asset turnover ratio** measures a company's efficiency using all of its assets to generate revenue. The **receivables turnover ratio** offers an indication of how quickly a company is able to collect its accounts receivable. A convenient extension of the receivables turnover ratio is the **average collection period**. This measure is computed by dividing 365 days by the turnover ratio. The result is an approximation of the number of days the average accounts receivable balance is outstanding. The **inventory turnover ratio** measures a company's efficiency in managing its investment in inventory. Similar to the receivables turnover, we can divide the inventory turnover ratio into 365 days to compute the **average days in inventory**. This measure indicates the number amount of days it normally takes to sell inventory.

Profitability Ratios

Profitability ratios assist in evaluating various aspects of a company's profit-making activities. Three common profitability measures are (1) the **profit margin on sales,** (2) the **return on assets,** and (3) the **return on shareholders' equity.** These ratios are calculated as follows:

Profit margin on sales	$=$	$\dfrac{\text{Net income}}{\text{Net sales}}$
Return on assets	$=$	$\dfrac{\text{Net income}}{\text{Average total assets}}$
Return on shareholders' equity	$=$	$\dfrac{\text{Net income}}{\text{Average shareholders' equity}}$

The **profit margin on sales** measures the amount of net income achieved per sales dollar. **Return on assets** indicates a company's overall profitability by measuring the amount of profit generated by total assets employed. The **return on shareholders' equity** measures the return to suppliers of equity capital.

The DuPont framework provides a convenient framework that breaks return on equity into three key components:

Return on equity $\quad=\quad$ Profit margin $\quad\times\quad$ Asset turnover $\quad\times\quad$ Equity multiplier

ROE :

$$\frac{\text{Net income}}{\text{Ave. total equity}} = \frac{\text{Net income}}{\text{Total sales}} \times \frac{\text{Total sales}}{\text{Ave. total assets}} \times \frac{\text{Ave. total assets}}{\text{Ave. total equity}}$$

ROA is determined by profit margin and asset turnover, so another way to compute ROE is by multiplying return on assets by the equity multiplier:

Return on equity $\quad=\quad$ Return on assets $\quad\times\quad$ Equity multiplier

$$\frac{\text{Net income}}{\text{Ave. total equity}} = \frac{\text{Net income}}{\text{Ave. total assets}} \times \frac{\text{Ave. total assets}}{\text{Ave. total equity}}$$

This version of the DuPont framework that the effect of ROA on ROE depends on how much debt (or leverage) the company has in its capital structure. All else equal, using debt to purchase assets provides more ROA for equity holders.

APPENDIX 5: INTERIM REPORTING

Interim reports are issued for periods of less than a year, typically as quarterly financial statements. Companies registered with the SEC, which include most public companies, must submit quarterly reports. Interim reporting serves to enhance the timeliness of financial information. With only a few exceptions, the same accounting principles applicable to annual reporting are used for interim reporting.

Complete financial statements are not required for interim period reporting. Minimum disclosures include the following:

- Sales, income taxes, extraordinary items, cumulative effect of accounting principle changes, and net income.
- Earnings per share.
- *Seasonal* revenues, costs, and expenses.
- Significant changes in estimates for income taxes.
- Discontinued operations, extraordinary items, and unusual or infrequent items.
- Contingencies.
- Changes in accounting principles or estimates.
- Significant changes in financial positions.

SELF-STUDY QUESTIONS AND EXERCISES

Concept Review

1. The realization principle states that revenue be recognized only after the earnings process is _____ and there is _____ of collection.

2. The product delivery date occurs when _____ to the goods passes from seller to buyer.

3. Revenue recognition is delayed until after the product has been delivered in situations involving significant uncertainty as to the collectibility of the cash to be received, caused either by the possibility of the product being _____ or, with credit sales, the possibility of _____ .

4. The _____ method allocates a share of a long-term project's revenues and expenses to each reporting period during the contract period.

5. The _____ method recognizes gross profit by applying the gross profit percentage on the sale to the amount of cash actually received.

6. The _____ method defers all gross profit recognition until cash equal to the cost of the item sold has been received.

7. Because the return of merchandise can retroactively negate the benefits of having made a sale, several criteria should be satisfied before revenue is recognized in situations when the _____ exists.

8. For a long-term construction project, the completed contract method records all costs of construction in an asset (inventory) account called _____ ; no income is recognized until _____.

9. With the percentage-of-completion method, progress to date usually is assumed to be the proportion of the project's cost incurred to date divided by_____.

10. The completed contract method should be used only in situations where the company is unable to make dependable estimates of _____ necessary to apply the percentage of completion method.

11. The billings on construction contract account is a valuation (contra) account to the asset _____ .

12. Disclosure of the method used to account for long-term contracts will appear in the _____.

13. An estimated loss on a long-term contract is fully recognized in the _____ the loss is anticipated, regardless of the revenue recognition method used.

14. GAAP require that the franchisor has _____ the services promised in the franchise agreement and that the collectibility of the initial franchise fee is before _____ the fee can be recognized as revenue.

15. Activity ratios measure a company's efficiency in managing its _____ .

16. The _____ ratio is calculated by dividing a period's net credit sales by the average net accounts receivable.

17. The _____ indicates the average age of accounts receivables.

18. The _____ ratio shows the number of times the average inventory balance is sold during a reporting period.

19. The _____ ratio measures a company's efficiency using assets to generate revenue.

20. The profit margin on sales measures the amount of net income achieved per _____.

21. The _____ ratio expresses income as a percentage of the average total assets available to generate that income.

22. The return on shareholders' equity ratio is obtained by dividing _____ by average _____ .

Question 23 is based on Appendix 5.

23. _____ reporting serves to enhance the timeliness of financial information.

Answers:
1. virtually complete, reasonable certainty **2.** legal title **3.** returned, bad debts
4. percentage-of-completion method **5.** installment sales **6.** cost recovery **7.** right of return
8. construction in progress, project completion **9.** total estimated costs **10.** future costs
11. construction in progress **12.** summary of significant accounting policies **13.** first period
14. substantially performed, reasonably assured **15.** assets **16.** receivables turnover
17. average collection period **18.** inventory turnover **19.** asset turnover **20.** sales dollar
21. return on assets **22.** net income, shareholders' equity **23.** Interim

REVIEW EXERCISES

Exercise 1
On August 1, 2009, the Slezenger Sporting Goods Company sold inventory to Jack's Golfing Hamlet for $100,000. Terms of the sale called for a down payment of $20,000 and two annual installments of $40,000 due on each August 1, beginning August 1, 2010. Each installment also will include interest on the unpaid balance applying an appropriate interest rate. The inventory cost Foster $60,000.

Required:
1. Compute the amount of gross profit to be recognized from the installment sale in 2009, 2010, and 2011 using point of delivery revenue recognition. Ignore interest charges.

2. Repeat requirement 1 applying the installment sales method.

3. Repeat requirement 1 applying the cost recovery method.

Solution:
Requirement 1

2009:	$40,000 ($100,000 – 60,000)
2010:	- 0 -
2011:	- 0 -

Requirement 2
Gross profit percentage = 40% ($40,000 ÷ $100,000)

2009:	40% × $20,000 = $ 8,000
2010:	40% × $40,000 = $16,000
2011:	40% × $40,000 = $16,000

Requirement 3

2009:	- 0 -
2010:	- 0 -
2011:	$40,000

Exercise 2

In the year 2009 Vitelli Brothers Construction contracted to build an office building for $6,000,000. Data relating to the contract are as follows ($ in thousands):

	2009	2010
Costs incurred during the year....................	$1,000	$3,000
Estimated costs to complete as of year-end	3,000	-
Billings during the year	3,000	3,000
Cash collections during the year.................	2,500	3,500

Required:
1. Determine the gross profit that Vitelli Brothers should recognize in both 2009 and 2010 using (1) the **completed contract method** and (2) the **percentage-of-completion method**.

Completed contract method:

Percentage-of-completion method:

2. Show the **2009** year-end balance sheet presentation for the construction-related accounts by the *percentage-of-completion method* only.

Solution:
Requirement 1
Completed contract method:

2009:	$0
2010:	$2,000 ($6,000 – 4,000)

Percentage-of-completion method:

2009: $\dfrac{\$1,000}{\$4,000} = 25\% \times \$2,000 = \$500$

2010: $2,000 – 500$ (2009 gross profit) = $1,500

Requirement 2

	2009
Current assets:	
Accounts receivable	$ 500
Current liabilities:	
Billings ($3,000) in excess of costs	
and profit ($1,500)	$1,500

Income Measurement and Profitability Analysis

Exercise 3

Financial statements for Kiplinger Corporation for the year 2009 are shown below:

2009 Income Statement

	($ in 000s)
Sales	$6,000
Cost of goods sold	(4,200)
Gross profit	1,800
Operating expenses	(1,100)
Interest expense	(150)
Tax expense	(200)
Net income	$ 350

Comparative Balance Sheets

	December 31 2009	December 31 2008
Assets:		
Cash	$ 500	$ 350
Accounts receivable	500	300
Inventory	600	400
Property, plant, and equipment (net)	1,400	1,350
Total assets	$3,000	$2,400
Liabilities and Shareholders' Equity:		
Current liabilities	$750	$ 500
Bonds payable	1,000	1,000
Paid-in capital	400	400
Retained earnings	850	500
Total liabilities and shareholders' equity	$3,000	$2,400

Required:

Calculate the following ratios for 2009:

1. Inventory turnover ratio

2. Average days in inventory

3. Receivables turnover ratio

4. Average collection period

5. Asset turnover ratio

6. Profit margin on sales

7. Return on assets

8. Equity multiplier

9. Return on shareholders' equity

10. Use the DuPont framework to show return on shareholders' equity as a function of profit margin, asset turnover and equity multiplier.

Income Measurement and Profitability Analysis

Solution:

1.	Inventory turnover ratio	$4,200 \div ([\$600 + 400] \div 2) = 8.4$
2.	Average days in inventory	$365 \div 8.4 = 43.45$ days
3.	Receivables turnover ratio	$6,000 \div ([\$500 + 300] \div 2) = 15.0$
4.	Average collection period	$365 \div 15.0 = 24.33$ days
5.	Asset turnover ratio	$6,000 \div ([\$3,000 + 2,400] \div 2) = 2.22$
6.	Profit margin on sales	$350 \div \$6,000 = 5.83\%$
7.	Return on assets	$350 \div ([\$3,000 + 2,400] \div 2) = 12.96\%$
8.	Equity multiplier	$([\$3,000 + 2,400] \div 2) / ([\$1,250 + 900] \div 2) = 2.51$
9.	Return on shareholders' equity	$350 \div ([\$1,250 + 900] \div 2) = 32.56\%$
10.	DuPont framework	$32.5\% = 5.83\% \times 2.22 \times 2.51$

MULTIPLE CHOICE

Enter the letter corresponding to the response that **best** completes each of the following statements or questions.

_____ 1. In general, revenue is recognized as earned when there is reasonable certainty as to the collectibility of the asset to be received and:
   a. The sales price has been collected.
   b. The earnings process is virtually complete.
   c. Production is completed.
   d. A purchase order has been received.

_____ 2. Western Appliance Company, which began business on January 1, 2009, appropriately uses the installment sales method of accounting. The following data are available for 2009:

Installment sales	$350,000
Cash collections on installment sales	150,000
Gross profit on sales	40%

The **gross profit** on installment sales for 2009 should be:

	Realized	**Deferred**
a.	$60,000	$80,000
b.	$80,000	$60,000
c.	$140,000	$80,000
d.	$140,000	60,000

_____3. The Pattison Company began operations on January 2, 2009, and appropriately uses the installment sales method of accounting. The following data are available for 2009 and 2010:

	2009	2010
Installment sales	$600,000	$750,000
Cash collections from:		
2009 sales	200,000	250,000
2010 sales		300,000
Gross profit on sales	30%	40%

The **deferred gross profit** that would appear in the 2010 balance sheet is:
a. $180,000
b. $200,000
c. $285,000
d. $225,000

_____4. For profitable long-term contracts, income is recognized in each year under the:

	Completed contract method	Percentage-of-completion method
a.	No	No
b.	Yes	No
c.	Yes	Yes
d.	No	Yes

_____5. When accounting for a long-term construction contract using the percentage-of-completion method, gross profit is recognized in any year is debited to:
a. Construction in progress.
b. Billings on construction contract
c. Deferred income
d. Accounts receivable

_____6. Hollywood Construction Company uses the percentage-of-completion method of accounting for long-term construction contracts. During 2009, Hollywood began work on a $3,000,000 fixed-fee construction contract, which was completed in 2012. The accounting records disclosed the following data at year-end:

	Cumulative contract costs incurred	Estimated costs to complete at end of year
2009	$ 200,000	$1,800,000
2010	1,100,000	1,100,000
2011	2,000,000	400,000

For the 2011 year, Hollywood should have recognized gross profit on this contract of:
   a. $100,000
   b. $500,000
   c. $266,667
   d. $225,000

_____ 7. Sandlewood Construction Inc. uses the percentage-of-completion method of accounting for long-term construction contracts. In 2009, Sandlewood began work on a $10,000,000 construction contract, which was completed in 2010. The accounting records disclosed the following data at the end of 2009:

Costs incurred	$5,400,000
Estimated cost to complete	3,600,000
Progress billings	4,100,000
Cash collections	3,200,000

How much gross profit should Sandlewood have recognized in 2009?
   a. $700,000
   b. $1,000,000
   c. $600,000
   d. $0

_____ 8. Based on the same data in question 7, in addition to accounts receivable, what would appear in the 2009 balance sheet related to the construction accounts?
   a.   A current asset of $1,300,000
   b.   A current liability of $900,000
   c.   A current asset of $900,000
   d.   A current asset of $1,900,000

_____ 9. The Simpson Construction Company uses the percentage-of-completion method of accounting for long-term construction contracts. In 2009, Simpson began work on a construction contract. Information on this contract at the end of 2009 is as follows:

Cost incurred during the year	$1,500,000
Estimated additional cost to complete	6,000,000
Gross profit recognized in 2009	250,000

What is the contract price (total revenue) on this contract?
   a. $7,000,000
   b. $8,750,000
   c. $7,500,000
   d. $9,000,000

_____10. Smith Company earns a 12% return on assets. If net income is $720,000, average total assets must be:
   a. $86,400
   b. $6,000,000
   c. $6,086,400
   d. $3,000,000

_____11. The Esquire Company reported sales of $1,600,000 and cost of goods sold of $1,122,000 for the year ended December 31, 2009. Ending inventory for 2008 and 2009 was $420,000 and $460,000, respectively. Esquire's inventory turnover for 2009 is:
   a. 2.44
   b. 2.55
   c. 3.64
   d. 3.48

The following data for the McQuire Corporation apply to questions 12 and 13:

Income statement:	**2009**	
Sales	$2,500,000	
Cost of goods sold	1,300,000	
Net income	200,000	

Balance sheets:	**2009**	**2008**
Accounts receivable	$ 300,000	$ 200,000
Total assets	2,000,000	1,800,000
Total shareholders' equity	900,000	700,000

_____12. The accounts receivable turnover for 2009 is:
   a. 10.0
   b. 8.33
   c. 5.2
   d. 4.33

_____13. The return on shareholders' equity for 2009 is:
   a. 20%
   b. 8%
   c. 22.22%
   d. 25%

Question 14 is based on Appendix 5.

_____14. Which of the following is **not** a required disclosure for interim period reporting?
    a.   Earnings per share.
    b.   Extraordinary items.
    c.   General and administrative expenses.
    d.   Sales.

Answers:

1.	b.	6.	a.	11.	b.
2.	a.	7.	c.	12.	a.
3.	d.	8.	d.	13.	d.
4.	d.	9.	b.	14.	c.
5.	a.	10.	b.		

Time Value of Money Concepts

LEARNING OBJECTIVES

After studying this chapter, you should be able to:
1. Explain the difference between simple and compound interest.
2. Compute the future value of a single amount.
3. Compute the present value of a single amount.
4. Solve for either the interest rate or the number of compounding periods when present value and future value of a single amount are known.
5. Explain the difference between an ordinary annuity and an annuity due situation.
6. Compute the future value of both an ordinary annuity and an annuity due.
7. Compute the present value of an ordinary annuity, an annuity due, and a deferred annuity.
8. Solve for unknown values in annuity situations involving present value.
9. Briefly describe how the concept of the time value of money is incorporated into the valuation of bonds, long-term leases, and pension obligations.

CHAPTER HIGHLIGHTS

PART A: BASIC CONCEPTS

The **time value of money** means that money can be invested today to earn interest and grow to a larger dollar amount in the future. **Interest** is the rent paid for the use of money for some period of time. For example, if you invested $10,000 today in a savings account, it would grow to a larger dollar amount in the future.

Future Value of a Single Amount

Simple interest is computed by multiplying the initial investment times both the applicable interest rate and the period of time for which the money is used. For example, if the $10,000 above were invested in a savings account at *10%* for *one year*, the *interest* would be $10,000 × 10%, or $1,000. This interest would increase the investment to $11,000, referred to as the **future value** of $10,000 invested at 10% for 1 year.

Compound interest includes interest not only on the initial investment but also on the accumulated interest in previous periods. As shown above, the future value of $10,000 invested at 10% for *one* year is $10,000 × (1.10), or $11,000. If invested for *two* years, the future value is $10,000 × (1.10) × (1.10), or $12,100, and if invested for three years, the future value is $10,000 × (1.10) × (1.10) × (1.10), or $13,310. The future value of any amount invested for *n* periods at interest rate *I* is computed as that amount times $(1+i)^n$.

Table 1, located at the back of the text, contains the future value (**FV**) of $1 invested for various periods of time, *n*, and at various rates, *i*. The future value of any invested amount, I, can be easily determined by multiplying that amount by the table value. For example, in the 10% column (*i* = 10%) and 3 period row (*n* = 3), Table 1 shows the future value of $1 to be 1.331. Multiplying this future value by $10,000 yields $13,310:

$$FV = I \times FV \text{ factor}$$
$$FV = \$10,000 \times 1.331^* = \$13,310$$

* Future value of $1: *n* = 3, *i* = 10% (from Table 1)

Present Value of a Single Amount

Because the future value of a present amount is the present amount *times* $(1 + i)^n$, logically, then, that computation can be reversed to find the *present value* of a future amount to be the future amount *divided by* $(1 + i)^n$. In the future value formula, FV + I × $(1+i)^n$, we substitute present value (**PV**) for I (invested amount) and solve for PV:

$$PV = \frac{FV}{(1+i)^n}$$

In our example,

$$PV = \frac{\$13,310}{(1+.10)^3} = \frac{\$13,310}{1.331} = \$10,000$$

As with future value, these computations are simplified by using present value tables. Of course, dividing by $(1 + i)^n$ is the same as multiplying by its reciprocal, $\frac{1}{(1+i)^n}$. Table 6 in the text provides the solutions of $\frac{1}{(1+i)^n}$ for various interest rates (*i*) and compounding periods (*n*). These amounts represent the present value (PV) of $1 to be received at the *end* of the different periods. The present value factor for *i* = 10% and *n* = 3 is .75131 and we can simply multiply this amount by future value to determine present value:

$$PV = FV \times PV \text{ factor}$$
$$PV = \$13,310 \times .75131^* = \$10,000$$

* Present value of $1: *n*=3, *i*=10% (from Table 2)

Graphically, the relation between the present value and the future value can be viewed this way:

	End of year 1	End of year 2	End of year 3
0			

$1,000 $1,100 $1,210

$10,000 $13,310

PV _____ FV

To better understand the relationship between future value and present value, consider the following two illustrations:

ILLUSTRATION

FUTURE VALUE

Assume you deposit $10,000 in a savings account that pays 8% interest at the end of each year. What will be your account balance after 3 years?

> **Computation:**
>
> $$FV = \underset{\substack{\text{invested} \\ \text{amount}}}{\$10,000} \times 1.25971^* = \$12,597 \text{ (rounded)}$$
>
> * Future value of $1: $n = 3$, $i = 8\%$ (from Table 1)

The accuracy of this computation is shown in the following demonstration:

Date	Interest	Year-end Balance
Initial deposit		$10,000
Year 1	$10,000 × 8% = $800	10,800
Year 2	10,800 × 8% = $864	11,664
Year 3	11,664 × 8% = $933 (rounded)	12,597

ILLUSTRATION

PRESENT VALUE

Assume you are offered an automobile for which the salesperson says you can pay $12,597, at the end of three years. This amount includes interest at 8% annually. What price would you be paying for the automobile if you accept the offer?

Computation:

$$PV = \$12,597 \times .79383^* = \$10,000 \text{ (rounded)}$$

future

amount

* Present value of $1: $n = 3$, $i = 8\%$ (from Table 2)

The $12,597 you would be paying for the $10,000 automobile includes $2,597 for three years' interest at 8%.

In some situations, the interest rate or the number of periods may be the unknown value. The solution requires that the *future value* be divided by the *present value* (or vice versa) to derive a table value. Locating this table value in Table 1 (or Table 2) relative to the known value, n or i, determines the corresponding unknown value, n or i.

Expected Cash Flow Approach

Present value measurement has long been integrated with accounting valuation and is specifically addressed in several accounting standards. SFAC No. 7 provides a framework for using future cash flows as the basis for accounting measurement and asserts that the objective in valuing an asset or liability using present value is to approximate the fair value of that asset or liability. Key to that objective is determining the present value of future cash flows associated with the asset or liability, *taking into account any uncertainty concerning the amounts and timing of the cash flows.* Although future cash flows in many instances are contractual and certain, the amounts and timing of cash flows are less certain in other situations.

Traditionally, the way uncertainty has been considered in present value calculations has been by discounting the "best estimate" of future cash flows applying a discount rate that has been adjusted to reflect the uncertainty or risk of those cash flows. With the approach described by SFAC No. 7 the adjustment for uncertainty or risk of cash flows is applied to the cash flows, not the discount rate. This *expected cash flow approach* incorporates specific probabilities of cash flows into the analysis.

ILLUSTRATION

EXPECTED CASH FLOW APPROACH

Trident Exploration Corporation faces the likelihood of having to pay an uncertain amount in four years for the restoration of land in connection with a mining operation. The future cash flow estimate is in the range of $130 million to $240 million with the following estimated probabilities:

Loss amount	Probability
$130 million	30%
$200 million	45%
$240 million	25%

Computation:

The expected cash flow is $189 million:

$130 × 30% = $ 39 million
200 × 45% = 90 million
240 × 25% = 60 million
$189 million

Assuming a risk-free interest rate of 6%, Trident Exploration would report a liability for the expected restoration costs of $149.7 million, the present value of the expected cash outflow:

$189 million × .79209* = $149.7 million

* Present value of $1, $n = 4$, $i = 6\%$ (from Table 2)

PART B: BASIC ANNUITIES

An **annuity** is a series of equal-sized cash flows occurring over equal intervals of time. In an **ordinary annuity** cash flows occur at the *end* of each period. In an **annuity due**, cash flows occur at the *beginning* of each period. The following time diagrams illustrate the distinction between an ordinary annuity and an annuity due for a three-period, $10,000 annuity beginning on 1/1/09. This annuity is then used to illustrate future and present values of annuities.

	1/1/09	12/31/09	12/31/10	12/31/11
Ordinary Annuity				
		$10,000 1st payment	$10,000 2nd payment	$10,000 3rd payment

	1/1/09	12/31/09	12/31/10	12/31/11
Annuity Due				
	$10,000 1st payment	$10,000 2nd payment	$10,000 3rd payment	

Future Value of an Ordinary Annuity

Table 3 in the text contains the future values of ordinary annuities (**FVA**) of $1 invested at the *end* of n periods at various interest rates, i. The future value of the $10,000 annuity depicted in the ordinary annuity graph above is calculated as follows, assuming an interest rate of 10%:

$$\text{FVA} = \underset{\substack{\text{annuity} \\ \text{amount}}}{\$10,000} \times 3.31^*$$

* Future value of an ordinary annuity of $1: $n = 3$, $i = 10\%$ (from Table 3)

$$\text{FVA} = \$33,100$$

If you deposited $10,000 at the *end* of *each* of three years in a savings account paying 10% annually, the account balance at the end of the three years would grow to $33,100. Of course, since the third deposit is made on the last day of year three, it earns no interest. This can be seen by determining the total future value by calculating the future value of each of the individual deposits as follows:

	Deposit		FV of $1 $i=10\%$		Future Value (at the end of year 3)	n
First deposit	$10,000	×	1.21	=	$12,100	2
Second deposit	10,000	×	1.10	=	11,000	1
Third deposit	10,000	×	1.00	=	10,000	0
	Total		3.31		$33,100	

Future Value of an Annuity Due

Table 5 in the text contains the future values of annuities due (**FVAD**) of $1 invested at the *beginning* of n periods at various interest rates, i. The future value of the $10,000 annuity depicted in the annuity due graph above is calculated as follows, assuming an interest rate of 10%:

$$\text{FVAD} = \underset{\substack{\text{annuity} \\ \text{amount}}}{\$10,000} \times 3.641^{*}$$

* Future value of an annuity due of $1: $n = 3$, $i = 10\%$ (from Table 5)

$$\text{FVAD} = \$36,410$$

The account balance at the end of three years, the future value, is higher than in the ordinary annuity case because the deposits are made at the beginning of the year thus earning higher interest. This same amount can be determined by calculating the future value of each of the individual deposits as follows:

	Deposit		FV of $1 $i=10\%$		Future Value (at the end of year 3)	n
First deposit	$10,000	×	1.331	=	$13,310	3
Second deposit	10,000	×	1.210	=	12,100	2
Third deposit	10,000	×	1.100	=	11,000	1
	Total		3.641		$36,410	

Present Value of an Ordinary Annuity

Table 4 in the text contains the present values of ordinary annuities (**PVA**) of $1 invested at the *end* of n periods at various interest rates, i. The present value of the $10,000 annuity depicted in the ordinary annuity graph above is calculated as follows, assuming an interest rate of 10%:

$$\text{PVA} = \underset{\substack{\text{annuity} \\ \text{amount}}}{\$10,000} \times 2.48685^{*}$$

* Present value of an ordinary annuity of $1: $n = 3$, $i = 10\%$ (from Table 4)

$$\text{PVA} = \$24,868.50$$

The present value can be interpreted as the amount you would need to deposit into a savings account today, earning 10% annually, in order to *withdraw* $10,000 from the account at the *end* of each of the next three years. This same total present value can be determined by calculating the present value of each of the individual withdrawals as follows:

	Withdrawal		PV of $1 i=10%		Present Value (at the beginning of year 1)	n
First withdrawal	$10,000	×	.90909	=	$ 9,090.90	1
Second withdrawal	10,000	×	.82645	=	8,264.50	2
Third withdrawal	10,000	×	.75131	=	7,513.10	3
	Total		2.48685		$24,868.50	

Table 2

Present Value of an Annuity Due

Table 6 in the text contains the present values of annuities due **(PVAD)** of $1 invested at the *beginning* of n periods at various interest rates, i. The present value of the $10,000 annuity depicted in the annuity due graph above is calculated as follows, assuming an interest rate of 10%:

$$\text{PVAD} = \underset{\substack{\text{annuity} \\ \text{amount}}}{\$10,000} \times 2.73554^{*}$$

[*] Present value of an annuity due of $1: $n = 3$, $i = 10\%$ (from Table 6)

$$\text{PVAD} = \$27,355.40$$

The present value can be interpreted as the amount you would need to deposit into a savings account today, earning 10% compounded annually, in order to withdraw $10,000 from the account at the *beginning* of each of the next three years. This same present value can be determined by calculating the present value of each of the individual withdrawals as follows:

	Withdrawal		PV of $1 i=10%		Present Value (at the beginning of year 1)	n
First withdrawal	$10,000	×	1.00000	=	$10,000.00	0
Second withdrawal	10,000	×	.90909	=	9,090.90	1
Third withdrawal	10,000	×	.82645	=	8,264.50	2
	Total		2.73554		$27,355.40	

Table 2

To better understand the relationship between *future* value and *present* value and between an *ordinary* annuity and an annuity *due*, consider the following illustrations.

ILLUSTRATION

FUTURE VALUE OF AN ORDINARY ANNUITY

Assume that you deposit $10,000 at the *end* of each of the next five years to a savings account that pays annual interest at the rate of 8% annually. What will be your account balance at the end of the five-year period?

Computation:

$$FVA = \underset{\substack{\text{invested} \\ \text{amount}}}{\$10,000} \times 5.8666^* = \$58,666$$

* Future value of an ordinary annuity of $1: $n = 5$, $i = 8\%$ (from Table 3)

ILLUSTRATION

FUTURE VALUE OF AN ANNUITY DUE

Assume your annual deposits in the previous illustration are made at the *beginning* of each year. What will be your account balance at the end of the five-year period?

Computation:

$$FVAD = \underset{\substack{\text{invested} \\ \text{amount}}}{\$10,000} \times 6.3359^* = \$63,359$$

* Future value of an annuity due of $1: $n = 5$, $i = 8\%$ (from Table 5)

Notice that the account balance in this illustration is greater than in the previous illustration. This is due to the fact that deposits are made sooner, and thus earn interest for a longer period of time.

ILLUSTRATION

PRESENT VALUE OF AN ORDINARY ANNUITY

Assume that a friend offered to sell you a lakeside cabin in exchange for five, $10,000 installment payments to be made at the *end* of each of the next five years. These payments include interest at 8%. What price would you be paying for the cabin?

Computation:

$$\text{PVA} = \underset{\substack{\text{annuity} \\ \text{amount}}}{\$10,000} \times 3.99271^* = \$39,927 \text{ (rounded)}$$

* Present value of an ordinary annuity of $1: $n = 5$, $i = 8\%$ (from Table 4)

Since you would pay $50,000 over the five years for the $39,927 cabin, the remaining $10,073 represents interest paid for financing the purchase over the five years.

ILLUSTRATION

PRESENT VALUE OF AN ANNUITY DUE

Assume your installment payments in the previous illustration are made at the *beginning* of each year. What would be the price of the cabin?

Computation:

$$\text{PVAD} = \underset{\substack{\text{annuity} \\ \text{amount}}}{\$10,000} \times 4.31213^* = \$43,121 \text{ (rounded)}$$

* Present value of an annuity due of $1: $n = 5$, $i = 8\%$ (from Table 6)

Notice that the price of the cabin in this illustration is greater than in the previous illustration. This is due to the fact that payments are made sooner and thus you are giving up more.

Present Value of a Deferred Annuity

A deferred annuity exists when the first cash flow occurs more than one period after the date the agreement begins. The following time diagram depicts a situation where a three-period, $10,000 annuity agreement begins on 1/1/09 requiring annual cash flows to begin on 12/31/11:

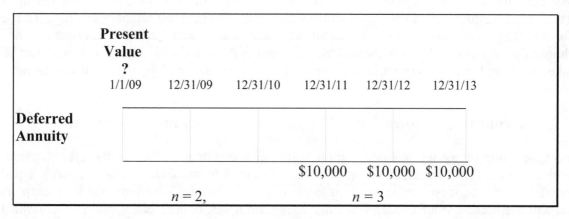

The present value of this annuity can be calculated numerous ways. For example, we could sum the present values of the three individual cash flows each discounted to 1/1/09. Or, a more efficient way involves a two-step process that first calculates the present value of the annuity as of the beginning of the annuity period (12/31/10) and then discounts this single amount to its present value as of today (1/1/09). Assuming an interest rate of 10%, this two-step process determines the present value to be $20,553:

$$\text{PVA} \quad = \quad \underset{\substack{\text{annuity} \\ \text{amount}}}{\$10,000} \quad \times \quad 2.48685^* \quad = \quad \$24,868.50$$

* Present value of an ordinary annuity of $1: $n = 3$, $i = 10\%$ (from Table 4)

This is the present value as of *December 31, 2010*. This single amount is then reduced to present value as of January 1, 2009, by making the following calculation:

$$\text{PV} \quad = \quad \underset{\substack{\text{future} \\ \text{amount}}}{\$24,868.50} \quad \times \quad .82645^* \quad = \quad \$20,553 \text{ (rounded)}$$

* Present value of $1: $n = 2$, $i = 10\%$ (from Table 2)

In some cases, the present value (or future value) is known and the annuity payments are to be determined. For example, in a later chapter you will determine the lease payments required in each of a specified number of periods to recover a specified investment, a present value. In these cases, the known present value (or future value) is *divided by* the table value (for the appropriate number of periods and the appropriate interest rate) to derive the required periodic payments. In other situations, the interest rate or the number of periods may be the unknown value. The solution requires that the present value (or future value) be divided by the *payment amount* to derive a table value. Locating this table value in Table 4 (or Table 3) relative to the known value, n or i, determines the corresponding unknown value, n or i.

Financial Calculators and Excel

Financial calculators can be used to solve future and present value problems. Also, many professionals choose to use spreadsheet software, such as Excel, to solve time value of money problems. These spreadsheets can be used in a variety of ways. A template can be created using the formulas or you can use the software's built-in financial functions. For example, Excel has a function called PV that calculates the present value of an ordinary annuity. To use the function, you would select the pull-down menu for "Insert," click on "Function" and choose the category called "Financial." Scroll down to PV and double click. You will then be asked to input the necessary variables - interest rate, the number of periods, and the payment amount

Accounting Applications of Present Value Techniques - Annuities

The time value of money has many applications in accounting. Most of these applications involve the concept of present value. Because financial instruments typically specify equal periodic payments, these applications quite often involve annuity situations. In later chapters you will use present value concepts to value long-term notes, bonds, leases, and postretirement obligations.

Summary

The following table summarizes the time value of money concepts discussed in Chapter 6:

Concept	Summary	Formula	Table
Future value (FV) of $1	The amount of money that a dollar will grow to at some point in the future	$FV = \$1(1 + i)^n$	1
Present value (PV) of $1	The amount of money today that is equivalent to a given amount to be received or paid in the future	$PV = \dfrac{\$1}{(1 + i)^n}$	2
Future value of an ordinary annuity (FVA) of $1	The future value of a series of equal-sized cash flows with the first payment taking place at the end of the first compounding period	$FVA = \dfrac{(1+i)^n - 1}{i}$	3
Present value of an ordinary annuity (PVA) of $1	The present value of a series of equal-sized cash flows with the first payment taking place at the end of the first compounding period	$PVA = \dfrac{1 - \dfrac{1}{(1+i)^n}}{i}$	4
Future value of an annuity due (FVAD) of $1	The future value of a series of equal-sized cash flows with the first payment taking place at the beginning of the annuity period	$FVAD = \left[\dfrac{(1+i)^n - 1}{i}\right] \times (1+i)$	5
Present value of an annuity due (PVAD) of $1	The present value of a series of equal sized-cash flows with the first payment taking place at the beginning of the annuity period	$PVAD = \left[\dfrac{1 - \dfrac{1}{(1+i)^n}}{i}\right] \times (1+i)$	6

SELF-STUDY QUESTIONS AND EXERCISES

Concept Review

1. The _____ of money means that money can be invested today to earn interest and grow to a larger dollar amount in the future.

2. _____ is the amount of money paid or received in excess of the amount borrowed or lent.

3. _____ interest is computed by multiplying an initial investment times both the applicable interest rate and the period of time for which the money is used.

4. _____ interest includes interest not only on the initial investment but also on the accumulated interest in previous periods.

5. The _____ is the rate at which money actually will grow during a full year.

6. The _____ value of a single amount is the amount of money that a dollar will grow to at some point in the future.

7. The _____ value of a single amount is today's equivalent to a particular amount in the future.

8. The calculation of future value requires the _____ of interest, while the calculation of present value requires the _____ of interest.

9. _____ include money and claims to receive money, the amount of which is fixed or determinable.

10. _____ are obligations to pay amounts of cash, the amount of which is fixed or determinable.

11. The _____ approach incorporates specific probabilities of cash flows into a present value calculation.

12. An _____ is a series of equal sized cash flows occurring over equal intervals of time.

13. In an ordinary annuity cash flows occur at the _____ of each period.

14. In an annuity due cash flows occur at the _____ of each period.

15. In the future value of an ordinary annuity, the _____ cash payment will not earn any interest.

16. In the present value of an annuity due, no interest needs to be removed from the _____ cash payment.

17. A _____ annuity exists when the first cash flow occurs more than one period after the date the agreement begins.

18. In situations requiring the determination of the unknown annuity *amount*, we divide the _____ by the _____.

19. For long-term leases, we calculate present value to remove the portion of the payments that represents interest, leaving the portion that represents payment for the _____.

20. Valuing pension obligations involves calculating a _____ annuity.

Answers:
1. time value **2.** Interest **3.** Simple **4.** Compound **5.** effective yield **6.** future **7.** present **8.** addition, removal **9.** Monetary assets **10.** Monetary liabilities **11.** expected cash flow **12.** annuity **13.** end **14.** beginning **15.** last **16.** first **17.** deferred **18.** present value, annuity factor **19.** asset **20.** deferred

REVIEW EXERCISES

Exercise 1
Using the appropriate table located at the back of the text, answer each of the following independent questions:

1. What is the future value of $5,000 three years from now invested at 9%?

2. What is the future value of an annuity of $4,000 invested at the *beginning* of each of the next three periods at 6% interest?

3. What is the present value of $20,000 to be received five years from now assuming an interest rate of 10%?

4. What is the present value of an annuity of $6,000 to be received at the *end* of each of the next 10 years assuming an interest rate of 10%?

Solution:

1. $\text{FV} = \$5,000\,(1.29503^*) = \$6,475$

   * Future value of $1: n=3, i=9\% (from Table 1)

2. $\text{FVAD} = \$4,000\,(3.3746^*) = \$13,498$

   * Future value of an annuity due of $1: n=3, i=6\% (from Table 5)

3. $\text{PV} = \$20,000\,(.62092^*) = \$12,418$

   * Present value of $1: n=5, i=10\% (from Table 2)

4. $\text{PVA} = \$6,000\,(6.14457^*) = \$36,867$

   * Present value of an ordinary annuity of $1: n=10, i=10\% (from Table 4)

Exercise 2

Larry Dobby wants to accumulate $80,000 to be used for his daughter's college education. He would like to have the amount available on December 31, 2015. Assume that the funds will accumulate in a certificate of deposit paying 7% interest compounded annually.

Required:

Answer each of the following independent questions:

1. If Larry were to deposit a single amount, how much would he have to invest on December 31, 2009?

2. If Larry were to make six equal deposits on each December 31, beginning on December 31, 2010, what is the required deposit?

3. If Larry were to make six equal deposits on each December 31, beginning on December 31, 2009, what is the required deposit?

Solution:

1. PV = $80,000 (.66634*) = $53,307
    * Present value of $1: n=6, i=7% (from Table 2)

2. Annuity amount = $\dfrac{\$80,000}{7.1533^*}$
    * Future value of an ordinary annuity of $1: n=6, i=7% (from Table 3)

    Annuity amount = $11,184

3. Annuity amount = $\dfrac{\$80,000}{7.6540^*}$
    * Future value of an annuity due of $1: n=6, i=7% (from Table 5)

    Annuity amount = $10,452

Exercise 3

Lucy and Vinnie Esposito purchased a new automobile for $16,000. They made a down payment of $4,000 and agreed to pay the remaining amount in four, equal annual installments beginning one year from today. Assuming an interest rate of 8%, calculate the amount of the required annual installment payment.

Solution:

$16,000 – 4,000 = $12,000 = Present value of annuity payments

Annuity amount = $\dfrac{\$12,000}{3.31213^*}$
* Present value of an ordinary annuity of $1: n=4, i=8% (from Table 4)

Annuity amount = $3,623

MULTIPLE CHOICE

Enter the letter corresponding to the response that **best** completes each of the following statements or questions.

_____ 1. The Sanchez Company purchased a delivery truck on February 1, 2009. The purchase agreement required Sanchez to pay the total amount due of $15,000 on February 1, 2010. Assuming an 8% rate of interest, the calculation of the price of the truck would involve multiplying $15,000 by the:
   a. Future value of an ordinary annuity of $1.
   b. Present value of $1.
   c. Present value of an ordinary annuity of $1.
   d. Future value of $1.

_____ 2. Sandra wants to calculate how much money she needs to deposit today into a savings account which earns 5% in order to be able to withdraw $3,000 at the end of each of the next 6 years. She should use which present value concept?
   a. Present value of $1 for 6 periods.
   b. Present value of an annuity due of $1 for 6 periods.
   c. Present value of an ordinary annuity of $1 for 6 periods.
   d. Future value of $1 for 6 periods.

_____ 3. The Richards Company purchased a machine for $5,000 down and $300 a month payable at the end of each of the next 36 months. How would the cash price of the machine be calculated, assuming the annual interest rate is given?
   a. $5,000 plus the present value of $10,800 ($300 × 36).
   b. $5,000 plus the present value of an annuity due of $300 for 36 periods.
   c. $15,800.
   d. $5,000 plus the present value of an ordinary annuity of $300 for 36 periods.

_____ 4. Given a set of present value tables, an annual interest rate, the dollar amount of equal payments made, and the number of semiannual payments, what other information is necessary to calculate the *present value* of the series of payments?
   a. The future value of the annuity.
   b. The timing of the payments (whether they are at the beginning or end of the period).
   c. The rate of inflation.
   d. No other information is required.

_____ 5. Wellman Company is considering investing in a two-year project. Wellman's required rate of return is 10%. The present value of $1 for one period at 10% is .909 and for two periods at 10% is .826. The project is expected to create cash flows, net of taxes, of $80,000 in the first year, and $100,000 in the second year. Wellman should invest in the project if the project's cost is less than or equal to:
   a. $180,000
   b. $163,620
   c. $155,320
   d. $148,680

_____ 6. The Bello Corporation wishes to accumulate $2,000,000 for plant expansion. The funds are required on January 1, 2014. Bello intends to make five equal annual deposits in a fund that will earn interest at 7% compounded annually. The first deposit is made on January 1, 2009. Present value and future value facts are as follows:

Present value of $1 at 7% for 5 periods   .713
Present value of an ordinary annuity of $1 at 7% for 5 periods   4.10
Future value of an ordinary annuity of $1 at 7% for 5 periods   5.75
Future value of an annuity due of $1 at 7% for 5 periods   6.15

What is the amount of the required annual deposit?
a. $325,203
b. $347,826
c. $487,805
d. $426,000

_____ 7. The Jamison Corporation agrees to pay an employee $10,000 a year for five years beginning three years from today and decides to fund the payments by depositing one lump sum in a savings account today. The company should use which present value concept to determine the required deposit?
a. Future value of $1.
b. Present value of a deferred annuity.
c. Future value of a deferred annuity.
d. None of the above.

_____ 8. Harry Morgan plans to make 30 quarterly deposits of $200 into a savings account. The first deposit will be made immediately. The savings account pays interest at an annual rate of 8%, compounded quarterly. How much will Harry have accumulated in the savings account at the end of the seven and a half-year period? (Use the appropriate table in the text.)
a. $ 8,114
b. $24,469
c. $ 6,000
d. $ 8,276

_____ 9. Assume the same data as in question 8, except that Harry will make the quarterly deposits at the end of the quarter. How much will Harry have accumulated in the savings account at the end of the seven and a half-year period? (Use the appropriate table in the text.)
a. $ 8,114
b. $24,469
c. $ 6,000
d. $ 8,276

_____10. The Strug Company purchased office furniture and equipment for $8,600 and agreed to pay for the purchase by making five annual installment payments beginning one year from today. The installment payments include interest at 8%. What is the required annual installment payment? (Use the appropriate table in the text.)
   a. $1,720
   b. $2,154
   c. $1,994
   d. $1,466

_____11. Assume the same data as in question 10, except that the installment payments begin immediately. What is the required annual installment payment? (Use the appropriate table in the text.)
   a. $1,720
   b. $2,154
   c. $1,994
   d. $1,466

_____12. On March 31, 2009, the Freeman Company leased a machine. The lease agreement requires Freeman to pay 10 annual payments of $6,000 on each March 31, with the first payment due on March 31, 2009. Assuming an interest rate of 10% and that this lease is treated as an installment sale, Freeman will initially value the machine by multiplying $6,000 by which of the following factors?
   a. Present value of $1 at 10% for 10 periods.
   b. Present value of an ordinary annuity of $1 at 10% for 10 periods.
   c. Present value of an annuity due of $1 at 10% for 10 periods.
   d. Future value of an annuity due of $1 at 10% for 10 periods.

_____13. The Stacey Mack Corporation used the expected cash flow approach to determine the present value of a future obligation to be paid in four years. Estimated future payment possibilities were as follows:

Possible payment	Probability
$50 million	20%
70 million	40%
90 million	40%

The risk-free interest rate is 5%. What is the estimated present value of the future obligation?
   a. $57.589 million.
   b. $60.880 million.
   c. $74.043 million.
   d. $70 million.

Time Value of Money Concepts

Answers:

1.	b.	6.	a.	11.	c.
2.	c.	7.	b.	12.	c.
3.	d.	8.	d.	13.	b.
4.	b.	9.	a.		
5.	c.	10.	b.		

Cash and Receivables

LEARNING OBJECTIVES

After studying this chapter, you should be able to:
1. Define what is meant by internal control and describe some key elements of an internal control system for cash receipts and disbursements.
2. Explain the possible restrictions on cash and their implications for classification in the balance sheet.
3. Distinguish between the gross and net methods of accounting for cash discounts.
4. Describe the accounting treatment for merchandise returns.
5. Describe the accounting treatment of anticipated uncollectible accounts receivable.
6. Describe the two approaches to estimating bad debts.
7. Describe the accounting treatment of short-term notes receivable.
8. Differentiate between the use of receivables in financing arrangements accounted for as a secured borrowing and those accounted for as a sale.
9. Describe the variables that influence a company's investment in receivables and calculate the key ratios used by analysts to monitor that investment.

CHAPTER HIGHLIGHTS

PART A: CASH AND CASH EQUIVALENTS

Cash includes currency and coins, balances in checking accounts, and items acceptable for deposit in these accounts, such as checks and money orders received from customers. **Cash equivalents** include such things as certain money market funds, treasury bills, and commercial paper. To be classified as cash equivalents, these investments must have a maturity date no longer than three months from the date of purchase. Cash and cash equivalents usually are combined and reported as a single amount in the current asset section of the balance sheet.

Cash that is *restricted* in some way and not available for current use usually is reported as *investments and funds* or *other assets*. For example, banks frequently ask borrowers to maintain a specified balance in a low-interest or noninterest-bearing account at the bank. These are known as compensating balances. The classification of these balances depends on the nature of the restriction and the classification of the related debt.

Internal Control of Cash

A system of internal control refers to a company's plan to (a) encourage adherence to company policies and procedures, (b) promote operational efficiency, (c) minimize errors and theft, and (d) enhance the reliability and accuracy of accounting data. Since cash is the most liquid asset and the asset most easily expropriated, a system of internal control of cash is a key issue.

The *Sarbanes-Oxley Act of 2002* requires that companies not only document their internal controls and assess their adequacy, but that their auditors must provide an opinion on management's assessment. The Public Company Accounting Oversight Board's *Auditing Standard No. 2* further requires the auditor to express its own opinion on whether the company has maintained effective internal control over financial reporting

A critical aspect of an internal control system is the *separation of duties*. Employees involved in recordkeeping should not also have physical access to assets. For example, in the cash area, the employee or employees who receive checks and make deposits should not be the same as the employee who enters the receipts in the accounting records. Periodic bank reconciliations and the use of a petty cash system are other important control procedures involving cash. These two topics are covered in the appendix to the chapter.

PART B: CURRENT RECEIVABLES

Receivables represent a company's claim to the future collection of cash, other assets, or services. **Accounts receivable** result from the sale of goods or services on account. When a receivable, trade or nontrade, is accompanied by a formal promissory note, it's referred to as a **note receivable**.

Initial Valuation of Accounts Receivable

The typical account receivable is initially valued at the exchange price agreed upon by the buyer and seller. **Trade discounts** are reductions in list prices of goods and services to arrive at the exchange price. **Cash discounts**, often called sales discounts, on the other hand, reduce the agreed upon exchange price if remittance is made within a specified short period of time. For example, terms of 2/10, n/30 mean that a 2% discount is available to the buyer if paid within 10 days, otherwise full payment is due within 30 days.

There are two ways to record cash discounts, the **gross method** and the **net method**.

ILLUSTRATION

McQuire Company sold merchandise on credit. The invoice price was $5,000, subject to a 2% cash discount if paid within 10 days.

To record the sale and cash collection using the Gross Method:

To record the sale:

Accounts receivable	5,000	
Sales revenue		5,000

To record cash collection if made within discount period:

Cash	4,900	
Sales discounts (2% × $5,000)	100	
Accounts receivable		5,000

To record cash collection if made after discount period:

Cash	5,000	
Accounts receivable		5,000

To record the sale and cash collection using the Net Method:

To record the sale:

Accounts receivable	4,900	
Sales revenue		4,900

To record cash collection if made within discount period:

Cash	4,900	
Accounts receivable		4,900

To record cash collection if made after discount period:

Cash	5,000	
Accounts receivable		4,900
Interest revenue (2% × $5,000)		100

Subsequent Valuation of Accounts Receivable — Sales Returns

If sales revenue is recognized at delivery of a product, recognizing sales returns when they occur could result in an overstatement of income in the period of sale. If returns are material, they should be estimated and recorded in the same period as the related sale. This is accomplished by recording adjusting journal entries at the end of an accounting period. For example, if at the end of 2009 a company anticipated that returns in early 2010 from year 2009 sales would be $20,000 (merchandise cost $12,000), the following adjusting entries are recorded:

Sales returns	20,000	
Allowance for sales returns		20,000
Inventory - estimated returns	12,000	
Cost of goods sold		12,000

Sales returns are a reduction in sales revenue and the allowance for sales returns is a contra account to accounts receivable. When returns occur in the next period, the allowance account is reduced (debited) and accounts receivable also is reduced (credited).

Subsequent Valuation of Accounts Receivable — Uncollectible Accounts Receivable

If material amounts of bad debts are anticipated, the **allowance method** should be used. The allowance method attempts to *estimate* future bad debts and match them with the related sales revenue. An adjusting entry records a debit to bad debt expense and a credit to allowance for uncollectible accounts, a contra account to accounts receivable. Actually, bad debt write-offs reduce both accounts receivable and the allowance account.

There are two ways commonly used to arrive at the estimate of future bad debts, the **income statement approach** and the **balance sheet approach**. Using the income statement approach, we estimate bad debt expense as a percentage of each period's credit sales. Using the balance sheet approach, we determine bad debt expense by estimating the net realizable value of accounts receivable to be reported in the balance sheet. In other words, the allowance for uncollectible accounts is determined and bad debt expense is an indirect outcome of adjusting the allowance account to the desired balance. An aging of accounts receivable often is used to determine net realizable value.

ILLUSTRATION

The Zeltech Company uses the allowance method to account for bad debts. At the beginning of 2009, the allowance account had a credit balance of $23,000. Credit sales for 2009 totaled $1,200,000 and the year-end accounts receivable balance was $245,000. During the year, $21,000 in receivables was determined to be uncollectible.

The Income Statement Approach

Assuming that Zeltech anticipates that 3% of all credit sales will ultimately become uncollectible, the following adjusting entries record the write-off of accounts receivable and bad debt expense:

Allowance for uncollectible accounts	21,000	
Accounts receivable		21,000
Bad debt expense (3% × $1,200,000)..	36,000	
Allowance for uncollectible accounts...		36,000

Notice that in recording bad debt expense net realizable value was not a determining factor.

The Balance Sheet Approach

Assume that at the end of 2009, an aging of accounts receivable indicated a net realizable value of $205,000. This means that the allowance account at the end of 2009 must have a credit balance of $40,000 to reduce gross accounts receivable of $245,000 to net realizable value of $205,000. After the year 2009 write-offs, the allowance account has a credit balance of only $2,000 ($23,000 beginning balance less write-offs of $21,000). Therefore, bad debt expense for 2009 is $38,000 ($40,000 - 2,000).

Allowance for uncollectible accounts	21,000	
Accounts receivable		21,000
Bad debt expense	38,000	
Allowance for uncollectible accounts ($40,000 – 2,000)....................		38,000

Notice that the allowance account is determined directly, and bad debt expense is an indirect outcome of adjusting the allowance account to the desired balance

Accounts receivable is reported in the balance sheet net of the allowance for uncollectible accounts. Using the balance sheet approach from above, Zeltech would report the following in the current asset section of the year 2009 balance sheet:

Accounts receivable	$245,000
Less: Allowance for uncollectible accounts	(40,000)
Net accounts receivable	$205,000

When a receivable that has been written off is subsequently collected, the receivable and allowance should be reinstated. The collection is then recorded the usual way as a debit to cash and a credit to accounts receivable.

If uncollectible accounts are not anticipated or are immaterial, or if it's not possible to reliably estimate uncollectible accounts, the allowance method need not be used. Any bad debts that do arise simply are written off as bad debt expense. This approach is known as the **direct write-off method**.

Notes Receivable

Notes receivable are formal credit arrangements between a creditor (lender) and a debtor (borrower). Notes receivable are classified as either current or noncurrent depending on the expected payment date(s).

Interest-Bearing Notes

The typical note receivable requires the payment of a specified face amount, also called principal, and interest at a stated percentage of the face amount. These are referred to as interest-bearing notes. Interest on notes is calculated as:

$$\text{Face amount} \times \text{Annual rate} \times \text{Time to maturity}$$

ILLUSTRATION

Masterson Carpet Company's fiscal year end is December 31. On March 31, 2009, the company sold carpeting to Jacobsen Home Builders. Masterson agreed to accept a $300,000, 12-month, 10% note in payment for the carpeting. Interest is payable at maturity. The following entries record the note and related sales revenue, the accrual of interest on December 31, 2009, and the payment of the note:

March 31, 2009

Note receivable	300,000	
Sales revenue		300,000

December 31, 2009

Interest receivable	22,500	
Interest revenue ($300,000 \times 10\% \times {}^{9}/_{12}$)		22,500

March 31, 2010

Cash [$300,000 + ($300,000 \times 10\%)]	330,000	
Interest revenue ($300,000 \times 10\% \times {}^{3}/_{12}$)		7,500
Interest receivable		22,500
Note receivable		300,000

Noninterest-Bearing Notes

Sometimes a receivable assumes the form of a so-called **noninterest-bearing note**. The name is a misnomer, though. Noninterest-bearing notes actually do bear interest, but the interest is deducted from the face amount to determine the cash proceeds available to the borrower at the outset. For example, the Masterson Carpet Company note in the illustration on the previous page could be packaged as a $300,000 noninterest-bearing note with a 10% discount rate. In that case, the $30,000 of interest would be discounted at the outset and the selling price of the carpet would have been $270,000.

March 31, 2009		
Note receivable	300,000	
Discount on note receivable ($300,000 × 10%)		30,000
Sales revenue		270,000
December 31, 2009		
Discount on note receivable	22,500	
Interest revenue ($300,000 × 10% × $^9/_{12}$)................................		22,500
March 31, 2010		
Discount on note receivable	7,500	
Interest revenue ($300,000 × 10% × $^3/_{12}$)...............................		7,500
Cash	300,000	
Note receivable		300,000

Financing With Receivables

Financial institutions have developed a wide variety of methods for companies to use their receivables to obtain immediate cash. Despite this diversity, any of these methods can be described as either:

1. A secured borrowing.
2. A sale of receivables.

When a company chooses between a borrowing and a sale, the critical element is the extent to which it (the transferor) is willing to *surrender control over the assets transferred*. The distinction for some arrangements is not always obvious. For such situations the FASB has provided guidelines. Specifically, the transferor is determined to have surrendered control over the receivables if and only three conditions are met. If not met, the transferor treats the transaction as a *secured borrowing*. In that case the company records a liability with the receivables serving as collateral. If the conditions are met, the transferor treats the transaction as a *sale*.

1) Isolated from transferor
2) Transferee can pledge or exchange it
3) Transferor has no control to repurchase or make transferee to return it

Secured Borrowing

These arrangements basically involve the use of receivables as collateral for a loan. You may already be familiar with the concept of **assigning** or **pledging** receivables as collateral if you or someone you know has a mortgage on a home. The bank or other financial institution holding the mortgage will require that, if the homeowner defaults on the mortgage payments, the home be sold and the proceeds used to pay off the mortgage debt. Similarly, in the case of an assignment of receivables, nonpayment of a debt will require the proceeds from collecting the assigned receivables to go directly toward repayment of the debt.

Usually, the amount borrowed is less than the amount of receivables assigned. The difference provides some protection for the lender to allow for possible uncollectible accounts. Also, the assignee (transferee) usually charges the assignor an up-front finance charge in addition to stated interest on the collateralized loan. The receivables might be collected either by the assignor or the assignee, depending on the details of the arrangement.

ILLUSTRATION

On November 1, 2009, the Weintrob Wholesale Fur Company borrowed $300,000 from a local finance company and signed a promissory note. Interest at 10% is payable monthly. Weintrob assigned $350,000 of its receivables as collateral for the loan. The finance company charges a finance fee equal to 2% of the receivables assigned.

Weintrob records the borrowing as follows:

Cash (difference)..	293,000	
Finance charge expense* (2% × $350,000)	7,000	
Liability – financing arrangement		300,000

Weintrob will continue to collect the receivables, record any discounts, sales returns, and bad debt write-offs, but will remit the cash to the finance company, usually on a monthly basis. If $250,000 of the receivables assigned are collected in November, Weintrob records the following entries:

Cash..	250,000	
Accounts receivable...		250,000
Interest expense ($300,000 × 10% × $1/12$).......................	2,500	
Liability – financing arrangement	250,000	
Cash..		252,500

*In theory, this fee should be allocated over the entire period of the loan rather than recorded as expense in the initial period. However, amounts usually are small and the loan period usually is short. For expediency, then, we expense the entire fee immediately.

Sale of Receivables

The two most common types of selling arrangements are **factoring** and **securitization**. The specific accounting treatment for the sale of receivables using factoring and securitization arrangements depends on the amount of risk the factor assumes, in particular whether it buys the receivables **without recourse** or **with recourse**.

When a company sells accounts receivable without recourse, the buyer assumes the risk of uncollectibility. This means the buyer has no *recourse* to the seller if customers don't pay the receivables. In that case, the seller simply accounts for the transaction as a sale of an asset.

ILLUSTRATION

The Weintrob Wholesale Fur Company factors its accounts receivable to a local finance company. On November 1, 2009, Weintrob factored $350,000 of accounts receivable. The transfer was made *without recourse*. The finance company remits 90% of the factored receivables and retains 10%. When the finance company collects the receivables, it remits to Weintrob the retained amount, less a 4% fee (4% of the total factored amount). Weintrob records the transfer as follows:

November 1, 2009		
Cash (90% × $350,000)..	315,000	
Loss on sale of receivables (4% × $350,000)	14,000	
Receivable from factor (10% × $350,000 = $35,000 – 14,000 fee)	21,000	
Accounts receivable (balance sold)......................................		350,000

When a company sells accounts receivable *with* recourse, the seller retains the risk of uncollectibility. In effect, the seller guarantees that the buyer will be paid even if some receivables prove to be uncollectible. In the above illustration, even if the receivables were sold with recourse, as long as the three conditions for sale treatment are met, Weintrob would still account for the transfer as a sale. The only difference would be the additional requirement that Weintrob record the estimated fair value of the recourse obligation as a liability. The recourse obligation is the estimated amount that Weintrob will have to pay the finance company as a reimbursement for uncollectible receivables. Assuming that this amount is estimated at $5,000, the entry recorded by Weintrob would be as follows:

November 1, 2009		
Cash (90% × $350,000)..	315,000	
Loss on sale of receivables (4% × $350,000 + 5,000).............	19,000	
Receivable from factor (10% × $350,000 = $35,000 – 14,000 fee)	21,000	
Recourse liability		5,000
Accounts receivable (balance sold)......................................		350,000

Discounting a Note Receivable

The transfer of a note receivable to a financial institution is called **discounting.** The financial institution accepts the note and gives the seller cash equal to the maturity value of the note reduced by a discount. The discount is computed by applying a discount rate to the maturity value and represents the financing fee the financial institution charges for the transaction. Similar to accounts receivable, if the three conditions for sale treatment are met, the transferor would account for the transfer as a sale. If the conditions are not met, it is treated as a secured borrowing.

ILLUSTRATION

On January 31, 2009, the Weintrob Wholesale Fur Company lent a customer $100,000. The note requires the payment of the principal amount plus interest at 8% on January 31, 2010. On April 30, 2009, Weintrob discounted the note at a local bank. The bank's discount rate is 10%. The three conditions for treatment as a sale are met. The appropriate journal entries are:

January 31, 2009

Note receivable...	100,000	
Cash..		100,000

April 30, 2009
Step 1 - Accrue interest earned on the note prior to its being discounted.

Interest receivable...	2,000	
Interest revenue ($100,000 × 8% × $^3/_{12}$)		2,000

Steps 2 and 3 - Add interest to maturity to calculate maturity value and deduct discount to calculate cash proceeds.

$100,000	Face amount
8,000	Interest to maturity ($100,000 × 8%)
108,000	Maturity value
(8,100)	Discount ($108,000 × 10% × $^9/_{12}$)
$ 99,900	Cash proceeds

Cash (proceeds determined above)	99,900	
Loss on sale of note receivable (difference)	2,100	
Note receivable (face amount)		100,000
Interest receivable (accrued interest determined above)		2,000

Decision Makers' Perspective

A company's investment in receivables is influenced by several variables, including the level of sales, the nature of the product or service sold, and credit and collection policies. Management must evaluate the costs and benefits of any change in credit and collection policies. The ability to use receivables as a method of financing also offers alternatives to management.

Investors and creditors can monitor a company's investment in receivables with the **receivables turnover ratio** and the related **average collection period**. These ratios are calculated as follows:

$$\text{Receivables turnover ratio} = \frac{\text{Net sales}}{\text{Average accounts receivable (net)}}$$

$$\text{Average collection period} = \frac{365 \text{ days}}{\text{Receivables turnover ratio}}$$

The receivables turnover ratio indicates the number of times during a period that the average accounts receivable balance is collected. The average collection period is an approximation of the number of days the average accounts receivable balance is outstanding.

APPENDIX 7: CASH CONTROLS

Bank Reconciliation

Since all cash receipts are deposited into the bank account and cash disbursements are made by check, the bank account provides a separate record of cash. Therefore, a comparison of the bank account with the cash account, **bank reconciliation**, is an important procedure in the control of cash. The *first step* in the reconciliation is to adjust the bank balance to the corrected cash balance for deposits in transit, outstanding checks, and bank errors. *Step 2* adjusts the book balance to the corrected cash balance for timing differences involving transactions already reflected by the bank of which the company is unaware (for example, service charges and NSF checks) and for company errors. Each of the adjustments in step 2 requires a journal entry to correct the book balance.

Step 1:	Bank Balance	Step 2:	Book Balance
	+ Deposits outstanding		+ Collections by bank
	− Checks outstanding		− Service charges
	± Errors		− NSF checks
			± Errors
	Corrected balance		**Corrected balance**

Petty Cash

Petty cash funds are used to pay for low cost items such as postage, office supplies, delivery charges, and entertainment expenses. A petty cash fund is established and then managed by the petty cash custodian. The custodian disburses cash from the fund when the appropriate documentation is presented (for example, a receipt for the purchase of office supplies). The documentation is then used as a basis for replenishing the fund. For example:

To record the establishment of a $200 petty cash fund:

Petty cash	200	
Cash (checking account)		200

To record $170 in expenses and to replenish the fund:

Postage expense...	40	
Delivery expense	60	
Entertainment expense...	70	
Cash (checking account)		170

SELF-STUDY QUESTIONS AND EXERCISES

Concept Review

1. _____ include such things as certain money market funds, treasury bills, and commercial paper.

2. A critical aspect of an internal control system is the _____ of duties. Employees involved in _____ should not also have physical access to assets.

3. Cash that is restricted in some way and not available for current use usually is reported as _____ or _____ .

4. Accounts receivable initially are valued at the _____ price agreed upon by the buyer and seller.

5. _____ reduce the amount to be paid if remittance is made within a specified period of time.

6. The _____ method views cash discounts not taken as part of sales revenue. The _____ method considers cash discounts not taken as interest revenue.

7. Recognizing sales returns when they occur, could result in an _____ of income in the period of the related sale.

8. The _____ method attempts to estimate future bad debts and match them with the related sales revenue.

9. Using the _____ approach, we estimate bad debt expense as a percentage of each period's net credit sales.

10. Using the _____ approach to estimate future bad debts, we determine bad debt expense by estimating the net realizable value of accounts receivable.

11. The write-off of an account receivable reduces both _____ and the _____ , thus having no effect on income and financial position.

12. _____ are formal credit arrangements between a creditor (lender) and a debtor (borrower).

13. An _____ involves the pledging of specific accounts receivable as collateral for a debt.

14. When notes receivable are transferred, the transaction is referred to as _____ notes receivable.

15. The buyer assumes the risk of uncollectibility when accounts receivable are factored _____ .

16. The transfer of receivables with recourse is accounted for as a _____ if the transferor surrenders control over the receivables transferred. Otherwise, the transfer is accounted for as a _____ .

17. The first step in recording a discounting of a note is to _____ on the note receivable prior to its being discounted.

18. The _____ ratio shows the number of times during a period that the average accounts receivable balance is collected.

Questions 19 and 20 are based on Appendix 7.

19. Bank reconciliations include adjustments to the balance per _____ for timing differences involving transactions already reflected in the company's accounting records that have not yet been processed by the bank.

20. A _____ provides a more efficient way to pay for low cost items such as postage, office supplies, and delivery charges.

Answers:

1. Cash equivalents **2.** separation, recordkeeping **3.** investments and funds, other assets
4. exchange **5.** Cash discounts **6.** gross, net **7.** overstatement **8.** allowance **9.** income statement
10. balance sheet **11.** receivables, allowance for uncollectible accounts **12.** Notes receivable
13. assignment **14.** discounting **15.** without recourse **16.** sale, secured borrowing
17. accrue interest earned **18.** receivables turnover **19.** bank **20.** petty cash fund

REVIEW EXERCISES

Exercise 1

Eastern Digital Corporation began 2009 with accounts receivable of $1,240,000 and a credit balance in allowance for uncollectible accounts of $36,000. During 2009, credit sales totaled $5,190,000 and cash collected from customers totaled $5,380,000. Also, actual write-offs of accounts receivable in 2009 were $33,000. At end of the year, an accounts receivable aging schedule indicated a required allowance of $32,300. No accounts receivable previously written off were collected.

Required:

1. Determine the balance in accounts receivable at the end of 2009.

2. Prepare the entry to record the write-off of accounts receivable during the year and the year-end adjusting entry to record bad debt expense.

Solution:
Requirement 1

Beginning balance	$1,240,000
Add: Credit sales	5,190,000
Less: Cash collections	(5,380,000)
Write-offs	(33,000)
Ending balance	$1,017,000

Requirement 2

To record the write-off of accounts receivable:

Allowance for uncollectible accounts	33,000	
Accounts receivable		33,000

To record bad debt expense:

Bad debt expense..	29,300	
Allowance for uncollectible accounts (determined below)............		29,300

Required allowance		$32,300
Allowance account:		
Beginning balance	$36,000	
Less: Write-offs	(33,000)	
Balance before year-end adjusting entry		(3,000)
Year-end adjustment		$29,300

Exercise 2

Midwestern Electric obtained a $40,000 note from a customer on April 1, 2009. The note plus interest at 9% is due on April 1, 2010. On July 31, 2009, Midwestern discounted the note at a local bank. The bank's discount rate is 12%.

Required:

Prepare the journal entries required on July 31, 2009, to accrue interest and to record the discounting for Midwestern. Assume that the discounting is accounted for as a sale.

Solution:

To accrue interest:

Interest receivable	1,200	
Interest revenue ($40,000 × 9% × $^4/_{12}$)		1,200

To record the discounting:

Cash (proceeds determined below)..	40,112	
Loss on sale of note receivable (difference)	1,088	
Note receivable (face amount)..		40,000
Interest receivable (determined above)		1,200

$40,000	Face amount
3,600	Interest to maturity ($40,000 × 9%)
43,600	Maturity value
(3,488)	Discount ($43,600 × 12% × $^8/_{12}$)
$40,112	Cash proceeds

Exercise 3 (Based on Appendix 7)

You have been given the following information pertaining to the checking account of North Coast Milling Company:

Bank statement:

Balance, March 1, 2009	$ 63,255
Deposits	322,200
Checks processed	(344,500)
Collection of note by bank	12,000
Service charges recorded	(80)
NSF checks	(200)
Balance, March 31, 2009	$ 52,675

General ledger cash account:

Balance, March 1, 2009	$ 61,250
Deposits	330,200
Checks written	(350,200)
Balance, March 31, 2009	$ 41,250

In addition, you determine that there were no deposits outstanding at the end of February and that all outstanding checks at the end of February were processed by the bank in March.

Required:

Prepare a bank reconciliation for the month of March.

Intermediate Accounting, 5/e

Solution:

Step 1:	**Bank Balance to Corrected Balance**	
	Balance per bank statement	$52,675
	Add: Deposits outstanding ($330,200 – 322,200)	8,000
	Deduct: Checks outstanding	(7,705) *
	Corrected cash balance	$52,970

Step 2:	**Book Balance to Corrected Balance**	
	Balance per books	$41,250
	Add: Note collected by bank	12,000
	Deduct:	
	Service charges	(80)
	NSF checks	(200)
	Corrected cash balance	$52,970

*Checks written in March		$350,200
Checks processed by the bank in March	$344,500	
Less outstanding checks at the end of February ($63,255 – 61,250)	(2,005)	
March checks processed in March		(342,495)
Checks still outstanding		$ 7,705

MULTIPLE CHOICE

Enter the letter corresponding to the response that **best** completes each of the following statements or questions.

_____ 1. Which of the following might be classified as a cash equivalent?
    a.   Cash in a checking account.
    b.   30-day treasury bill.
    c.   Money orders waiting to be deposited.
    d.   120-day treasury bill.

_____ 2. An internal control system is designed to do all but which of the following?
    a.   Promote operational efficiency.
    b.   Safeguard assets.
    c.   Encourage adherence to company policies.
    d.   Assure the promotion of the most qualified employees.

_____ 3. A company uses the gross method to account for cash discounts offered to its customers. If payment is made *before* the discount period expires, which of the following is correct?
  a. Sales discounts is debited for the amount of discounts taken by customers.
  b. Sales discounts is credited for the amount of discounts taken by customers.
  c. Interest expense is debited for the amount of discounts taken by customers.
  d. Accounts receivable is credited for the amount of discounts taken by customers.

_____ 4. Allister Company does not use the allowance method to account for bad debts and instead any bad debts that do arise are written off as bad debt expense. What problem might this create if bad debts are material?
  a. Receivables likely will be understated.
  b. No problems are created.
  c. Receivables likely will be overstated.
  d. The matching principle is violated when the write-off occurs in the same period that the receivable is initially recorded.

_____ 5. Jasper Company uses the allowance method to account for bad debts. During 2009, the company recorded bad debt expense of $9,000 and wrote off as uncollectible accounts receivable totaling $5,000. These transactions caused a decrease in working capital (current assets minus current liabilities) of:
  a. $ 7,000
  b. $ 5,000
  c. $ 9,000
  d. $14,000

_____ 6. The Reingold Hat Company uses the allowance method to account for bad debts. During 2009, the company recorded $800,000 in credit sales. At the end of 2009, account balances were: Accounts receivable, $120,000; Allowance for uncollectible accounts, $3,000 (credit). If bad debt expense is estimated to be 3% of credit sales, the appropriate adjusting entry will include a debit to bad debt expense of:
  a. Zero.
  b. $27,000
  c. $21,000
  d. $24,000

_____ 7. Enchill Company accrues bad debt expense during the year at an amount equal to 3% of credit sales. At the end of the year, a journal entry adjusts the allowance for uncollectible accounts to a desired amount based on an aging of accounts receivable. At the beginning of 2009, the allowance account had a credit balance of $18,000. During 2009, credit sales totaled $480,000 and receivables of $14,000 were written off. The year-end aging indicated that a $21,000 allowance for uncollectible accounts was required. Enchill's bad debt expense for 2009 would be:
  a. $17,000
  b. $ 2,600
  c. $21,000
  d. $14,400

_____8. Harmon Sporting Goods received a $60,000, 6-month, 10% note from a customer. Four months after receiving the note, it was discounted at a local bank at a 12% discount rate. The cash proceeds received by Harmon were:
a. $63,000
b. $64,680
c. $61,740
d. $67,200

_____9. At the end of June, the Marquess Company factored $200,000 in accounts receivable with Homemark Finance. The transfer is made *without recourse*. Homemark charges a fee of 3% of receivables factored. During July, $150,000 of the factored receivables are collected. What amount of loss on sale of receivables would Marquess record in June?
a. $6,000
b. $4,500
c. $1,500
d. Zero.

_____10. In question 9, if the transfer were made *with recourse* but is still accounted for as a sale, what amount of loss on sale of receivables would the company record in June assuming the estimated recourse liability is $2,000?
a. $6,500
b. $8,000
c. $4,000
d. Zero.

_____11. The following data are available for the Hunting Balloon Company:

Sales for the current year	$1,500,000
Cost of goods sold for the current year	1,200,000
Accounts receivable, beginning of year	140,000
Accounts receivable, end of year	160,000

The accounts receivable turnover ratio for the current year is:
a. 8.00
b. 10.71
c. 10.00
d. 9.375

Questions 12 through 15 are based on Appendix 7.

_____ 12. The replenishment of a petty cash fund might include which of the following?
    a.   A debit to cash.
    b.   A debit to petty cash.
    c.   A debit to office supplies expense.
    d.   A credit to petty cash.

_____ 13. In a bank reconciliation, deposits outstanding are:
    a.   Subtracted from the bank balance.
    b.   Added to the book balance.
    c.   Added to the bank balance.
    d.   Subtracted from the book balance.

_____ 14. In a bank reconciliation, NSF checks are:
    a.   Subtracted from the bank balance.
    b.   Added to the book balance.
    c.   Added to the bank balance.
    d.   Subtracted from the book balance.

_____ 15. Alvin Electronics is in the process of reconciling its bank account for the month of November. The following information is available:

Balance per bank statement	$8,325
Outstanding checks	2,400
Deposits outstanding	1,215
Bank service charges for November	35
Check written by Alvin for $300 but recorded incorrectly by Alvin as a $30 disbursement.	

What should be the corrected cash balance at the end of November?
    a. $6,870
    b. $7,140
    c. $6,835
    d. $7,105

Answers:

1.	b.	6.	d.	11.	c.
2.	d.	7.	a.	12.	c.
3.	a.	8.	c.	13.	c.
4.	c.	9.	a.	14.	d.
5.	c.	10.	b.	15.	b.

Inventories: Measurement

LEARNING OBJECTIVES

After studying this chapter, you should be able to:
1. Explain the difference between a perpetual inventory system and a periodic inventory system.
2. Explain which physical quantities of goods should be included in inventory.
3. Determine the expenditures that should be included in the cost of inventory.
4. Differentiate between the specific identification, FIFO, LIFO, and average cost methods used to determine the cost of ending inventory and cost of goods sold.
5. Discuss the factors affecting a company's choice of inventory method.
6. Understand supplemental LIFO disclosures and the effect of LIFO liquidations on net income.
7. Calculate the key ratios used by analysts to monitor a company's investment in inventories.
8. Determine ending inventory using the dollar-value LIFO inventory method.

CHAPTER HIGHLIGHTS

PART A: RECORDING AND MEASURING INVENTORY

Types of Inventory

Inventory refers to the assets a company (1) intends to sell in the normal course of business, and (2) has in production for future sale (work in process), or (3) uses currently in the production of goods to be sold (raw materials). Inventory for a manufacturing company consists of raw materials, work in process, and finished goods. Wholesale and retail companies purchase goods that are primarily in finished form. Therefore, their inventory consists only of finished goods, often referred to as merchandise inventory. In this course we focus primarily on merchandising companies (wholesalers and retailers).

Perpetual and Periodic Inventory Systems

There are two accounting systems used to record transactions involving inventory: the **perpetual inventory system** and the **periodic inventory system**. The **perpetual inventory system** continuously tracks and records both changes in inventory quantity and inventory cost. Inventory is increased (debited) when merchandise is purchased or returned by a customer, and decreased (credited) when merchandise is sold or returned to a supplier.

The **periodic inventory system** adjusts inventory and records cost of goods sold only at the end of each period. Merchandise purchases, purchase returns, purchase discounts, and freight-in (purchases plus freight-in less returns and discounts equals net purchases) are recorded in temporary accounts and the period's cost of goods sold is determined at the end of the period by combining the temporary accounts with the inventory account:

Beginning inventory + Net purchases – Ending inventory = Cost of goods sold

Ending inventory usually is determined by a physical count and then assigning costs to the quantities determined.

The ability to track inventory quantities from their acquisition to their sale is an important internal control feature of the perpetual system, thus providing more timely information. However, a perpetual system is generally more expensive to implement than a periodic system. The periodic system is less costly to implement during the period but requires a physical count before ending inventory and cost of goods sold can be determined.

ILLUSTRATION

The Johnson & Sons Wholesale Meat Company began 2009 with merchandise inventory of $60,000. During the year, additional merchandise was purchased at a cost of $350,000. Sales for the year, all on account, totaled $440,000.

PERPETUAL INVENTORY SYSTEM

Summary inventory transactions assuming cost of goods sold for the year totaled $280,000.

To record the purchase of merchandise:		
Inventory	350,000	
Accounts payable...		350,000
To record sales on account:		
Accounts receivable...	440,000	
Sales		440,000
To record cost of goods sold:		
Cost of goods sold	280,000	
Inventory		280,000

PERIODIC INVENTORY SYSTEM

Summary inventory transactions assuming an ending inventory of $130,000.

To record the purchase of merchandise:		
Purchases	350,000	
Accounts payable...		350,000
To record sales on account:		
Accounts receivable...	440,000	
Sales		440,000
To record cost of goods sold at the end of the year:		
Cost of goods sold	280,000	
Inventory (ending)	130,000	
Inventory (beginning)		60,000
Purchases		350,000

What Is Included in Inventory?

Physical Quantities Included In Inventory

Typically, determining the physical quantity that should be included in inventory is a simple matter because it consists of items in the possession of the company. Three possible exceptions are goods in transit, goods on consignment, and sales returns. For **goods in transit**, ownership depends on the terms of the agreement between the purchaser and the seller. Inventory shipped *f.o.b. shipping point* (purchaser is responsible for the shipping costs) is included in the purchaser's inventory as soon as the merchandise is shipped. Inventory shipped *f.o.b. destination* (seller is responsible for the shipping costs) is included in the purchaser's inventory only after it reaches the purchaser's location. **Goods on consignment** are included in the inventory of the consignor until sold by the consignee. Recall from our discussions in previous chapters that when the right of return exists, a seller must be able to estimate those returns before revenue can be recognized. The adjusting entry for estimated **sales returns** reduces sales revenue and accounts receivable. At the same time, cost of goods sold is reduced and inventory is increased. As a result, a company includes in inventory the cost of merchandise it anticipates will be returned.

Expenditures Included In Inventory

In general, expenditures necessary to bring inventory to its *condition* and *location* for sale or use are included in its cost. Obviously, the cost includes the purchase price of the goods but also freight charges paid by the purchaser (**freight-in**) and insurance costs paid by the purchaser while the goods are in transit. The cost of inventory is reduced when merchandise is returned to the supplier (**purchase returns**). Shipping charges on outgoing goods are related to the selling activity and are reported as a selling expense when incurred, not as part of inventory cost.

Inventories: Measurement

Purchase discounts represent reductions in the amount to be paid by the purchaser if remittance is made within a designated period of time. As with the seller, the buyer can record purchase discounts using either the **gross method** or the **net method**.

ILLUSTRATION

Fitzgerald Company purchased merchandise on credit. The invoice price was $5,000, subject to a 2% cash discount if paid within 10 days.

To record the purchase and cash payment using the Gross Method:

To record the purchase:		
Purchases *	5,000	
Accounts payable..		5,000
To record cash payment if made within the discount period:		
Accounts payable..	5,000	
Purchase discounts * (2% × $100)		100
Cash		4,900
To record cash payment if made after the discount period:		
Accounts payable	5,000	
Cash		5,000

* The inventory account is used in a perpetual system.

To record the purchase and cash payment using the Net Method:

To record the purchase:		
Purchases * (98% × $5,000)...	4,900	
Accounts payable..		4,900
To record cash payment if made within the discount period:		
Accounts payable..	4,900	
Cash		4,900
To record cash payment if made after the discount period:		
Accounts payable	4,900	
Interest expense (2% × $5,000).......................................	100	
Cash		5,000

* The inventory account is used in a perpetual system.

Inventory Cost Flow Assumptions

Regardless of the inventory system used, it's necessary to assign dollar amounts to physical quantities of goods sold and goods remaining in ending inventory. If a perpetual system is used, each time merchandise is sold we need to determine the cost of the items sold. If a periodic system is used, we need to apportion the cost of goods available for sale (beginning inventory + net purchases) between ending inventory and cost of goods sold at the end of the period.

Specific Identification

It's sometimes possible for each unit sold during the period or each unit on hand at the end of the period to be matched with its *actual cost*. The **specific identification method**, however, is not feasible for many types of products either because items are not uniquely identifiable or because it's too costly to match a specific purchase price with each item sold or each item remaining in ending inventory. Most companies use cost flow methods based on assumptions about how inventory might flow in and out of a company. It's important to note that the actual flow of a company's inventory does not have to correspond to the cost flow assumption employed.

Average Cost

The **average cost method** assumes that items sold and items in ending inventory come from a mixture of all the goods available for sale. The average unit cost is applied to goods sold or to ending inventory. In a periodic system, the weighted-average unit cost is determined as follows:

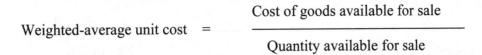

$$\text{Weighted-average unit cost} \quad = \quad \frac{\text{Cost of goods available for sale}}{\text{Quantity available for sale}}$$

In perpetual system, the weighted-average unit cost becomes a moving average unit cost. A new weighted-average unit cost is calculated each time that additional units are produced.

First-in, First-out (FIFO)

The **first-in, first-out (FIFO) method** assumes that items sold are those that were acquired first. Therefore, ending inventory applying FIFO consists of the most recently acquired items. The same ending inventory and cost of goods sold amounts are always produced in a perpetual inventory system as in a periodic inventory system when FIFO is used. This is because the same units and costs are first in and first out whether cost of goods sold is determined as each sale is made or at the end of the period as a residual amount.

Last-in, First-out (LIFO)

The **last-in, first-out (LIFO) method** assumes that items sold are those that were most recently acquired. Therefore, ending inventory applying LIFO consists of the items acquired first. Unlike FIFO, applying LIFO in a perpetual inventory system will generally result in a different ending inventory and cost of goods sold from the allocation arrived at applying LIFO in a periodic system. Periodic LIFO applies the last in, first out concept to total sales and total purchases only at the conclusion of the reporting period. Perpetual LIFO applies the same concept, but many times during the period — every time a sale is made.

ILLUSTRATION

The Pringle Beverage Company began 2009 with 10,000 units of inventory on hand. These units cost $15 each. The following transactions related to the company's merchandise inventory occurred during the first quarter of 2009:

January 22	—	Purchased	5,000 units for $16 each =	$ 80,000
February 14	—	Purchased	6,000 units for $17 each =	102,000
March 25	—	Purchased	4,000 units for $18 each =	72,000
Total purchases			15,000 units	$254,000

All unit costs include the purchase price and freight charges borne by Pringle. During the quarter ending March 31, 2009, sales in units totaled 17,000 units leaving 8,000 units in ending inventory. The company uses the periodic inventory system. Ending inventory at March 31 and cost of goods sold for the quarter using the various cost flow assumptions are determined as follows:

Average Cost

Beginning inventory (10,000 units @ $15)	$150,000
Plus: Purchases (15,000 units @ various prices)	254,000
Cost of goods available for sale (25,000 units)	404,000
Less: Ending inventory (determined below)	(129,280)
Cost of goods sold (17,000 units)	$274,720

Cost of ending inventory:

$$\text{Weighted-average unit cost} = \frac{\$404,000}{25,000 \text{ units}} = \$16.16$$

8,000 units × $16.16 = **$129,280**

Cost of goods sold could have been determined directly by multiplying the weighted-average unit cost of $16.16 by the number of units sold ($16.16 × 17,000 = $274,720).

First-in, First-out (FIFO)

Beginning inventory (10,000 units @ $15)			$150,000
Plus: Purchases (15,000 units @ various prices)			254,000
Cost of goods available for sale (25,000 units)			404,000
Less: Ending inventory (determined below)			(140,000)
Cost of goods sold (17,000 units)			$264,000

Cost of ending inventory:

Date of Purchase	Units	Unit Cost	Total Cost
Feb. 14	4,000	$17	$ 68,000
March 15	4,000	18	72,000
Total	8,000		$140,000

The 17,000 units sold could be costed directly as follows:

Date of Purchase	Units	Unit Cost	Total Cost
Beg. inv.	10,000	$15	$150,000
Jan. 22	5,000	16	80,000
Feb. 14	2,000	17	34,000
Total	17,000		$264,000

Last-in, First-out (LIFO)

Beginning inventory (10,000 units @ $15)			$150,000
Plus: Purchases (15,000 units @ various prices)			254,000
Cost of goods available for sale (25,000 units)			404,000
Less: Ending inventory (determined below)			(120,000)
Cost of goods sold (17,000 units)			$284,000

Cost of ending inventory:

Date of Purchase	Units	Unit cost	Total cost
Beg. inv.	8,000	$15	$120,000
Total	8,000		$120,000

The 17,000 units sold could be costed directly as follows:

Date of Purchase	Units	Unit cost	Total cost
Beg. inv.	2,000	$15	$ 30,000
Jan. 22	5,000	16	80,000
Feb. 14	6,000	17	102,000
March 25	4,000	18	72,000
Total	17,000		$284,000

Decision Makers' Perspective—Factors Influencing Method Choice

There are several factors that influence managers when choosing an inventory method. If a company wanted to choose a method that most closely approximates specific identification, then the actual **physical flow** of inventory in and out of the company would motivate the choice. Remember, however, that a company is not required to choose an inventory method that approximates actual physical flow.

If the unit cost of inventory changes during a period, the inventory method chosen can have a significant effect on the amount of **net income** reported by the company and also on the amount of **income taxes** paid. If a company uses LIFO to measure its taxable income, IRS regulations require that LIFO also be used to measure income reported to investors and creditors (the **LIFO conformity rule**). Therefore, the effect of method choice on income taxes is a significant factor affecting method choice. For example, when costs rise and inventory quantities are not decreasing, LIFO produces a higher cost of goods sold, lower net income, and a lower current tax bill than the other methods. Many companies choose LIFO to reduce income taxes in periods when costs are rising. LIFO companies are allowed to report in a note the effect of using another method on inventory valuation rather than LIFO.

Proponents of LIFO argue that it results in a better *match* of revenues and expenses because the most recent costs are included in cost of goods sold which are then matched with revenue measured at current selling prices. However, inventory costs in the balance sheet with LIFO generally are out of date because they reflect old purchase transactions. This distortion could carry over to the income statement as well if inventory layers are liquidated (if inventory quantity declines). If costs have been rising, LIFO liquidations produce higher net income than would have resulted if the liquidated inventory were included in cost of goods sold at current costs. The paper profits caused by including out of date, low costs in cost of goods sold is referred to as the effect on income of liquidations of LIFO inventory.

For example, in the example above illustrating the various cost flow assumptions, inventory quantity declined from 10,000 units in beginning inventory to 8,000 units in ending inventory. This means that 2,000 units of beginning inventory purchased at $15 each are included in cost of goods sold. If the company had purchased 2,000 additional units during the period at the period-end price of $18, cost of goods sold would have been higher by $6,000 ($18 − 15 = $3 × 2,000 units). This is the before-tax **LIFO liquidation profit**. A company must disclose in a note any material effect of a LIFO liquidation on net income.

Decision Makers' Perspective—Inventory Management

The inventory method also could affect the analysis of a company's liquidity and profitability by investors, creditors, and financial analysts. Analysts must make adjustments when evaluating companies that use different inventory methods. When one or more of the companies involved use LIFO, supplemental LIFO disclosures can be used to make these adjustments by converting LIFO inventory and cost of goods sold amounts to another method.

Two important ratios used involving inventory used by analysts are the gross profit ration and the inventory turnover ratio. The **gross profit ratio** indicates the percentage of each sales dollar available to cover other expenses and provide a profit. The **inventory turnover ratio** measures a company's efficiency in managing its investment in inventory. These two ratios are calculated as follows:

Gross profit ratio	=	$\dfrac{\text{Gross profit}}{\text{Net sales}}$
Inventory turnover ratio	=	$\dfrac{\text{Cost of goods sold}}{\text{Average inventory}}$

A convenient extension of the inventory turnover ratio is the **average days in inventory**, which is calculated by dividing 365 days by the turnover ratio. This measure indicates the number of days it normally takes to sell inventory.

The choice of inventory method also affects earnings quality, particularly in times of rapidly changing prices. For example, a LIFO liquidation profit (or loss) reduces the quality of current period earnings. Fortunately for analysts, companies must disclose these profits or losses, if material. In addition, LIFO cost of goods sold determined using a periodic inventory system is more susceptible to manipulation than is FIFO. Year-end purchases can have a dramatic effect on LIFO cost of goods sold in rapid cost-change environments.

PART B: METHODS OF SIMPLIFYING LIFO

The recordkeeping costs of unit LIFO can be significant. Another disadvantage of unit LIFO is the possibility of LIFO liquidation. One way to simplify recordkeeping and reduce the risk of LIFO layer liquidations is to group inventory into *pools* based on physical similarities. The average cost for all of the pool purchases during the period is applied to the current year's LIFO layer. However, grouping inventory based on physical similarities presents problems, particularly when items in the pool are discontinued and have to be replaced. The dollar-value LIFO approach helps overcome these problems.

Dollar-Value LIFO

The dollar-value LIFO (DVL) approach extends the concept of inventory pools by allowing a company to combine a large variety of goods into a pool. Physical units are not used in calculating ending inventory. Instead, the inventory is viewed as a quantity of *value* instead of a physical quantity of goods. Instead of layers of units from different purchases, the DVL inventory pool is viewed as being comprised of *layers of dollar value* from different years. DVL simplifies recordkeeping and minimizes the possibility of LIFO liquidation through the aggregation of many types of inventory into larger pools.

Under DVL, we determine whether a new LIFO inventory layer was added by comparing the ending dollar amount with the beginning dollar amount after deflating inventory amounts to base year with the aid of a cost index. The base year is the year in which the DVL method is adopted and the layer year is any subsequent year in which an inventory layer is created. The cost index for the base year is set at 1.00. Subsequent years' indices reflect cost changes relative to the base year.

The starting point in DVL is determining the current year's ending inventory valued at year-end cost. A three-step process is then used to determine ending inventory and cost of goods sold:

Step 1: Convert ending inventory valued at year-end cost to base year cost. This is accomplished by dividing the ending inventory at year-end cost by the current year's cost index.

Step 2: Identify the layers of ending inventory and the years they were created.

Step 3: Convert each layer's base year cost to layer year cost using the cost index for the year it was acquired.

ILLUSTRATION

Koch Industries, Inc. has only one inventory pool. On December 31, 2009, Koch adopted the dollar-value LIFO inventory method. The inventory on that date using the dollar-value LIFO method was $162,000. Inventory data for the following three years are as follows:

Year Ended December 31	Inventory at Year-End Costs	Cost Index
2010	$183,750	1.05
2011	201,960	1.08
2012	203,500	1.10

Ending inventory for each of the years is determined as follows:

Date	Step 1 Ending Inventory at Base Year Cost	Step 2 Inventory Layers at Base Year Cost	Step 3 Inventory Layers Converted to Cost	Ending Inventory DVL Cost
12/31/09	$\dfrac{\$162,000}{1.00} = \$162,000$	$162,000 (base)	$162,000 × 1.00 = $162,000	$162,000
12/31/10	$\dfrac{\$183,750}{1.05} = \$175,000$	$162,000 (base) 13,000 (2010)	$162,000 × 1.00 = $162,000 13,000 × 1.05 = 13,650	**175,650**
12/31/11	$\dfrac{\$201,960}{1.08} = \$187,000$	$162,000 (base) 13,000 (2010) 12,000 (2011)	$162,000 × 1.00 = $162,000 13,000 × 1.05 = 13,650 12,000 × 1.08 = 12,960	**188,610**
12/31/12	$\dfrac{\$203,500}{1.10} = \$185,000$	$162,000 (base) 13,000 (2010) 10,000 (2011)	$162,000 × 1.00 = $162,000 13,000 × 1.05 = 13,650 10,000 × 1.08 = 10,800	**186,450**

SELF-STUDY QUESTIONS AND EXERCISES

Concept Review

1. Inventory for a manufacturing company consists of _____ , _____ , and _____ .

2. A _____ inventory system continuously tracks and records both changes in inventory quantity and inventory cost.

3. A _____ inventory system adjusts inventory and records cost of goods sold only at the end of each reporting period.

4. Inventory shipped _____ is included in the purchaser's inventory as soon as the merchandise is shipped.

5. Inventory shipped _____ is included in the purchaser's inventory only after it reaches the purchaser's location.

6. Goods held on consignment are included in the inventory of the consignor until _____ .

7. Purchase discounts not taken are included as _____ using the gross method and as _____ using the net method.

8. By either the gross or net method of accounting for purchase discounts, _____ is reduced by discounts taken.

9. The _____ method matches a specific purchase price with each item sold or each item remaining in ending inventory.

10. The _____ method assumes that items sold and items in ending inventory come from a mixture of all the goods available for sale.

11. The weighted-average unit cost in a perpetual inventory system becomes a moving average unit cost. A new weighted-average unit cost is calculated each time additional units are _____ .

12. The _____ method assumes that items sold are those that were acquired first.

13. Ending inventory applying the _____ method consists of the items acquired first.

14. If unit costs are _____ , LIFO will result in a higher cost of goods sold and lower ending inventory than FIFO.

15. IRS regulations require that if a company uses LIFO to measure _____ , the company also must use LIFO for _____ .

16. If costs have been rising, LIFO liquidations produce _____ net income than would have resulted if the liquidated inventory were included in cost of goods sold at current costs.

17. The _____ indicates the percentage of each sales dollar available to cover expenses and provide a profit.

18. Dollar-value LIFO views inventory as a quantity of _____ instead of a physical quantity of goods.

19. The starting point in dollar-value LIFO is determining the current year's ending inventory valued at _____ costs.

20. Step 3 of the dollar-value LIFO technique converts each layer's base year cost to layer year cost using the _____ .

Answers:
1. raw materials, work in process, finished goods **2.** perpetual **3.** periodic **4.** f.o.b. shipping point **5.** f.o.b. destination **6.** sold by the consignee **7.** purchases, interest expense
8. net purchases **9.** specific identification **10.** average cost **11.** purchased **12.** first-in, first-out
13. LIFO **14.** increasing **15.** taxable income, external financial reporting **16.** higher
17. gross profit ratio **18.** value **19.** year-end **20.** cost index for the year it was acquired

REVIEW EXERCISES

Exercise 1

The following information is available for the Lawler Wholesale Clothing Company for 2009:

Beginning inventory	$150,000
Merchandise purchases (all on account)	550,000
Freight charges on purchases paid in cash	16,000
Ending inventory	176,000
Sales (all on account)	923,000
Cost of goods sold	?

The company uses the net method to account for purchase discounts. Terms of all purchases were 2/10, n/30 and all of the purchases were paid for within the discount period.

Required:

1. Applying the periodic inventory system, prepare summary journal entries to account for merchandise purchases, payment to suppliers, freight charges, sales, and the year-end adjusting entry to record cost of goods sold.

   Merchandise purchases:

   Payment to suppliers:

   Freight charges:

   Sales:

   Adjusting entry to record cost of goods sold:

Inventories: Measurement

2. Applying the perpetual inventory system, prepare summary journal entries to account for merchandise purchases, payment to suppliers, freight charges, and sales. Use the cost of goods sold amount determined in requirement 1.

Merchandise purchases:

Payment to suppliers:

Freight charges:

Sales:

Solution:
Requirement 1
Merchandise purchases:
Purchases ($550,000 × 98%) .... | 539,000 |
    Accounts payable... | | 539,000

Payment to suppliers:
Accounts payable .... | 539,000 |
    Cash... | | 539,000

Freight charges:
Freight-in .... | 16,000 |
    Cash .... | | 16,000

Sales:
Accounts receivable .... | 923,000 |
    Sales .... | | 923,000

Adjusting entry to record cost of goods sold:
Cost of goods sold (determined below) .... | 529,000 |
Inventory (ending) .... | 176,000 |
    Purchases .... | | 539,000
    Freight-in .... | | 16,000
    Inventory (beginning) .... | | 150,000

Beginning inventory		$150,000
Plus net purchases:		
Purchases	$539,000	
Freight-in	16,000	555,000
Cost of goods available		705,000
Less: Ending inventory		(176,000)
Cost of goods sold		$529,000

Requirement 2
Merchandise purchases:
Inventory ($550,000 × 98%)... | 539,000 |
    Accounts payable... | | 539,000

Payment to suppliers:
Accounts payable .... | 539,000 |
    Cash... | | 539,000

Freight charges:
Inventory .... | 16,000 |
    Cash .... | | 16,000

Sales:
Accounts receivable .... | 923,000 |
    Sales .... | | 923,000

Cost of goods sold .... | 529,000 |
    Inventory .... | | 529,000

Exercise 2

The following merchandise inventory transactions occurred during the month of September for the Atrax Corporation:

September 1 — Inventory on hand, 5,000 units at a cost $3.23 each
       6 — Sold 2,000 units.
    16 — Purchased 4,000 units at $3.50 each.
    20 — Sold 5,000 units.
    25 — Purchased 4,000 unit at $4.00 each.
    30 — Inventory on hand, 6,000 units.

Required:
1. Determine ending inventory at September 30 and cost of goods sold for the month using a periodic inventory system and each of the following cost flow methods:
   a. Average cost.
   b. First-in, first-out (FIFO).
   c. Last-in, first-out (LIFO).

a. Average cost:

b. First-in, first-out (FIFO):

c. Last-in, first-out (LIFO)

2. Assume that Atrax uses the perpetual inventory system. What would be the *cost of goods sold* for the September 20th sale applying the average cost method and the LIFO method?

   Average cost method (perpetual):

   LIFO method (perpetual):

Solution:
Requirement 1

Cost of goods available for sale:		
Beginning inventory (5,000 × $3.23)		$16,150
Purchases:		
4,000 × $3.50	$14,000	
4,000 × $4.00	16,000	30,000
Cost of goods available for sale (13,000 units)		$46,150

a. Average cost:

Cost of goods available for sale	$46,150
Less: Ending inventory (determined below)	(21,300)
Cost of goods sold	**$24,850**

Cost of ending inventory:

$$\text{Weighted-average unit cost} = \frac{\$46,150}{13,000 \text{ units}} = \$3.55$$

6,000 units × $3.55 = **$21,300**

Solution (continued):
b. First-in, first-out (FIFO):

Cost of goods available for sale			$46,150
Less: Ending inventory (determined below)			(23,000)
Cost of goods sold			**$23,150**

Cost of ending inventory:

Date of Purchase	Units	Unit Cost	Total cost
Sept. 16	2,000	$3.50	$ 7,000
Sept. 25	4,000	4.00	16,000
	6,000		**$23,000**

c. Last-in, first-out (LIFO):

Cost of goods available for sale			$46,150
Less: Ending inventory (determined below)			(19,650)
Cost of goods sold			**$26,500**

Cost of ending inventory:

Date of Purchase	Units	Unit Cost	Total cost
Beg. inv.	5,000	$3.23	$16,150
Sept. 16	1,000	3.50	3,500
	6,000		**$19,650**

Requirement 2

Average cost method (perpetual):
The weighted-average unit cost for the September 20th sale would be:

	3,000 units ×	$3.23 =	$ 9,690
+	4,000 units ×	3.50 =	14,000
	7,000 units		$23,690 ÷ 7,000 units = $3.38

Cost of units sold = 5,000 units × $3.38 = **$16,900**

Last-in, first-out (LIFO) method:
Cost of units sold:

	4,000 units ×	$3.50 =	$14,000
+	1,000 units ×	3.23 =	3,230
			$17,230

Exercise 3

The Carter Company has only one inventory pool. On December 31, 2009, Carter adopted the dollar-value LIFO inventory method. The inventory on that date using the dollar-value LIFO method was $450,000. Inventory data for the next two years are as follows:

Year Ended December 31	Inventory at Year-End Costs	Inventory at Base Year Costs
2010	$469,200	$460,000
2011	509,250	485,000

Required:
Compute the ending inventory at December 31, 2010 and 2011, using the dollar-value LIFO method.

Solution:

Date	Ending Inventory at Base Year Cost		Inventory Layers at Base Year Cost	Inventory Layers Converted to Cost	Ending Inventory DVL Cost
12/31/09	$\dfrac{\$450,000}{1.00} = \$450,000$		$450,000 (base)	$450,000 × 1.00 = $450,000	$450,000
12/31/10	$\dfrac{\$469,200}{\text{Index}} = \$460,000$	Index = 1.02			
			$450,000 (base)	$450,000 × 1.00 = $450,000	
			10,000 (2010)	10,000 × 1.02 = 10,200	**460,200**
12/31/11	$\dfrac{\$509,250}{\text{Index}} = \$485,000$	Index = 1.05			
			$450,000 (base)	$450,000 × 1.00 = $450,000	
			10,000 (2010)	10,000 × 1.02 = 10,200	
			25,000 (2011)	25,000 × 1.05 = 26,250	**486,450**

MULTIPLE CHOICE

Enter the letter corresponding to the response that **best** completes each of the following statements or questions.

_____1. In a perpetual inventory system, if merchandise is returned to a supplier:
a. Purchase returns is credited.
b. Inventory is credited.
c. Purchase discounts is credited.
d. Inventory is debited.

_____2. The Hamlet Company uses the periodic inventory system. Information for 2009 is as follows:

Sales	$2,650,000
Beginning inventory	680,000
Purchases	1,200,000
Purchase returns	12,000
Ending inventory	740,000

Hamlet's cost of goods sold for 2009 is:
a. $1,522,000
b. $1,188,000
c. $1,140,000
d. $1,128,000

_____3. Symington Corporation uses the periodic inventory system. At December 31, 2009, the end of the company's fiscal year, a physical count of inventory revealed an ending inventory balance of $320,000. The following items were *not* included in the physical count:

Goods held on consignment at Murphy Corporation	$23,000
Merchandise shipped to a customer on 12/30 f.o.b. destination	
(merchandise arrived at customer's location on 1/3/10)	12,000
Merchandise shipped to a customer on 12/29 f.o.b. shipping point	
(merchandise arrived at customer's location on 1/2/10)	6,000
Merchandise purchased from a supplier, shipped f.o.b. destination	
on 12/29, in transit at year-end	24,000

Symington's 2009 ending inventory should be:
a. $320,000
b. $379,000
c. $355,000
d. $332,000

_____4. By the *gross method* of accounting for purchase discounts, a discount *not* taken is recorded as:
a. Purchases.
b. Interest expense.
c. A reduction in sales revenue.
d. None of the above.

_____5. By the *net method* of accounting for purchase discounts, a discount *not* taken is recorded as:
a. Purchases.
b. Interest expense.
c. A reduction in sales revenue.
d. None of the above.

_____6. Identify the statement below concerning the *LIFO* inventory method that is *untrue*.
a. In the absence of changes in costs, the results of using LIFO would be identical to those obtained by FIFO.
b. LIFO will provide a close matching of current revenues with current costs since the most recent costs are expensed first.
c. The ending inventory under LIFO will tend to approximate replacement cost.
d. In periods of declining costs, cost of goods sold using LIFO will produce a lower cost of goods sold than FIFO.

Questions 7, 8, 9, and 10 are based on the following data:

Sanfillipo, Inc., had 800 units of inventory on hand at March 1, 2009, costing $20 each. Purchases and sales of inventory during the month of March were as follows:

Date	Purchases	Sales
March 8		600 units
15	400 units @ $22 each	
22	400 units @ $24 each	
27		400 units

Sanfillipo uses the periodic inventory system. According to a physical count, 600 units were on hand at the end of March.

_____7. The cost of inventory at the end of March applying the *FIFO* method is:
   a. $12,900
   b. $14,400
   c. $12,000
   d. $14,000

_____8. The cost of inventory at the end of March applying the *LIFO* method is:
   a. $12,900
   b. $14,400
   c. $12,000
   d. $14,000

_____9. The cost of inventory at the end of March applying the *average cost* method is:
   a. $12,900
   b. $14,400
   c. $12,000
   d. $14,000

_____10. If Sanfillipo instead used the perpetual inventory system, cost of goods sold for the month of March applying the LIFO inventory method would be:
   a. $22,400
   b. $21,500
   c. $21,600
   d. $24,000

_____11. In a period of declining costs, the use of which of the following inventory cost methods would result in the highest ending inventory?
   a. FIFO.
   b. LIFO.
   c. Average cost.
   d. Weighted-average cost.

_____12. LIFO liquidation profits occur when:
   a. Costs are rising and inventory quantity increases.
   b. Costs decline.
   c. Costs increase.
   d. Costs are rising and inventory quantity declines.

_____13. For its 2009 fiscal year, the King Pharmaceutical Company reported sales of $10,500,000, cost of goods sold of $6,300,000, and net income of $525,000. The company's gross profit ratio for the year is:
   a. 40%
   b. 60%
   c. 5%
   d. 67%

_____14. On December 31, 2009, the Charlie Company adopted the dollar-value LIFO inventory method. Inventory at the end of 2009 for its only inventory pool was $500,000 under the dollar-value LIFO method. At the end of 2010 inventory at year-end cost is $672,000 and the cost index is 1.05. Inventory at the end of 2010 at dollar-value LIFO cost is:
   a. $625,000
   b. $640,000
   c. $647,000
   d. $672,000

_____15. J.T. Rider and Sons uses the dollar-value LIFO inventory method. At the end of 2010 the cost index is 1.25 and the ending inventory at base year cost is $360,000. If 2010 beginning inventory at base year cost was $300,000, 2010 ending inventory at dollar-value LIFO cost is:
   a. $300,000
   b. $450,000
   c. $360,000
   d. $375,000

Answers:

1.	b.	6.	c.	11.	b.
2.	d.	7.	d.	12.	d.
3.	c.	8.	c.	13.	a.
4.	a.	9.	a.	14.	c.
5.	b.	10.	c.	15.	d.

Intermediate Accounting, 5/e

Inventories: Additional Issues

LEARNING OBJECTIVES

After studying this chapter, you should be able to:
1. Understand and apply the lower-of-cost-or-market rule used to value inventories.
2. Estimate ending inventory and cost of goods sold using the gross profit method.
3. Estimate ending inventory and cost of goods sold using the retail inventory method, applying the various cost flow methods.
4. Explain how the retail inventory method can be made to approximate the lower-of-cost-or-market rule.
5. Determine ending inventory using the dollar-value LIFO retail inventory method.
6. Explain the appropriate accounting treatment required when a change in inventory method is made.
7. Explain the appropriate accounting treatment required when an inventory error is discovered.

CHAPTER HIGHLIGHTS

PART A: REPORTING — LOWER OF COST OR MARKET

To avoid reporting inventory at an amount greater than the benefits it can provide, the **lower-of-cost-or-market (LCM)** approach to valuing inventory was developed. Reporting inventories at LCM allows losses to be recognized when the value of inventory declines below its cost, rather than in the period in which the goods ultimately are sold.

Determining Market Value

GAAP define market value for LCM purposes as replacement cost (by purchase or reproduction) except that market should not:

a. Exceed the net realizable value (i.e., estimated selling price in the ordinary course of business less reasonably predictable costs of completion and disposal).

b. Be less than net realizable value reduced by an allowance for an approximately normal profit margin.

Inventories: Additional Issues

In effect, we have a ceiling and a floor between which market (that is, replacement cost) must fall. **Net realizable value (NRV)** represents the upper limit and **net realizable value less a normal profit margin (NRV-NP)** provides the lower limit. If **replacement cost (RC)** is within the range, it represents market; if it is above the ceiling or below the floor, the ceiling or the floor becomes market. *As a result, the designated market value is the number that falls in the middle of the three possibilities; RC, NRV, and NRV-NP.* The designated market value is compared with cost, and the lower of the two is used to value inventory.

Applying Lower of Cost or Market

The LCM rule can be applied to individual items, logical inventory categories, or the entire inventory. Each approach is acceptable but should be applied consistently from one period to another.

Adjusting Cost to Market

When the LCM rule is applied and a material write-down of inventory is required, the preferable method of recording the reduction is to recognize the loss as a separate item in the income statement as follows:

Loss on reduction to LCM	xxx
Inventory..	xxx

This method is conceptually more appealing than the alternative method of including the loss in cost of goods sold. The latter approach distorts the relationship between sales and cost of goods sold.

ILLUSTRATION

The Shaffer Company has three products in its ending inventory. Specific per unit data for each of the products are as follows:

	Product 1	Product 2	Product 3
Cost	$50	$80	$35
Replacement cost	42	75	32
Selling price	65	120	40
Disposal costs	5	10	4
Normal profit margin	15	25	5

Applying the LCM rule to its ending inventory, Shaffer would use the following unit values:

Product	(1) RC	(2) Ceiling NRV (*)	(3) Floor NRV-NP (**)	(4) Designated Market Value [Middle value of (1)-(3)]	(5) Cost	Per Unit Inventory Value [Lower of (4) or (5)]
1	$42	$ 60	$45	$45	$50	$45
2	75	110	85	85	80	80
3	32	36	31	32	35	32

* Selling price less disposal costs.

** NRV less normal profit margin

If Shaffer applies the LCM rule to individual products, the inventory of Products 1 and 3 require write-downs to market. For example, if 5,000 units of each product are on hand at the end of the period, the following entry records the write-down:

Loss on reduction to LCM (determined below) 40,000
    Inventory... 40,000

Required inventory write-down:
Product 1 — 5,000 units × $5 ($50 – 45)   = $25,000
Product 3 — 5,000 units × $3 ($35 – 32)   =   15,000
                                         $40,000

PART B: INVENTORY ESTIMATION TECHNIQUES

An important disadvantage of the periodic inventory system is the costly procedure of counting inventory at the end of each period to determine ending inventory and cost of goods sold. Fortunately, companies can estimate inventory by either the gross profit method or the retail method.

The Gross Profit Method

The **gross profit method** estimates cost of goods sold, which is then subtracted from cost of goods available for sale to obtain an estimate of ending inventory. The estimate of cost of goods sold relies on the historical relationship among (a) net sales, (b) cost of goods sold, and (c) gross profit. If we know net sales, and if we know what percentage of net sales the gross profit is, we can estimate cost of goods sold.

ILLUSTRATION

The following information is available for the Rocklin Office Supply Company:

Inventory, October 1, 2009	$240,000
Net purchases for the month of October	750,000
Net sales for the month of October	950,000
Gross profit ratio (historical)	30%

Ending inventory and cost of goods sold for the month can be estimated using the gross profit method as follows:

Beginning inventory	(from records)		$240,000
Plus: Net purchases	(from records)		750,000
Goods available for sale			990,000
Less: Cost of goods sold:			
Net sales		$950,000	
Less: Estimated gross profit of 30%		(285,000)	
Estimated cost of goods sold			(665,000)
Estimated ending inventory			$325,000

Alternatively, cost of goods sold can be calculated as $950,000 \times (1 - .30) = $665,000

The gross profit method provides only an estimate and is not acceptable for the preparation of annual financial statements. However, the technique can be valuable in a number of situations such as in determining the cost of inventory that has been lost, stolen, or destroyed, or in estimating inventory and cost of goods sold for interim reports.

The Retail Inventory Method

The **retail inventory method** is similar to the gross profit method in that it relies on the relationship between cost and selling price to estimate ending inventory and cost of goods sold. As the name implies, many retail companies use the method.

The retail method tends to provide a more accurate estimate than the gross profit method because it's based on the *current* **cost-to-retail percentage** (the reciprocal of the gross profit ratio) rather than an historical gross profit ratio. The increased reliability in the estimate of the cost percentage is achieved by comparing cost of goods available for sale with goods available for sale *at current selling prices*. So, to use the technique, a company must maintain records of inventory and purchases not only at cost, but also at current selling price. Because of this increased reliability, the retail inventory method can be used for financial reporting and income tax purposes.

In its simplest form, the retail inventory method estimates the amount of ending inventory (at retail) by subtracting sales (at retail) from goods available for sale (at retail). This estimated ending inventory at retail is then converted to *cost* by multiplying it by the cost-to-retail percentage. This ratio is found by dividing goods available for sale at *cost* by goods available for sale at *retail*. For example, if goods available for sale is $260,000 at cost and $400,000 at retail, and net sales for the period totaled $340,000, ending inventory and cost of goods sold can be estimated as follows:

$$\text{Cost-to-retail percentage} = \frac{\$260,000}{\$400,000} = 65\%$$

Goods available for sale at retail	$400,000
Less: Net sales	(340,000)
Estimated ending inventory at retail	$ 60,000
Multiplied by the cost-to-retail percentage	65%
Estimated ending inventory at cost	$ 39,000

Estimated cost of goods sold is then determined by subtracting ending inventory from cost of goods available for sale ($260,000 – 39,000 = $221,000).

Retail Terminology

When merchandise is purchased, retail records register the purchase at current selling prices. Subsequent changes in the selling prices of merchandise must be included in the determination of ending inventory at retail. **Net markups** (markups less markup cancellations) are added in the retail column and **net markdowns** (markdowns less markup cancellations) are subtracted in the retail column to determine ending inventory at retail.

Cost Flow Methods

An advantage of the retail inventory method is its ability to be modified to estimate ending inventory and cost of goods sold to approximate average cost, lower-of-average-cost-or-market, and LIFO. A FIFO approximation is possible, but rarely used in practice.

To approximate **average cost**, the cost-to-retail percentage is calculated by dividing the total cost of goods available for sale by total goods available for sale at retail. Net markups and markdowns both are included in the determination of goods available for sale at retail.

To approximate the **lower-of-average-cost-or-market**, referred to as the **conventional retail method**, markdowns are subtracted in the retail column *after* the calculation of the cost-to-retail percentage. By not including net markdowns in the calculation, the percentage is lower, thus producing a lower estimate of ending inventory. The logic for using this approximation is that a markdown is evidence of a reduction in the utility of inventory.

Inventories: Additional Issues

In applying **LIFO** to the retail method in the simplest way, we assume that the *retail prices of goods remained stable during the period*. This assumption, which is relaxed later, allows us to look at the beginning and ending inventory in dollars to determine if inventory quantity has increased or decreased. If quantity has increased, ending inventory includes the beginning inventory as well as an additional LIFO layer added during the period. When there's a net decrease in inventory quantity, LIFO layer(s) are liquidated. When using the LIFO retail method, we assume no more than one inventory layer is added per year if inventory increases. Each year's LIFO layer will carry its own cost-to-retail percentage. Therefore, beginning inventory is excluded when calculating the current year's cost-to-retail percentage.

ILLUSTRATION

The Patel Paint Company uses the retail inventory method. The following data for 2009 are available.

	Cost	Retail
Beginning inventory	$20,000	$34,000
Purchases	161,000	264,000
Freight-in	4,000	
Purchase returns	5,000	8,000
Net markups		10,000
Net markdowns		3,705
Net sales		210,000

Estimates of ending inventory and cost of goods sold using the *conventional retail method* are determined as follows:

Conventional (Average, LCM)

		Cost	Retail
Beginning inventory		$ 20,000	$ 34,000
Plus:	Purchases	161,000	264,000
	Freight-in	4,000	
Less:	Purchase returns	(5,000)	(8,000)
Plus:	Net markups		10,000
			300,000

Cost-to-retail percentage: $\dfrac{\$180,000}{\$300,000} = 60\%$

		Cost	Retail
Less:	Net markdowns		(3,705)
Goods available for sale		180,000	296,295
Less:	Net sales		(210,000)
Estimated ending inventory **at retail**			$ 86,295
Estimated ending inventory **at cost** (60% × $86,295)		(51,777)	
Estimated cost of goods sold		$128,223	

Estimates of ending inventory and cost of goods sold using the *LIFO method* are determined as follows:

LIFO		Cost	Retail
Beginning inventory		$ 20,000	$ 34,000
Plus: Purchases		161,000	264,000
Freight-in		4,000	
Net markups			10,000
Less: Purchase returns		(5,000)	(8,000)
Net markdowns			(3,705)
Goods available for sale (excluding beg. inventory)		160,000	262,295
Goods available for sale (including beg. inventory)		180,000	296,295

Cost-to-retail percentage: $\dfrac{\$160,000}{\$262,295} = 61\%$

Less: Net sales			(210,000)
Estimated ending inventory at retail			$ 86,295

Estimated ending inventory at cost:

	Retail	Cost	
Beginning inventory	$34,000	$20,000	
Current period's layer	52,295 × 61% =	31,900	
Total	$86,295	$51,900	(51,900)
Estimated cost of goods sold			$128,100

Other Issues Pertaining to the Retail Method

Some key elements of the retail method can complicate the process. The previous illustration demonstrates how freight-in and purchase returns affect the cost and retail columns. Other elements include employee discounts and shortages. If sales are recorded net of *employee discounts*, to arrive at the correct amount of ending inventory at retail, the discounts must be added back to net sales before sales are deducted in the retail column. Also, we need to reduce the retail column for shortages caused by spoilage, breakage, or theft. *Normal shortages* are deducted in the retail column *after* the calculation of the cost-to-retail percentage while *abnormal shortages* are deducted in both the cost and the retail columns *before* the calculation of the percentage.

PART C: DOLLAR-VALUE LIFO RETAIL

In our earlier illustration of the LIFO retail method, we assumed that the retail prices of the inventory remained stable during the period. But, this isn't necessarily true. To see if there's been a real increase in quantity, we need a way to eliminate the effect of any price changes before we compare the ending inventory with the beginning inventory. Fortunately, we can accomplish this by combining two methods we've already discussed — the LIFO retail method and dollar-value LIFO (Chapter 8). The combination is called the **dollar-value LIFO retail method**.

We follow the LIFO retail procedure up to the point of comparing the ending inventory with the beginning inventory. A three-step process is then used to convert ending inventory at year-end retail prices to LIFO cost:

In **step 1**, ending inventory at current year-end retail prices is converted to base year retail prices by dividing by the current year's retail price index (relative to the base year). In **step 2**, ending inventory at base year retail is then apportioned into layers, each at base year retail. In **step 3**, each layer is then converted to layer year cost using the layer year's unique price index and cost-to-retail percentage.

ILLUSTRATION

On January 1, 2009, the Patel Paint Company adopted the dollar-value LIFO retail inventory method. The following data for 2009 are available:

	Cost	Retail
Beginning inventory	$20,000	$34,000
Purchases	161,000	264,000
Freight-in	4,000	
Purchase returns	5,000	8,000
Net markups		10,000
Net markdowns		3,705
Net sales		210,000
Retail price index, 12/31/09		1.03

Estimates of ending inventory and cost of goods sold using the *dollar-value LIFO retail method* are determined as follows:

	Cost	Retail
Beginning inventory	$ 20,000	$ 34,000
Plus: Purchases	161,000	264,000
Freight-in	4,000	
Net markups		10,000
Less: Purchase returns	(5,000)	(8,000)
Net markdowns		(3,705)
Goods available for sale (excluding beginning inventory)	160,000	262,295
Goods available for sale (including beginning inventory)	180,000	296,295

Base year cost-to-retail percentage: $\dfrac{\$20,000}{\$34,000} = 58.823\%$

2009 cost-to-retail percentage: $\dfrac{\$160,000}{\$262,295} = 61\%$

Less: Net sales	(210,000)
Estimated ending inventory at **current** year **retail** prices	$ 86,295
Estimated ending inventory at cost (below)	(51,278)
Estimated cost of goods sold	$128,722

Ending Inventory at Year-end Retail Prices	Step 1 Ending Inventory at Base Year Retail Prices	Step 2 Inventory Layers at Base Year Retail Prices	Step 3 Inventory Layers Converted to Cost
$86,295 (above)	$\dfrac{\$86,295}{1.03} = \$83,782$	$34,000$ (base) $\times 1.00 \times 58.823\%$ $\underline{49,782}$ (2009) $\times 1.03 \times 61\%$ $\$83,782$	$= \$20,000$ $= \underline{\ \ 31,278}$

Total ending inventory at dollar-value LIFO retail cost $51,278

PART D: CHANGE IN INVENTORY METHOD AND INVENTORY ERRORS

Change in Inventory Method

Most Inventory Changes

A change in inventory method *other than a change to LIFO* is treated as a normal change in accounting principle. This means reporting all previous periods' financial statements as if the new method had been used in all prior periods. The first step is to revise prior years' financial statements. In the second step, we adjust the appropriate accounts, and the final step is to provide a disclosure note that includes clear justification that the change in inventory method is appropriate. The note also would indicate the effects of the change on items not reported on the face of the primary statements, as well as any per share amounts affected for the current period and all prior periods presented.

Changes to the LIFO Method

Accounting records usually are inadequate for a company changing *to LIFO* to report the cumulative income effect. Instead, the LIFO method simply is used from that point on. The base year inventory for all future LIFO determinations is the beginning inventory in the year the LIFO method is adopted. A disclosure note is needed to explain (a) the nature of and justification for the change, (b) the effect of the change on current year's income and earnings per share, and (c) why retrospective application is impracticable.

Inventory Errors

If an inventory error is discovered in the same accounting period it occurred, the original erroneous entry should simply be reversed and the appropriate entry recorded. If a *material* inventory error is discovered in an accounting period subsequent to the period in which the error was made, any previous years' financial statements that were incorrect as a result of the error are *retrospectively restated* to reflect the correction. And, of course, any account balances that are incorrect as a result of the error are corrected by journal entry. If, due to an error affecting net income, retained earnings is one of the incorrect accounts, the correction is reported as a *prior period adjustment* to the beginning balance in the statement of shareholders' equity. In addition, a disclosure note is needed to describe the nature of the error and the impact of its correction on net income, income before extraordinary item, and earnings per share.

ILLUSTRATION

The Flint Company uses the periodic inventory system. At the end of 2009 inventory costing $200,000 held on consignment by another company was incorrectly omitted from Flint's ending inventory balance. The consignee sold the inventory in 2010. The error was discovered in 2011 after the 2010 financial statements were issued. The effect of the error on financial elements can be analyzed as follows:

Analysis:	U = Understated	O = Overstated

2009		**2010**	
Beginning inventory		Beginning inventory	U
Plus: Net purchases		Plus: Net purchases	
Less: Ending inventory	U ↗	Less: Ending inventory	
Cost of goods sold	O	Cost of goods sold	U
Revenues		Revenues	
Less: Cost of goods sold	O	Less: Cost of goods sold	U
Less: Other expenses		Less: Other expenses	
Net income	U	Net income	O
↓		↓	
Retained earnings	U	Retained earnings	**corrected**

Because 2009's ending inventory is 2010's beginning inventory, by the end of 2010 the error has self-corrected and no prior period adjustment entry to retained earnings is needed. However, both the 2009 and 2010 financial statements are retroactively restated to reflect the correct cost of goods sold and net income even though no correcting entry would be needed. Also, a disclosure note in Flint's annual report should describe the nature of the error and the impact of its correction on each year's net income. Ignoring income taxes, net income would be understated in 2009 by $200,000 and overstated in 2010 by $200,000.

If the error had been discovered in 2010, an entry to correct the inventory and retained earnings balances would be necessary and only 2009's financial statements would require restatement.

APPENDIX 9: PURCHASE COMMITMENTS

Purchase commitments are contracts that obligate a company to purchase a specified amount of merchandise or raw materials at specified prices on or before specified dates. These contracts protect the buyer against price increases and provide a guaranteed supply of product. However, if the market price of the product decreases before the agreement is exercised, the company must still purchase the product at the agreed on higher contract price. This causes a loss on the commitment because the actual purchase must be recorded at the lower of the contract price or market price on the date the contract is executed.

ILLUSTRATION

On April 15, 2009, the Forman Company signed a purchase commitment agreement that requires Foreman to purchase inventory for $300,000 by October 15, 2009. The company uses the perpetual inventory system and its fiscal year-end is December 31.

If the market price is equal to or greater than the contract price at date of purchase:

Inventory...	300,000	
Cash (or accounts payable)...		300,000

If the market price is less than the contract price at date of purchase (say $270,000):

Inventory...	270,000	
Loss on purchase commitment	30,000	
Cash (or accounts payable)...		300,000

If the contract period extends beyond the fiscal year, and if the market price at year-end is less than the contract price for outstanding purchase commitments, a loss is recorded for the difference. This treatment complies with the lower-of-cost-or-market rule for valuing inventory. For example, in the above illustration, if the actual purchase date was sometime in 2010 and the year-end market price of the inventory to be purchased was $260,000, the following journal entry records the estimated loss and corresponding liability. The liability represents the obligation to the seller to purchase inventory at above market price.

December 31, 2009

Estimated loss on purchase commitment ($300,000 – 260,000)	40,000	
Estimated liability on purchase commitment..................................		40,000

If the market price on purchase date has not declined from the year-end price:

Inventory...	260,000	
Estimated liability on purchase commitment	40,000	
Cash (or accounts payable)...		300,000

If the market price on purchase date declines from the year-end price (to say $245,000):

Inventory	245,000	
Loss on purchase commitment ($260,000 – 245,000)	15,000	
Estimated liability on purchase commitment	40,000	
Cash (or accounts payable)...		300,000

SELF-STUDY QUESTIONS AND EXERCISES

Concept Review

1. The _____ approach to valuing inventory recognizes losses in the period when the value of inventory declines below its cost.

2. GAAP define market for LCM purposes as the inventory's current replacement cost, except that market should not exceed the _____, or be less than _____ .

3. Preferably, a loss from the write-down of inventory is reported as a _____ in the income statement.

4. The gross profit method is not acceptable for the preparation of _____ financial statements.

5. The retail inventory method uses the cost-to-retail percentage based on a current relationship between _____ and _____ .

6. A _____ is a reduction in selling price below the original selling price.

7. By the _____ retail inventory method, markdowns are subtracted in the retail column after the cost-to-retail percentage is calculated.

8. By the _____ retail inventory method, markdowns are subtracted in the retail column before the cost-to-retail percentage is calculated.

9. By the conventional retail inventory method, beginning inventory is included in the calculation of the _____ .

10. By the LIFO retail inventory method, beginning inventory is _____ in the calculation of the cost-to-retail percentage.

11. In the retail inventory method, _____ *shortage* is deducted in the retail column after the calculation of the cost-to-retail percentage.

12. In the retail inventory method, _____ *shortage* is deducted in both the cost and retail columns before the calculation of the cost-to-retail percentage.

13. In dollar-value retail LIFO, each layer year carries its unique _____ index and its unique _____ percentage.

14. For a change in inventory method other than to _____ , prior years' financial statements are revised.

15. Accounting records usually are inadequate for a company changing _____ to employ retrospective treatment.

16. If a material inventory error is discovered in an accounting period subsequent to the period in which the error is made, any previous years' financial statements that were incorrect as a result of the error are _____ to reflect the correction.

17. An overstatement of ending inventory in the current year will cause cost of goods sold in the subsequent year to be _____.

Answers:
1. lower-of-cost-or-market **2.** net realizable value, net realizable value reduced by a normal profit margin **3.** separate item **4.** annual **5.** cost, selling price **6.** markdown
7. conventional **8.** LIFO (or average cost) **9.** cost-to-retail percentage **10.** excluded
11. normal **12.** abnormal **13.** retail price, cost-to-retail **14.** LIFO **15.** to LIFO
16. retrospectively restated **17.** overstated

REVIEW EXERCISES

Exercise 1
The Bataille Corporation has four products in its inventory. Information about the December 31, 2009, inventory is as follows:

Product	Total Cost	Total Replacement Cost	Total Net Realizable Value
A	$ 52,000	$ 48,000	$ 45,000
B	180,000	170,000	220,000
C	30,000	20,000	25,000
D	45,000	42,000	75,000

The normal profit margin is 20% of cost.

Required:
1. Assuming the LCM rule is applied to individual products, determine the balance sheet carrying value at December 31, 2009, and the amount of the loss from inventory write-down to be recognized in the 2009 income statement.

2. Assuming the LCM rule is applied to the entire inventory, determine the balance sheet carrying value at December 31, 2009, and the amount of the loss from inventory write-down to be recognized in the 2009 income statement.

Solution:
Requirement 1

	(1)	(2) Ceiling	(3) Floor	(4)	(5)	
Product	RC	NRV	NRV-NP (NP = 20% x cost)	Designated Market Value [Middle value of (1)-(3)]	Cost	Inventory Value [Lower of (4) or (5)]
A	$48,000	$45,000	$34,600	$ 45,000	$ 52,000	$ 45,000
B	170,000	220,000	184,000	184,000	180,000	180,000
C	20,000	25,000	19,000	20,000	30,000	20,000
D	42,000	75,000	66,000	66,000	45,000	45,000
			Totals	$315,000	$307,000	$290,000

The balance sheet carrying value at December 31, 2009, would be $290,000 and the amount of the loss recognized in the 2009 income statement would be $17,000 ($307,000 – 290,000).

Requirement 2
The balance sheet carrying value at December 31, 2009, would be $307,000, the cost of the entire inventory, because the total inventory cost of $307,000 is less than the total inventory market value of $315,000. Therefore, there is no write-down required and no loss recognized in the 2009 income statement.

Exercise 2
The Farnsworth Company uses the retail inventory method. The following information is available for 2009:

	Cost	Retail
Beginning inventory	$138,860	$262,000
Net Purchases	239,000	413,020
Normal shortage		5,000
Net markups		12,000
Net markdowns		4,000
Net sales		390,000

Inventories: Additional Issues

Required:

1. Compute estimated ending inventory and cost of goods sold for 2009 applying the *conventional retail inventory method*.

2. Compute estimated ending inventory and cost of goods sold for 2009 applying the *dollar-value LIFO retail inventory method*. Assume that the company adopted the method at the beginning of 2009 and that the retail price index at the end of 2009 is 1.04.

Solution:
Requirement 1

			Cost	Retail
Beginning inventory			$138,860	$262,000
Plus:	Net purchases		239,000	413,020
	Net markups			12,000
				687,020
Cost-to-retail percentage:	$\dfrac{\$377,860}{\$687,020} = 55\%$			
Less:	Net markdowns			(4,000)
	Normal shortage			(5,000)
Goods available for sale			377,860	678,020
Less:	Net sales			(390,000)
Estimated ending inventory **at retail**				$288,020
Estimated ending inventory **at cost** (55% × $288,020)			(158,411)	
Estimated cost of goods sold			$219,449	

Solution (continued):
Requirement 2

	Cost	Retail
Beginning inventory	$138,860	$262,000
Plus: Net purchases	239,000	413,020
Net markups		12,000
Less: Net markdowns		(4,000)
Goods available for sale (excluding beginning inventory)	239,000	421,020
Goods available for sale (including beginning inventory)	377,860	683,020

Base year cost-to-retail percentage: $\dfrac{\$138,860}{\$262,000} = 53\%$

2009 cost-to-retail percentage: $\dfrac{\$239,000}{\$421,020} = 56.77\%$

Less: Net sales		(390,000)
Normal shortage		(5,000)
Estimated ending inventory at current year retail prices		$288,020

Estimated ending inventory at cost (below)	(147,682)	
Estimated cost of goods sold	$230,178	

Ending Inventory at Year-end Retail Prices	Step 1 Ending Inventory at Base Year Retail Prices	Step 2 Inventory Layers at Base Year Retail Prices	Step 3 Inventory Layers Converted to Cost
$288,020 (above)	$\dfrac{\$288,020}{1.04} = \$276,942$	$262,000 (base) × 1.00 × 53%	= $138,860
		14,942 (2009) × 1.04 × 56.77%	= 8,822
		$276,942	

Total ending inventory at dollar-value LIFO retail cost **$147,682**

Exercise 3

For each of the following inventory errors, determine the effect of the error on current year's cost of goods sold, net income, and retained earnings. Assume that the error is not discovered until the following year and that the periodic inventory system is used.

U = understated			
O = overstated			
NE = no effect	**Cost of Goods Sold**	**Net Income**	**Retained Earnings**

1. Overstatement of beginning inventory
2. Understatement of purchases
3. Understatement of beginning inventory
4. Freight-in charges are overstated
5. Understatement of ending inventory
6. Understatement of purchase returns
7. Overstatement of ending inventory
8. Overstatement of purchases +
   overstatement of ending inventory
   by the same amount

Solution:	**Cost of Goods Sold**	**Net Income**	**Retained Earnings**
1. Overstatement of beginning inventory	O	U	U
2. Understatement of purchases	U	O	O
3. Understatement of beginning inventory	U	O	O
4. Freight-in charges are overstated	O	U	U
5. Understatement of ending inventory	O	U	U
6. Understatement of purchase returns	O	U	U
7. Overstatement of ending inventory	U	O	O
8. Overstatement of purchases + overstatement of ending inventory by the same amount	NE	NE	NE

MULTIPLE CHOICE

Enter the letter corresponding to the response that **best** completes each of the following statements or questions.

_____1. When applying the lower-of-cost-or-market rule, market should not be *less than*:
   a.   Replacement cost.
   b.   Net realizable value.
   c.   Selling price.
   d.   Net realizable value less a normal profit margin.

_____2. The following information pertains to one item of inventory of the Simon Company:

	Per unit
Cost	$180
Replacement cost	150
Selling price	195
Disposal costs	5
Normal profit margin	30

Applying the lower-of-cost-or-market rule, this item should be valued at:
   a. $150
   b. $180
   c. $160
   d. $190

_____3. The gross profit method can be used in all of the following situations *except*:
   a.   In determining the cost of inventory destroyed in a fire.
   b.   In the preparation of annual financial statements.
   c.   In budgeting and forecasting.
   d.   The gross profit method can be used in all of the above situations.

_____4. The records of California Marine Products, Inc., revealed the following information related to inventory destroyed in an earthquake:

Inventory, beginning of period	$300,000
Purchases to date of earthquake	160,000
Net sales to date of earthquake	450,000
Gross profit ratio	30%

The estimated amount of inventory destroyed by the earthquake is:
   a. $325,000
   b. $145,000
   c. $ 10,000
   d.   None of the above.

_____5. The difference in the calculation of the cost-to-retail percentage applying the conventional retail method and the average cost method is that the average cost method:
   a. Excludes beginning inventory.
   b. Excludes markdowns.
   c. Includes markups.
   d. Includes markdowns.

_____6. The difference in the calculation of the cost-to-retail percentage applying the LIFO method and the average cost method is that the average cost method:
   a. Excludes beginning inventory.
   b. Excludes markdowns.
   c. Includes beginning inventory.
   d. Includes markdowns.

Questions 7, 8, 9, and 10 are based on the following data:

The Toso Company uses the retail inventory method. The following information is available for the year ended December 31, 2009:

	Cost	Retail
Inventory 1/1/09	$ 390,000	$ 650,000
Net purchases for the year	1,402,000	1,835,000
Net markups		75,000
Net markdowns		45,000
Net sales		1,845,000

_____7. Applying the *conventional retail inventory method*, Toso's inventory at December 31, 2009, is estimated at:
   a. $477,392
   b. $469,000
   c. $395,159
   d. $405,035

_____8. Applying the *average cost retail inventory method*, Toso's inventory at December 31, 2009, is estimated at:
   a. $477,392
   b. $469,000
   c. $395,159
   d. $405,035

_____9. Applying the *LIFO retail inventory method*, Toso's inventory at December 31, 2009, is estimated at:
   a. $477,392
   b. $469,000
   c. $395,159
   d. $405,035

_____10. Assume that on 1/1/09 Toso adopted the *dollar-value LIFO retail inventory method* and that the retail price index at the end of 2009 is 1.02. Toso's inventory at December 31, 2009, is estimated at:
   a. $477,392
   b. $469,000
   c. $395,262
   d. $405,035

_____11. In 2009, the Robinson Company switched its inventory method from FIFO to average cost. Inventories at the end of 2008 were reported in the balance sheet at $22 million. If the average cost method had been used, 2008 ending inventory would have been $20 million. The company's tax rate is 40%. The adjustment to 2009's beginning retained earnings would be:
   a.   Zero.
   b.   A $2 million decrease.
   c.   A $1.2 million increase.
   d.   A $1.2 million decrease.

_____12. In the question above, assume that 2009's ending inventory is $23 million using average cost, and would have been $26 million if the company had not switched from the FIFO method. The effect of the change in method on *2009* net income is a:
   a. $600,000 decrease.
   b. $1,000,000 decrease.
   c. $1,800,000 decrease.
   d. $3,000,000 decrease.

_____13. The Jackson Company incorrectly omitted $100,000 of merchandise from its 2009 ending inventory. In addition, a merchandise purchase of $40,000 was incorrectly recorded as a $4,000 debit to the purchases account. As a result of these errors, 2009 before-tax income is:
   a.   Overstated by $64,000.
   b.   Understated by $136,000.
   c.   Understated by $64,000.
   d.   Overstated by $136,000.

Answers:

1.	d.	6.	c.	11.	d.
2.	c.	7.	b.	12.	a.
3.	b.	8.	a.	13.	c.
4.	b.	9.	d.		
5.	d.	10.	c.		

Operational Assets: Acquisition and Disposition

LEARNING OBJECTIVES

After studying this chapter, you should be able to:
1. Identify the various costs included in the initial cost of property, plant, and equipment, natural resources, and intangible assets.
2. Determine the initial cost of individual operational assets acquired as a group for a lump-sum purchase price.
3. Determine the initial cost of an operational asset acquired in exchange for a deferred payment contract.
4. Determine the initial cost of operational assets acquired in exchange for equity securities or through donation.
5. Calculate the fixed-asset turnover ratio used by analysts to measure how effectively managers use property, plant, and equipment.
6. Explain how to account for dispositions and exchanges for other nonmonetary assets.
7. Identify the items included in the cost of a self-constructed asset and determine the amount of capitalized interest.
8. Explain the difference in the accounting treatment of costs incurred to purchase intangible assets versus the costs incurred to internally develop intangible assets.

CHAPTER HIGHLIGHTS

PART A: VALUATION AT ACQUISITION

Types of Operational Assets

For financial reporting purposes, operational assets typically are classified in two categories:

1. **Property, plant, and equipment.** Assets in this category include land, buildings, equipment, machinery, autos, and trucks. **Natural resources** such as oil and gas deposits, timber tracts, and mineral deposits also are included.

2. **Intangible assets.** Unlike other operational assets, these lack physical substance and the extent and timing of their future benefits typically are highly uncertain. They include patents, copyrights, trademarks, franchises, and goodwill.

Costs To Be Capitalized

The initial cost of an operational asset includes the purchase price and all expenditures necessary to bring the asset to its desired *condition* and *location* for use. Our objective in identifying the costs of an asset is to distinguish the expenditures that produce future benefits from those that produce benefits only in the current period. Costs are capitalized, rather than expensed, if they are expected to produce benefits beyond the current period.

Property, Plant, and Equipment

Equipment is a broad term that encompasses machinery used in manufacturing, computers and other office equipment, vehicles, furniture, and fixtures. The cost of equipment includes the purchase price plus any sales tax (less any discounts received from the seller), transportation costs paid by the buyer to transport the asset to the location in which it will be used, expenditures for installation, testing, legal fees to establish title, and any other costs of bringing the asset to its condition and location for use.

The cost of **land** includes the purchase price plus closing costs such as fees for attorneys, title and title search, recording fees, and any expenditure needed to get the land ready for its intended use. Land must be distinguished from **land improvements** (parking lots, driveways and private roads, fences, lawn and garden sprinkler systems) because land has an indefinite life and land improvements usually do not. The costs of land improvements are depreciated over periods benefited by their use.

The cost of acquiring a **building** includes the purchase price and closing costs such as realtor commissions and legal fees.

Natural resources include timber tracts, mineral deposits, and oil and gas deposits. They provide benefits through their physical *consumption* in the production of goods and services. The cost of a natural resource includes the **acquisition costs** for the use of land, the **exploration** and **development costs** incurred before production begins, and the estimated **restoration costs** to restore land to its original condition after extraction ends.

Restoration costs are one example of **asset retirement obligations (AROs)**. Sometimes a company incurs obligations associated with the disposition of an operational asset, often as a result of acquiring that asset. For example, an oil and gas exploration company might be required to restore land to its original condition after extraction is completed. *SFAS No. 143* requires that an existing legal obligation associated with the retirement of a tangible, long-lived asset be recognized as a liability and measured at fair value. When the liability is credited, the offsetting debit is to the related operational asset. These retirement obligations could arise in connection with several types operational assets but are most likely with natural resources.

A company recognizes the fair value of an ARO in the period it's incurred. The liability increases the valuation of the operational asset. Usually, the fair value is estimated by calculating the present value of estimated future cash outflows using the **expected cash flow approach** that incorporates specific probabilities of cash flows into the analysis. We use a discount rate equal to the *credit-adjusted risk free rate*. The higher a company's credit risk, the higher will be the discount rate. All other uncertainties or risks are incorporated into the cash flow probabilities.

Intangible Assets

Intangible assets generally represent exclusive rights that provide benefits to the owner. Purchased intangibles are valued at their original cost to include the purchase price and all other necessary costs to bring the asset to condition and location for use.

Included are such items as:

Patent	An exclusive right to manufacture a product or process.
Copyright	An exclusive right of protection given to a creator of a published work such as a song, film, painting, photograph, or book.
Trademark	An exclusive right to display a word, a slogan, a symbol, or an emblem that distinctively identifies a company, product, or a service.
Franchise	A contractual agreement under which the franchisor grants the franchisee the exclusive right to use the franchisor's trademark or tradename within a geographical area usually for a specified period of time.
Goodwill	Represents the unique value of the company as a whole over and above all identifiable tangible and intangible assets. It can only be purchased through the acquisition of another company and is calculated as the excess of the consideration exchanged (purchase price) over the fair value of the net assets (assets less liabilities) acquired.

Intangible assets with finite useful lives are amortized; intangible assets with indefinite useful lives are *not* amortized.

ILLUSTRATION

The Cybar Semiconductor Corporation began business in 2009. During the year ended December 31, 2009, the company made the following expenditures:

Purchase of machinery	345,000
Transportation costs for machinery	2,000
Installation and testing of machinery	3,400
Purchase of delivery vehicles (includes transportation)	60,000
First year license fees for vehicles	3,000
Purchase of a patent	50,000
Legal fees for filing the patent	1,000
Purchase of land	600,000
Title and recording fees for land	1,200
Purchase of building (includes $20,000 for removal of old building)	2,200,000

The various operational assets acquired would be initially valued as follows:

Property, plant, and equipment:	
Machinery ($345,000 + 2,000 + 3,400)	$ 350,400
Vehicles	60,000
Land ($600,000 + 1,200 + 20,000 cost of removal of old building)	621,200
Building ($2,200,000 – 20,000)	2,180,000
Intangible Assets:	
Patent ($50,000 + 1,000)	51,000
First year license fees for the vehicles are expensed, not capitalized.	

Lump-Sum Purchases

If a lump-sum purchase involves different assets, it's necessary to allocate the lump-sum acquisition price among the separate items, usually in proportion to the individual assets' relative fair values. The relative fair value percentages are multiplied by the lump-sum purchase price to determine the initial valuation of each of the separate assets.

Noncash Acquisitions

Companies sometimes acquire operational assets without paying cash but instead by issuing debt or equity securities, receiving donated assets, or by exchanging other operational assets. Assets acquired in noncash transactions usually are valued at the fair value of the assets given or the fair value of the assets received, whichever is more clearly evident.

Deferred Payments

Operational assets often are acquired in exchange for notes payable. We know from our discussion of the time value of money in Chapter 6 that most liabilities are valued at the present value of future cash payments, reflecting an appropriate time value of money. As long as the note payable explicitly contains a realistic interest rate, the present value will equal the face value, which also should be equal to the fair value of the operational asset acquired. However, if the note agreement specifies no interest (noninterest-bearing note) or interest at a lower than market rate, the operational asset and the note are valued at either the fair value of the note (its present value) or the fair value of the asset acquired. Both alternatives should lead to the same valuation.

Issuance of Equity Securities

Assets acquired by issuing stock are valued at the fair value of the securities or the fair value of the assets, whichever is more clearly evident.

Donated Assets

Assets donated by unrelated parties are recorded at their fair value based on either an available market price or an appraisal value. Upon receipt of the asset, the acquiring company generally records revenue at an amount equal to the value of the donated asset.

ILLUSTRATION

Listed below are several transactions of Celluloid Logic, Inc., that occurred during 2009:

1. On March 1 the company purchased machinery by paying $10,000 down and signing a noninterest-bearing note requiring $40,000 to be paid on March 1, 2012. If Celluloid had borrowed cash to buy the machinery, the bank would have required an interest rate of 8%.
2. On June 15 the local municipality donated land to the company. The land had an appraised value of $340,000.
3. On August 29 the company exchanged 20,000 shares of its nopar common stock for a patent. Celluloid's common stock had a market price of $20 per share on the date of the exchange.

Celluloid Logic would record the above transactions as follows:

March 1		
Machinery ($10,000 + 31,753[‡])	41,753	
Discount on note payable (difference)	8,247	
Cash		10,000
Notes payable (face amount)		40,000
June 15		
Land	340,000	
Revenue—donation of asset		340,000
August 29		
Patent	400,000	
Common stock (20,000 shares × $20)		400,000

Valuation of noninterest-bearing note payable:

[‡]$PV = \$40,000 \, (.79383^*) = \$31,753$ (rounded)

[*]Present value of $1: $n = 3$, $i = 8\%$ (from Table 2)

Decision Makers' Perspective

The operational asset acquisition decision is among the most significant decisions that management must make. These decisions, often referred to as **capital budgeting** decisions, require management to forecast all future net cash flows (cash inflows minus cash outflows) generated by the operational asset(s). These cash flows are then used in a model to determine if the future cash flows are sufficient to warrant the capital expenditure.

Operational Assets: Acquisition and Disposition

A key to profitability is how well a company manages and utilizes its assets. Operational assets — particularly property, plant, and equipment (PP&E) — usually are a company's primary revenue-generating assets. Their efficient use is critical to generating a satisfactory return to owners. A ratio that analysts often use to measure how effectively managers use PP&E is the **fixed-asset turnover ratio**. This ratio is calculated as follows:

$$\text{Fixed-asset turnover ratio} \quad = \quad \frac{\text{Net sales}}{\text{Average fixed assets}}$$

The ratio indicates the level of sales generated by the company's investment in fixed assets.

PART B: DISPOSITIONS AND EXCHANGES

Dispositions

When an operational asset is sold a gain or loss is recognized for the difference between the consideration received and the asset's book value (cost less accumulated depreciation, depletion, or amortization). Retirements and abandonments are treated similarly. The only difference is that there will be no monetary consideration received, so a loss is recorded for the remaining book value of the asset.

For example, Moncrief Manufacturing Company acquired machinery in 2007 for $130,000. At the end of 2009, after three years of depreciation at $30,000 per year had been recorded, the machinery is sold for $24,000. The following journal entry records the sale:

Cash	24,000	
Accumulated depreciation ($30,000 × 3 years)	90,000	
Loss (difference)	16,000	
Machinery (cost)...		130,000

When an operational assets is to be disposed of by *sale,* we classify it as "held for sale" and report it at the lower of its book value or fair value less any cost to sell. If the fair value less cost to sell is below book value, we recognize an impairment loss. Operational assets classified as held for sale are not depreciated or amortized.

Exchanges

Sometimes a company will acquire an operational asset in exchange for another operational asset. This frequently involves a trade-in by which a new asset is acquired in exchange for an old asset, and cash is given to equalize the fair values of the assets exchanged. The basic principle followed in these nonmonetary asset exchanges is to value the asset received at *fair value*. This can be the fair value of the asset(s) given up or the fair value of the asset(s) received plus (or minus) any cash exchanged. An exception to the fair value principle relates to certain exchanges that lack commercial substance. In this case, if a gain is indicated, it can't be recognized and the asset received is valued at the book value of the asset given. Another exception is situations when we can't determine the fair value of either the asset given up or the asset received. In these situations, the asset received is valued at the book value of the asset given.

ILLUSTRATION

Xavier Corporation acquires a new machine in exchange for an old machine. The old machine originally cost $26,000 and has a book value on the date of the exchange of $12,000 (accumulated depreciation of $14,000).

Situation 1: The fair value of the old machine is $10,000.

Situation 2: The fair value of the old machine is $18,000.

The exchange would be recorded as follows:

Situation 1		
Machine—new (fair value)..	10,000	
Accumulated depreciation	14,000	
Loss ($12,000 – 10,000)	2,000	
Machine—old		26,000
Situation 2		
Machine—new (fair value)..	18,000	
Accumulated depreciation	14,000	
Machine—old		26,000
Gain ($18,000 – 12,000)		6,000

If the fair values of the assets exchanged are not equal, cash is given/received to equalize the exchange. If cash is given, the valuation of the acquired asset is increased; if cash is received, the valuation of the acquired asset is decreased. For example, if $3,000 in cash is given in situation 1 above, the new machine is valued at $13,000 ($10,000 + 3,000).

PART C: SELF-CONSTRUCTED ASSETS AND RESEARCH AND DEVELOPMENT

Self-Constructed Assets

The cost of a self-constructed asset includes identifiable materials and labor and a portion of the company's manufacturing overhead costs. In addition, interest costs incurred during the construction period are eligible for capitalization.

Interest Capitalization

Interest is capitalized during the construction period for (a) assets built for a company's own use as well as for (b) assets constructed *as discrete projects* for sale or lease. This excludes from interest capitalization inventories that are routinely manufactured in large quantities on a repetitive basis and assets that already are in use or are ready for their intended use.

The capitalization period for a self-constructed asset starts with the first expenditure (materials, labor, or overhead) and ends either when the asset is substantially complete and ready for use or when interest costs no longer are being incurred. Interest costs incurred can pertain to borrowings other than those obtained specifically for the construction project. However, interest costs can't be imputed; actual interest costs must be incurred.

The *first step* in the capitalization procedure is to determine average accumulated expenditures. This amount approximates the average debt necessary for construction. If expenditures are made fairly evenly throughout the construction period, the average accumulated expenditures can be determined as a *simple* average of accumulated expenditures at the beginning and end of the period. If expenditures are not incurred evenly throughout the period, a *weighted* average is determined by time-weighting individual expenditures or groups of expenditures by the number of months from their incurrence to the end of the construction period or the end of the reporting period, whichever comes first.

The *second* step is to determine the amount of interest capitalized by multiplying an interest rate or rates by the average accumulated expenditures. The **specific interest method** uses rates from specific construction loans to the extent of specific borrowings and then applies the weighted-average rate on all other debt to any excess of average accumulated expenditures over specific construction borrowings. By the **weighted-average method**, the weighted-average interest rate on all debt, including construction-specific borrowings, is multiplied by average accumulated expenditures.

The *third* step in the procedure is to compare calculated capitalized interest with actual interest incurred during the period. Capitalized interest is limited to the amount of interest incurred.

If material, the amount of interest capitalized during the period must be disclosed in a note.

ILLUSTRATION

On January 3, 2009, the Maryland Corporation began construction of its own warehouse. For the year ended December 31, 2009, expenditures, which were incurred evenly throughout the year, totaled $5,000,000. In addition to a 10% construction loan of $2,000,000, Maryland also had outstanding for the entire year a $500,000, 9% long-term note payable and a $1,000,000, 12% mortgage payable. Maryland uses the *specific interest method* to determine capitalized interest as follows:

Step 1   Average accumulated expenditures = $5,000,000 ÷ 2 = $2,500,000

Step 2   Interest capitalized:

$$\begin{array}{lll}
\$2,000,000 & \times\ 10\% & =\quad \$200,000 \\
\underline{\quad 500,000} & \times\ 11\%* & =\quad \underline{\quad 55,000} \\
\underline{\$2,500,000} & & \quad\ \underline{\underline{\$255,000}}
\end{array}$$

Weighted-average interest rate of nonconstruction debt:

$$\begin{array}{lll}
\$\ \ 500,000 & \times\ 9\% & =\quad \$\ 45,000 \\
\underline{\ 1,000,000} & \times\ 12\% & =\quad \underline{\ 120,000} \\
\$1,500,000 & & \quad\ \underline{\$165,000}
\end{array}$$

*$165,000 ÷ $1,500,000 = **11%**

Step 3   Compare calculated capitalized interest to actual interest:

	Actual interest	Calculated interest
Nonconstruction debt (above)	$165,000	
Construction loan (above)	200,000	
	$365,000	$255,000

Use lower amount

Research and Development

Research and development (R&D) costs entail a high degree of uncertainty regarding future benefits and are difficult to match with future revenues. For these reasons, GAAP require all R&D costs to be charged to expense in the period incurred. *Research* is planned search or critical investigation aimed at the discovery of new knowledge and *development* is the translation of research findings or other knowledge into a plan or design for a new product or process or for significant improvement to an existing product or process.

R&D costs include labor, materials, and a reasonable allocation of indirect costs related to those activities. In addition, if an operational asset is purchased specifically for a single R&D project, its cost is considered R&D and expensed immediately even though the asset's useful life extends beyond the current year. However, the cost of an operational asset that has an alternative future use beyond the current R&D project is *not* a current R&D expense. Instead, the depreciation or amortization of these alternative-use assets is included as R&D expense in the current and future periods the assets are used for R&D activities.

In general, R&D costs pertain to activities that occur prior to the start of commercial production; costs of starting commercial production and beyond are not R&D costs. GAAP require disclosure of total R&D expense incurred during the period.

R&D costs incurred for others under contract are capitalized as inventory and carried forward into future years until the project is complete. Income can be recognized using either the percentage-of-completion method or the completed contract method.

As with R&D expenditures, a company must expense all of the costs related to a company's start-up activities in the period incurred, rather than capitalize those costs as an asset. Start-up costs also include **organization costs** related to organizing a new entity, such as legal fees and state filing fees to incorporate.

An exception to expensing all R&D costs in the period incurred exists for the computer software industry. Computer software companies expense R&D costs until **technological feasibility** is achieved. Costs incurred after technological feasibility but before the product is available for general release to customers are capitalized as an intangible asset. The periodic amortization of capitalized computer software development costs is the greater of (1) the ratio of current revenues to current and anticipated revenues or (2) the straight-line percentage over the useful life of the asset.

For business acquisitions, the purchase price is allocated to tangible and intangible assets as well as to in-process research and development. To do this, we must distinguish between developed technology (an intangible asset) and in-process R&D. Using terminology adopted in accounting for software development costs, if **technological feasibility** has been achieved, the value of that technology is considered "developed." The amount allocated to developed technology is capitalized and amortized as any other intangible asset. Beginning in 2009, the amount allocated to in-process R&D is capitalized as an *indefinite-life* intangible asset. As you will learn in Chapter 11, we don't amortize indefinite life intangibles. Instead, we test them for "impairment" at least annually. If the R&D project is completed successfully, we switch to the way we account for developed technology and amortize the capitalized amount over the estimated period the product or process developed will provide benefits. If the project instead is abandoned, we expense the entire balance immediately.

APPENDIX 10: OIL AND GAS ACCOUNTING

There are two generally accepted methods that companies can use to account for oil and gas exploration costs. The method used must be disclosed in a note.

1. The **successful efforts method** requires that exploration costs that are known *not* to have resulted in the discovery of oil or gas (sometimes referred to as dry holes) be included as expenses in the period the expenditures are made.

2. The **full-cost method** allows costs incurred in searching for oil and gas within a large geographical area to be capitalized as assets and expensed in the future as oil and gas from the successful wells are removed from that area.

SELF-STUDY QUESTIONS AND EXERCISES

Concept Review

1. Unlike other operational assets, _____ assets lack physical substance and the extent and timing of their future benefits typically are highly uncertain.

2. The initial cost of an operational asset includes the purchase price and all expenditures necessary to bring the asset to its desired _____ and _____ for use.

3. Costs are capitalized, rather than expensed, if they are expected to produce benefits _____ .

4. The costs of land improvements are capitalized and _____ .

5. The cost of a natural resource includes the acquisition cost for the use of the land, the _____ and _____ costs incurred before production begins, and restoration costs.

6. Intangible assets usually represent exclusive _____ that provide benefits to the owner.

7. A _____ is an exclusive right of protection given to a creator of a published work.

8. A _____ is an exclusive right to display a word, a slogan, a symbol, or an emblem.

9. Goodwill is the excess of the consideration exchanged over the _____ of the net assets acquired.

10. In lump-sum acquisitions involving different assets, the total purchase price is allocated in proportion to the relative _____ of the assets acquired.

11. Assets acquired in exchange for a noninterest-bearing note are valued either by (1) determining the fair value of the note payable by computing its _____ , or (2) by determining the _____ of the assets acquired.

12. Assets acquired by issuing equity securities are valued at the fair value of the _____ or the fair value of the _____ , whichever is more clearly evident.

13. On receipt of a donated asset, the company usually records _____ at an amount equal to the value of the donated asset.

14. If we cannot determine the fair value of either asset in a nonmonetary exchange, the asset received is valued at the _____ of the asset given.

15. In a nonmonetary exchange, a gain is indicated if the fair value of the asset given is higher than its _____ .

16. In exchanges of nonmonetary assets, the general rule is that the asset acquired is valued at _____ regardless of whether a gain or loss is indicated.

17. In exchanges of nonmonetary assets that lack commercial substance, the acquired asset is value at the _____ of the asset given up, plus (minus) cash given (received).

18. The _____ ratio measures a company's effectiveness in managing property, plant, and equipment.

19. _____ approximates the average debt necessary for construction.

20. The amount of interest capitalized is determined by multiplying an _____ by the _____ .

21. Interest capitalized is limited to _____ .

22. Most research and development costs are expensed _____ .

23. In general, R&D costs pertain to activities that occur prior to the start of _____ .

24. GAAP require the capitalization of software development costs incurred after _____ is established.

Question 25 is based on Appendix 10:

25. The _____ method requires that exploration costs that are known *not* to have resulted in the discovery of oil or gas be included as expenses in the period incurred.

Answers:
1. intangible 2. condition, location 3. beyond the current period 4. depreciated
5. exploration, development 6. rights 7. copyright 8. trademark 9. fair value 10. fair values
11. present value, fair value 12. securities, assets 13. revenue 14. book value 15. book value
16. fair value 17. book value 18. fixed-asset turnover 19. Average accumulated expenditures
20. interest rate, average accumulated expenditures 21. interest incurred
22. in the period incurred 23. commercial production 24. technological feasibility
25. successful efforts

REVIEW EXERCISES

Exercise 1

Caspar Machine Corporation began business early in 2009. During the year, the following transactions occurred:

1. Paid $5,000 in attorney fees related to organizing the corporation.
2. Purchased a manufacturing facility for $3,000,000 that included land, a building, and machinery. The fair values of the separate assets were as follows:

Land	$ 800,000
Building	2,000,000
Machinery	1,200,000
Total appraised value	$4,000,000

3. Paid research and development costs totaling $125,000.
4. Purchased all of the outstanding common stock of Zintec Corporation for $2,000,000. The fair values of Zintec's assets and liabilities on the date of purchase were as follows:

Receivables	$ 350,000
Inventories	500,000
Machinery	700,000
Patent	400,000
Total assets	$1,950,000
Notes payable assumed	$ 300,000

5. Paid $20,000 in legal fees for successful defense of the patent purchased from Zintec.

Required:

Prepare the journal entries for each of the above transactions.

Solution:		
Organization cost expense	5,000	
Cash		5,000
Land [($800,000 ÷ $4,000,000) × $3,000,000]	600,000	
Building [($2.000,000 ÷ $4,000,000) × $3,000,000]..................................	1,500,000	
Machinery [($1,200,000 ÷ $4,000,000) × $3,000,000].............................	900,000	
Cash		3,000,000
Research and development expense..	125,000	
Cash		125,000
Receivables	350,000	
Inventories	500,000	
Machinery	700,000	
Patent	400,000	
Goodwill (difference)	350,000	
Notes payable		300,000
Cash		2,000,000
Patent	20,000	
Cash		20,000

Exercise 2

During 2009, Starbird Company entered into two separate nonmonetary exchanges.

1. Exchanged equipment that cost $10,000 and had accumulated depreciation of $6,000 plus $10,000 in cash for new equipment. The fair value of the old equipment was $4,600.

2. Exchanged a machine that cost $40,000 and had accumulated depreciation of $20,000 for a new machine and $5,000 in cash. The fair value of the old machine was $25,000, which means the fair value of the new machine was $20,000 ($25,000 less cash received of $5,000).

Required:

1. Prepare the journal entry for the first exchange assuming the exchange has commercial substance.

2. Prepare the journal entry for the second exchange assuming the exchange has commercial substance.

Solution:

Requirement 1

Equipment—new (fair value + cash given = $4,600 + 10,000)	14,600		
Accumulated depreciation	6,000		
Equipment—old		10,000	
Cash		10,000	
Gain ($4,600 – 4,000)		600	

Requirement 2

Machine—new (fair value – cash received = $25,000 – 5,000)	20,000		
Cash	5,000		
Accumulated depreciation	20,000		
Machine—old		40,000	
Gain ($25,000 – 20,000)		5,000	

Exercise 3

On January 2, 2009, the Miles Company signed a contract with Jones Construction to build a new building for a total contract price of $1,200,000. The building will take one year to build, and both parties have approved the following progress payments:

Start of contract	$ 200,000
March 31, 2009	250,000
June 30, 2009	250,000
September 30, 2009	250,000
December 31, 2009	250,000
Total payments	$1,200,000

On January 2, 2009, Miles borrowed $500,000 at 12% specifically for the project. The note was due in 18 months. The company had no other short-term debt but there were two long-term notes payable outstanding for the entire year: $1,500,000 note with an interest rate of 10% and a $2,500,000 note with an interest rate of 6%.

Required:

1. Calculate the amount of interest Miles should capitalize in 2009 assuming that the *specific interest method* is used.

2. Calculate the amount of interest Miles should capitalize in 2009 assuming that the *weighted-average interest method* is used.

Operational Assets: Acquisition and Disposition

Solution:

Average accumulated expenditures:

Date of payment (expenditure)					
Start of contract	$200,000	×	$^{12}/_{12}$	=	$200,000
March 31	250,000	×	$^{9}/_{12}$	=	187,500
June 30	250,000	×	$^{6}/_{12}$	=	125,000
September 30	250,000	×	$^{3}/_{12}$	=	62,500
December 31	250,000	×	0/0	=	- 0 -
Average accumulated expenditures					$575,000

Requirement 1

$500,000	×	12%	=	$60,000	
75,000	×	7.5%*	=	5,625	
$575,000				$65,625	= Capitalized interest

Calculated interest is less than actual annual interest of $360,000 ($60,000 + 300,000).

Weighted-average interest rate of *nonconstruction* debt:

$1,500,000	×	10%	=	$150,000
2,500,000	×	6%	=	150,000
$4,000,000				$300,000

$$\frac{\$300,000}{\$4,000,000} = 7.5\%*$$

Requirement 2

$575,000	×	8%*	=	$46,000	= Capitalized interest

Calculated interest is less than actual annual interest of $360,000.

Weighted-average interest rate of *all* debt:

$ 500,000	×	12%	=	$ 60,000
1,500,000	×	10%	=	150,000
2,500,000	×	6%	=	150,000
$4,500,000				$360,000

$$\frac{\$360,000}{\$4,500,000} = 8\%*$$

MULTIPLE CHOICE

Enter the letter corresponding to the response that **best** completes each of the following statements or questions.

_____1. Each of the following would be considered an operational asset except:
   a. An oil well.
   b. A building.
   c. Inventories.
   d. A patent.

_____2. The initial cost of land would include all of the following except:
   a. The cost of grading.
   b. Title search costs.
   c. Recording fees.
   d. Property taxes for the current period.

_____3. The following expenditures relate to machinery purchased by Callabasas Manufacturing:

Purchase price	$16,000
Transportation costs	800
Installation	500
Testing	2,000
Repair of part broken during shipment	300

At what amount should Callabasas capitalize the machinery?
   a. $17,300
   b. $19,300
   c. $19,600
   d. $17,600

_____4. Goodwill is the excess of the purchase price of an acquired company over the:
   a. Fair value of the net assets acquired.
   b. Sum of the fair values of the assets acquired.
   c. Book value of the acquired company.
   d. None of the above.

_____5. The Piazza Baseball Bat Company acquired all of the outstanding common stock of Dierdorf Lumber for $3,500,000. The book values and fair values of Dierdorf's assets and liabilities on the date of purchase were as follows:

	Book Value	Fair Value
Current assets	$ 860,000	$ 830,000
Operational assets	2,300,000	2,940,000
Liabilities	600,000	600,000

Piazza should record goodwill of:
a. $0
b. $940,000
c. $340,000
d. $330,000

_____6. Cello Corporation purchased three patents at a total cost of $960,000. The appraised values of the individual patents were as follows:

Patent 1	$600,000
Patent 2	400,000
Patent 3	200,000

The costs that should be assigned to Patents 1, 2, and 3, respectively, are:
a. $320,000; $320,000; $320,000.
b. $480,000; $320,000; $160,000.
c. $600,000; $400,000; $200,000.
d. None of the above.

_____7. The City of San Martin gave a parcel of land to the Canova Company as part of an agreement requiring Canova to construct its office building on the donated land. The land cost the city $80,000 when purchased several years ago and had an appraised value of $200,000 on the date it was given to Canova. As a result of the donation, Canova should record:
a. A debit to land of $80,000.
b. A credit to revenue of $200,000.
c. A credit to paid-in capital of $200,000.
d. A credit to gain of $120,000.

_____8. Wolf Computer exchanged a machine with a book value of $40,000 and a fair value of $45,000 for a patent. In addition to the machine, $6,000 in cash was given. Wolf should recognize:
a. A gain of $11,000.
b. A loss of $1,000.
c. A gain of $5,000.
d. No gain or loss.

_____9. Assume the same facts as in question 8, except that the machine is exchanged for a similar machine rather than for a patent. Wolf should recognize:
   a. A gain of $11,000.
   b. A loss of $1,000.
   c. A gain of $5,000.
   d. No gain or loss.

_____10. The Ghirardi Company's fixed-asset turnover ratio for 2009 was 5 and average fixed assets employed during the year were $2,040,000. Ghirardi's net sales for the year were:
   a. $408,000.
   b. $10,200,000.
   c. $12,000,000
   d. None of the above.

_____11. The specific interest and the weighted-average interest methods for determining capitalized interest will yield the same results *except* when:
   a. Construction debt interest rates differ from the rates of other interest-bearing debt.
   b. There is no construction-related debt.
   c. There is no interest-bearing debt other than construction related.
   d. Construction debt interest rates are the same as the rates of other interest-bearing debt.

_____12. In January of 2009, the Falwell Company began construction of its own manufacturing facility. During 2009, $6,000,000 in costs were incurred evenly throughout the year. Falwell took out a $2,500,000, 10% construction loan at the beginning of the year. The company had no other interest-bearing debt. What amount of interest should Falwell capitalize in 2009?
   a. $0
   b. $600,000
   c. $300,000
   d. $250,000

_____13. Micro Tech, Inc. made the following cash expenditures during 2009 related to the development of a new technology which was patented at the end of the year:

Materials and supplies used	$ 38,000
R&D salaries	120,000
Patent filing fees	3,000
Payments to external consultants	50,000
Purchase of R&D equipment	140,000

The equipment purchased has no future use beyond the current project. $10,000 of the materials and supplies used and $32,000 in salaries relate to the construction of prototypes. In its 2009 financial statements Micro Tech should report research and development expenses of:

a. $306,000
b. $348,000
c. $351,000
d. $208,000

_____14. During 2009, the Balboa Software Company incurred development costs of $2,000,000 related to a new software project. Of this amount, $400,000 was incurred after technological feasibility was achieved. The project was completed in the middle of the year and the product was available for release to customers on July 1. Year 2009 revenues from the sale of the new software were $500,000 and the company anticipated future additional revenues of $4,500,000. The economic life of the software is estimated at four years. Year 2009 amortization of software development costs should be:

a. $40,000
b. $100,000
c. $50,000
d. $200,000

Answers:

1.	c.	6.	b.	11.	a.
2.	d.	7.	b.	12.	d.
3.	b.	8.	c.	13.	b.
4.	a.	9.	c.	14.	c.
5.	d.	10.	b.		

Operational Assets: Utilization and Impairment

LEARNING OBJECTIVES

After studying this chapter, you should be able to:
1. Explain the concept of cost allocation as it pertains to operational assets.
2. Determine periodic depreciation using both time-based and activity-based methods.
3. Calculate the periodic depletion of a natural resource.
4. Calculate the periodic amortization of an intangible asset.
5. Explain the appropriate accounting treatment required when a change is made in the service life or residual value of an operational asset.
6. Explain the appropriate accounting treatment required when a change in depreciation, amortization, or depletion method is made.
7. Explain the appropriate treatment required when an error in accounting for an operational asset is discovered.
8. Identify situations that involve a significant impairment of the value of operational assets and describe the required accounting procedures.
9. Discuss the accounting treatment of repairs and maintenance, additions, improvements, and rearrangements to operational assets.

CHAPTER HIGHLIGHTS

PART A: DEPRECIATION, DEPLETION, AND AMORTIZATION

Operational assets are purchased with the expectation that they will provide future benefits, usually for several years. The costs of acquiring the assets should be allocated to expense during the reporting periods benefited by their use. That is, their costs are matched with the revenues they help generate. However, very seldom is there a clear-cut relationship between the use of operational assets and revenue production. As a consequence, we must resort to arbitrary allocation methods to approximate a matching of expense with revenue.

Cost allocation for operational assets is known as **depreciation** for plant and equipment, **depletion** for natural resources, and **amortization** for intangibles. It is important to understand that depreciation, depletion and amortization are processes of cost allocation, not valuation. The cost of the asset, less any anticipated residual value, is allocated over its estimated useful life in a systematic and rational manner that attempts to match revenues with the *use* of the asset, not the decline in its value.

For assets used in the manufacture of a product, depreciation, depletion, or amortization is considered a product cost to be included as part of the cost of inventory. For assets *not* used in production, primarily plant and equipment and certain intangibles used in the selling and administrative functions of the company, periodic depreciation or amortization is reported as expense in the income statement.

Measuring Cost Allocation

The process of cost allocation for operational assets requires that three factors be established at the time the asset is put into use. These factors are:

1. **Service life** — The estimated use that the company expects to receive from the asset.

Service life, or *useful life*, can be expressed in units of time or in units of activity. For example, the estimated service life of a delivery truck could be expressed in terms of *years* or in terms of the number of *miles* that the company expects the truck to be driven before disposition.

2. **Allocation base** — The value of the usefulness that is expected to be consumed.

Allocation base (depreciable base, depletion base, and amortization base) is the difference between the cost of the asset and its anticipated **residual value**. Residual value, or salvage value, is the amount the company expects to receive for the asset at the end of its service life less any anticipated disposal costs.

3. **Allocation method** — The pattern by which the usefulness is expected to be consumed.

The allocation method used should be systematic and rational and correspond to the pattern of asset use. In practice, there are two general approaches that attempt to obtain this systematic and rational allocation. The first approach allocates the cost base according to the *passage of time*. Methods following this approach are referred to as **time-based** methods. The second approach allocates an asset's cost base using a measure of the asset's *output*. These are **activity-based** methods.

Depreciation of Operational Assets

Time-Based Depreciation Methods

By far the most easily understood and widely used depreciation method is **straight line**. By this approach, an equal amount of depreciable base is allocated to each year of the asset's service life. The depreciable base is simply divided by the number of years in the asset's life to determine annual depreciation.

$$\frac{\text{Depreciable base}}{\text{Service life}} = \text{Depreciation per year}$$

Accelerated depreciation methods produce a declining pattern of depreciation with higher depreciation in the early years of the asset's life and lower depreciation in later years. Two commonly used ways to achieve a declining pattern are the sum-of-the-years' digits method and declining balance methods.

The **sum-of-the-years'-digits (SYD) method** multiplies the depreciable base by a fraction that declines each year and results in depreciation that decreases by the same amount each year. The denominator of the fraction remains constant and is the sum of the digits from one to n, where n is the number of years in the asset's service life. For example, if there are five years in the service life, the denominator is the sum of 1, 2, 3, 4, and 5, which equals 15. The numerator decreases each year; it begins with the value of n in the first year and decreases by one each year until it equals one in the final year of the asset's estimated service life. The annual fractions for an asset with a five-year life are: $^5/_{15}$, $^4/_{15}$, $^3/_{15}$, $^2/_{15}$, and $^1/_{15}$.

Declining balance depreciation methods multiply beginning-of-year book value, not depreciable base, by a constant annual rate that is a multiple of the straight-line rate. The straight-line rate is simply one, divided by the number of years in the asset's service life. For example, the straight-line rate for an asset with a five-year life is one-fifth or 20%. Various multiples used in practice are 125%, 150%, or 200% of the straight-line rate. When 200% is used as the multiplier, the method is known as the **double-declining-balance (DDB) method** since the rate used is double the straight-line rate.

Activity-Based Depreciation Methods

Activity-based depreciation methods estimate service life in terms of some measure of productivity, either a measure of *output* (for example, the estimated number of units a machine will produce), or in terms of its *input* (for example, the number of hours a machine will operate). The most common activity-based method is called the **units-of-production method**, which computes a depreciation rate per measure of output and then multiplies this rate by actual output to determine periodic depreciation.

$$\frac{\text{Depreciable base}}{\text{Units of output}} = \text{Depreciation per unit of output}$$

Because we are estimating service life based on units produced rather than in years, depreciation is not constrained by time. However, total depreciation is constrained by the asset's cost and the anticipated residual value. In the last year of the asset's life, therefore, depreciation expense will usually be a residual amount necessary to bring the book value of the asset down to residual value.

ILLUSTRATION

On January 1, 2009, the Moncrief Manufacturing Company purchased machinery for $130,000. The estimated service life of the machinery is four years and the estimated residual value is $10,000. The equipment is expected to produce 480,000 units during its service life. Actual units produced were as follows:

Year	Units
2009	100,000
2010	130,000
2011	140,000
2012	105,000

Depreciation for the four-year life of the machinery using the straight-line, sum-of-the-years' digits, double-declining-balance, and units-of-production methods is as follows:

Straight-line method:

$$\frac{\$130,000 - 10,000}{4 \text{ years}} = \$30,000 \text{ per year}$$

Sum-of-the-years'-digits method:

Year	Depreciable Base	X	Depreciation Rate per Year	=	Depreciation
2009	$120,000		$\frac{4}{10}$		$ 48,000
2010	120,000		$\frac{3}{10}$		36,000
2011	120,000		$\frac{2}{10}$		24,000
2012	120,000		$\frac{1}{10}$		12,000
Total					$120,000

Double-declining-balance method:

Straight-line rate of 25% (1 ÷ 4 years) x 2 = 50% DDB rate.

Year	Book Value Beginning of Year	×	Depreciation Rate per Year	=	Depreciation	Book Value End of Year
2009	$130,000		50%		$65,000	$65,000
2010	65,000		50%		32,500	32,500
2011	32,500		50%		16,250	16,250
2012	16,250		*		6,250 *	10,000
Total					$120,000	

* Amount necessary to reduce book value to residual value

Units-of-production method:

$$\frac{\$130,000 - 10,000}{480,000 \text{ units}} = \$.25 \text{ per unit depreciation rate}$$

Year	Actual Units Produced	×	Depreciation Rate per Unit	=	Depreciation	Book Value End of Year
2009	100,000		$.25		$25,000	$105,000
2010	130,000		.25		32,500	72,500
2011	140,000		.25		35,000	37,500
2012	105,000		*		27,500 *	10,000
Totals	475,000				$120,000	

* Amount necessary to reduce book value to residual value

Decision Makers' Perspective—Selecting a Depreciation Method

Activity-based depreciation methods are theoretically superior to time-based methods but often are impractical to apply in practice. The most popular time-based method is the straight-line method. It is the easiest method to understand and apply, and it produces a higher net income than accelerated methods in the early years of an asset's life. On the other hand, accelerated methods usually are better for income tax purposes, reducing taxable income more in the early years of an asset's life than straight line.

Unlike the choice of inventory methods, there is no conformity rule with respect to depreciation methods. A company does not have to use the same depreciation method for both financial reporting and income tax purposes. As a result, most companies use the straight-line method for financial reporting and the Internal Revenue Service's prescribed accelerated method for income tax purposes.

Group and Composite Depreciation Methods

Group and composite depreciation methods aggregate assets in order to reduce the recordkeeping costs of determining periodic depreciation. The two methods are the same except for the way the collection of assets is aggregated for depreciation. The **group depreciation method** defines the collection as depreciable assets that share similar service lives and other attributes. For example, group depreciation could be used for fleets of vehicles or collections of machinery. The **composite depreciation method** is used when assets are physically dissimilar but are aggregated anyway to gain the convenience of group depreciation. For instance, composite depreciation can be used for all of the depreciable assets in one manufacturing plant, even though individual assets in the composite may have widely diverse service lives.

Both approaches involve applying a single straight-line rate, based on the average service lives of the assets in the group or composite, to the total cost of the group or composite. Because depreciation records are not kept on an individual asset basis, dispositions are recorded under the assumption that the book value of the disposed item exactly equals any proceeds received and no gain or loss is recorded.

Depletion of Natural Resources

Depletion of the cost of natural resources usually is determined using the units-of-production method. Service life is the estimated amount of natural resource to be extracted and depletion base is cost less any anticipated residual value. Residual value usually relates to the value of the land after the natural resource has been extracted.

As an example, if the depletion base of a mineral mine was $4,000,000, and the mining company estimated that 2,000,000 tons of mineral would be extracted, the depletion rate per ton of mineral would be $2:

$$\frac{\$4,000,000}{2,000,000 \text{ tons}} = \$2 \text{ per ton depletion rate}$$

For each ton of mineral extracted, $2 in depletion is recorded and the asset, mineral mine, is reduced by $2. Depletion is a product cost and is included in the inventory of the mineral.

Quite often, companies use the units-of-production method to calculate depreciation on assets used in the extraction of natural resources. The activity base used is the same as that used to calculate depletion, the estimated recoverable natural resource.

Amortization of Intangible Assets

Intangible Assets Subject to Amortization

For an intangible asset with a *finite* useful life, we allocate its capitalized cost less any estimated residual value to periods in which the asset is expected to contribute to the company's revenue-generating activities. This requires that we determine the asset's useful life, its amortization base (cost less estimated residual value), and the appropriate allocation method, similar to depreciating tangible assets.

Intangible assets usually have no residual value, so the amortization base is simply cost. Most intangibles have a legal life (for example, 20 years for a patent) or a contractual life (for example, the contractual life of a franchise agreement) that limits service life. The method of amortization should reflect the pattern of use of the asset in generating benefits. Most companies use the straight-line method.

Intangible Assets Not Subject to Amortization

An intangible asset that is determined to have an *indefinite* useful life is not subject to periodic amortization. Useful life is considered indefinite if there is no foreseeable limit on the period of time over which the asset is expected to contribute to the cash flows of the entity. Goodwill is the most common intangible asset with an indefinite useful life.

PART B: ADDITIONAL ISSUES

Partial Periods

Only in textbooks are operational assets purchased and disposed of at the very beginning or very end of a company's fiscal year. When acquisition and disposals occur at other times, a company theoretically must determine how much depreciation, depletion, and amortization to record for the part of the year that each asset actually is used. For example, in our previous illustration involving the machinery purchased by the Moncrief Manufacturing Company, if the acquisition date had been April 30, 2009, instead of January 1, the full-year time-based depreciation results must be multiplied by $2/3$ to determine depreciation for 2009:

Method	Full-year Depreciation	× $2/3$	Partial-year Depreciation
Straight line	$30,000		$20,000
SYD	48,000		32,000
DDB	65,000		43,333

For the accelerated methods, the remaining $1/3$ of the first year's depreciation is included in 2010 along with $2/3$ of the depreciation for the second year of the asset's life. This calculation is not necessary for the straight-line method since a full year's depreciation is the same for each year of the asset's life. In an activity-based method the rate per unit of output simply is multiplied by the actual output for the period, regardless of the length of that period.

Practically, most companies adopt a simplifying assumption, or convention, for computing partial year's depreciation and use it consistently. For example, a common convention, known as the **half-year convention**, records one-half of a full year's depreciation in the year of acquisition and another half year in the year or disposal.

Changes in Estimates

A change in an estimate of the service life or the residual value of an operational asset should be reflected in the financial statements of the current period and future periods. Prior years' financial statements are not restated. For example, if the Moncrief Manufacturing Company in our first illustration decided to use the straight-line method and, during year 2011, revised the estimated service life from four years to seven years, new annual depreciation would be determined by dividing book value at the beginning of the year of change less anticipated residual value by the remaining service life, as follows:

Cost	$130,000
Less: Accumulated depreciation ($30,000 × 2 years)	(60,000)
Undepreciated cost at beginning of 2011	70,000
Less: Residual value (unchanged)	(10,000)
Remaining depreciable base	60,000
Divided by remaining service life (7 years – 2 years)	÷ 5 yrs.
New annual depreciation	$ 12,000

A disclosure note is presented that describes the change in estimate and the effect of the change on income before extraordinary items, net income, and earnings per share. In the above example, the before-tax effect on income of the change in estimate is to increase income by $18,000 (old depreciation of $30,000 less new depreciation of $12,000).

Change in Depreciation, Amortization, or Depletion Method

A change in depreciation, amortization, or depletion method is considered a change in accounting estimate that is achieved by a change in accounting principle. We account for these changes prospectively, exactly as we would any other change in estimate. For example, referring once again to the Moncrief Manufacturing Company illustration, assume that the company originally chose the sum-of-the-years'-digits method but at the beginning of 2011 switched to the straight-line method. Estimates of service life and residual value remain unchanged. Depreciation for 2009 and 2010 using the sum-of-the-years'-digits method would be:

Year	SYD
2009	$48,000
2010	36,000
Totals	$84,000

Depreciation for 2011 is calculated as follows:

Cost	$130,000
Less: Accumulated depreciation (above)	(84,000)
Undepreciated cost at beginning of 2011	46,000
Less: Residual value (unchanged)	(10,000)
Remaining depreciable base	36,000
Divided by remaining service life (7 years – 2 years)	÷ 5 yrs.
New annual depreciation	$ 7,200

In addition, a disclosure note is required that reports the effect of the change on net income and earnings per share along with clear justification for changing depreciation methods.

Error Correction

If a material error involving an operational asset (for example, a computational error in the calculation of depreciation, depletion, or amortization) is discovered in an accounting period subsequent to the period in which the error is made, any previous years' financial statements that were incorrect as a result of the error are retroactively restated to reflect the correction. Any account balances that are incorrect as a result of the error are corrected by journal entry. If retained earnings is one of the incorrect accounts, the correction is reported as a *prior period adjustment* to the beginning balance in the statement of shareholders' equity. In addition, a disclosure note is needed to describe the nature of the error and the impact of its correction on net income, income before extraordinary item, and earnings per share.

Impairment of Value

An operational asset should be written down if there has been a *significant* impairment of value. The way we recognize and measure an impairment loss differs depending on whether the operational assets are to be held and used or are being held for sale.

Operational Assets: Utilization and Impairment

Operational Assets to Be Held and Used

For operational assets to be held and used, different guidelines apply to (1) tangible operational assets and intangible operational assets with finite useful lives (subject to depreciation, depletion, or amortization) and (2) intangible operational assets with indefinite useful lives (not subject to amortization).

Tangible operational assets and intangible operational assets with finite useful lives are tested for impairment only when events or changes in circumstances indicate book value may not be recoverable. The measurement of an impairment loss is a two-step process. Step 1 - An impairment loss is required only when the undiscounted sum of future cash flows is less than book value. The measurement of impairment loss—step 2—is the difference between the asset's book value and its fair value. If an impairment loss is recognized, the written-down book value becomes the new cost base for future cost allocation. Later recovery of an impairment loss is prohibited.

In step 2, fair value is the amount at which the asset could be bought or sold in a current transaction between willing parties. Quoted market prices could be used if they're available. If fair value is not determinable, it must be estimated. The present value of future cash flows often is used as a measure of fair value.

Indefinite life intangible assets should be tested for impairment annually, or more frequently if events or changes in circumstances indicate that the asset may be impaired. For indefinite life intangible assets *other than goodwill*, if book value exceeds fair value, an impairment loss is recognized for the difference.

For **goodwill**, an impairment loss is indicated – step 1 - when the fair value of the reporting unit is less than its book value. A reporting unit is an operating segment of a company or a component of an operating segment for which discrete financial information is available and segment management regularly reviews the operating results of that component. For step 2, a goodwill impairment loss is measured as the excess of the book value of the goodwill over its "implied" fair value. The implied fair value of goodwill is calculated in the same way that goodwill is determined in a business combination. That is, it's a residual amount measured by subtracting the fair value of all identifiable net assets from the consideration exchanged (purchase price) using the unit's previously determined fair value as the consideration exchanged.

ILLUSTRATION

The Zetrex Corporation acquired Calnet Corporation for $800 million. The fair value of the identifiable net assets of Calnet was $650 million. After the acquisition, Calnet continued to operate as a separate company and is considered a reporting unit. Zetrex performs a goodwill impairment test at the end of every fiscal year. At the end of 2009, the book value of Calnet's net assets is $620 million, including the $150 million in goodwill recorded on acquisition. On that date, the fair value of Calnet has dropped to $520 million and the fair value of all of its identifiable tangible and intangible assets, excluding goodwill, is $480 million.

Step 1. **Recoverability.** Because the book value of the net assets on the test date of $620 million exceeds the $520 million fair value of the reporting unit, an impairment loss is indicated.

Step 2. **Measurement of impairment loss.** The impairment loss is $110 million, determined as follows:

> **Determination of implied goodwill:**
>
> | | |
> |---|---|
> | Fair value of Calnet | $520 million |
> | Fair value of Calnet's net assets (excluding goodwill) | 480 million |
> | Implied value of goodwill | $ 40 million |
>
> **Measurement of impairment loss:**
>
> | | |
> |---|---|
> | Book value of goodwill | $150 million |
> | Implied value of goodwill | 40 million |
> | Impairment loss | $110 million |

Operational Assets to Be Sold

An operational asset or group of assets classified as held for sale is measured at the lower of its book value or fair value less cost to sell. An impairment loss is recognized for any write-down to fair value less cost to sell. We don't depreciate or amortize these assets while classified as held for sale and we report them separately in the balance sheet.

PART C: SUBSEQUENT EXPENDITURES AND DISPOSITION

Expenditures Subsequent to Acquisition

Many operational assets require expenditures to repair, maintain, or improve them. In general, expenditures that are expected to produce future benefits beyond the current year are capitalized. Expenditures that simply maintain a given level of benefits are expensed in the period they are incurred. In practice, many companies do not capitalize any expenditure unless it exceeds a predetermined amount that is considered material. Subsequent expenditures can be classified as follows:

Repairs and maintenance are expenditures made to maintain a given level of benefits and generally are expensed in the period incurred.

Additions involve adding a new major component to an existing asset and should be capitalized because future benefits are increased.

Improvements involve the replacement of a major component of an existing asset and usually are capitalized using one of the following methods:
1. By the substitution method, both the disposition of the old component and the acquisition of the new component are recorded.
2. The cost of the improvement sometimes is recorded without removing the original cost and accumulated depreciation of the original component.
3. Another way to record improvements is to reduce accumulated depreciation.

Rearrangements involve expenditures to restructure an asset without addition, replacement, or improvement. An example would be the rearrangement of the production line on the factory floor. The cost of material rearrangements should be capitalized if they clearly increase future benefits.

Finally, the costs incurred to *successfully* defend an intangible right, for example a patent, should be capitalized. The costs incurred to *unsuccessfully* defend an intangible right should be expensed.

APPENDIX 11A: COMPARISON WITH MACRS

The federal tax code allows taxpayers to compute depreciation for their tax returns on assets acquired after 1986 using the modified accelerated cost recovery system (MACRS). Under MACRS, each asset is classified with a recovery period category that determines the fixed rate depreciation schedule. MACRS depreciation is equivalent to applying the double-declining-balance method with a switch to the straight-line method in the year straight-line yields an equal or higher deduction than DDB and a half-year convention.

APPENDIX 11B: RETIREMENT AND REPLACEMENT DEPRECIATION

The **retirement depreciation method** records depreciation when assets are disposed of and measures depreciation as the difference between the proceeds received and cost. By the **replacement depreciation method**, depreciation is recorded when assets are replaced.

SELF-STUDY QUESTIONS AND EXERCISES

Concept Review

1. Cost allocation for operational assets is know as _____ for plant and equipment, _____ for natural resources, and _____ for intangibles.

2. Allocation base is the difference between the cost of an operational asset and its _____ .

3. Depreciation, depletion, and amortization for an asset used to manufacture a product is an _____ cost included in the cost of _____ .

4. The _____ depreciation method allocates an equal amount of depreciable base to each year of the asset's service life.

5. The _____ depreciation method multiplies the depreciable base by a declining fraction.

6. The _____ depreciation method computes a depreciation rate per measure of output and then multiplies this rate by actual output to determine periodic depreciation.

7. _____ depreciation methods are theoretically superior to time-based depreciation methods but often are impractical to apply in practice.

8. A company does not have to use the same depreciation method for both financial reporting and _____ purposes.

9. _____ depreciation methods aggregate assets to reduce the recordkeeping costs of determining periodic depreciation.

10. Depletion of the cost of natural resources usually is determined using the _____ method.

11. The cost of an intangible asset with an _____ useful life is not amortized.

12. The cost of an intangible asset usually is amortized by the _____ method.

13. A change in the estimate of the service life or residual value of an operational asset should be reflected in the financial statements of the ____ period and _____ periods.

14. A change in depreciation method is accounted for as a change in _____ .

15. Recognition of an impairment loss on a tangible operational asset is required if the book value of the asset exceeds the sum of _____ from the asset.

16. A goodwill impairment loss is indicated when the fair value of the _____ is less than its book value.

17. Additions involve adding a new major component to an existing asset and should be _____ .

18. Expenditures classified as _____ involve the replacement of a major component of an operational asset.

19. Expenditures made to restructure an asset without addition, replacement, or improvement are termed _____ .

20. The cost incurred to successfully defend an intangible right should be _____ .

Answers:
1. depreciation, depletion, amortization **2.** residual value **3.** overhead, inventory
4. straight-line **5.** sum-of-the-years' digits **6.** units-of-production **7.** Activity-based
8. income tax **9.** Group and composite **10.** units-of-production **11.** indefinite
12. straight-line **13.** current, future **14.** estimate **15.** undiscounted expected cash flows
16. reporting unit **17.** capitalized **18.** improvements **19.** rearrangements **20.** capitalized

REVIEW EXERCISES

Exercise 1

The King Company purchased a new machine on April 1, 2009, for $48,000. The machine is expected to have a life of five years and a residual value of $3,000. The company's fiscal year ends on December 31.

Required:

1. Determine the appropriate amount of depreciation for 2009 and 2010 applying each of the following methods:

Year	Straight-line	SYD	DDB
2009	_____	_____	_____
2010	_____	_____	_____

Computations:

2. Assume that King decided to use the straight-line method and that the machine was sold at the end of December 2010, for $27,000. Prepare the journal entry to record the sale.

Solution:
Requirement 1

Year	Straight-line	SYD	DDB
2009	$6,750	$11,250	$14,400
2010	9,000	12,750	13,440

Computations:
Straight line:

$$\frac{\$48,000 - \$3,000}{5\,years} = \$9,000 \text{ per year} \times {}^9/_{12} \text{ for } 2009 = \$6,750$$

SYD:

2009: $\$45,000 \times {}^5/_{15} = \$15,000 \times {}^9/_{12} =$ $\underline{\$11,250}$

2010: $\$45,000 \times {}^5/_{15} = \$15,000 \times {}^3/_{12} =$ $\$\ 3,750$

     $+\ 45,000 \times {}^4/_{15} = \$12,000 \times {}^9/_{12} =$ $\underline{\quad 9,000}$

    Total 2010 depreciation $\underline{\$12,750}$

DDB:

2009: $\$48,000 \times 40\%^* = \$19,200 \times {}^9/_{12} =$ $\underline{\$14,400}$

2010: $(\$48,000 - 14,400) \times 40\%^* =$ $\underline{\$13,440}$

*2 times the straight-line rate of 20% = 40%

Requirement 2

Cash	27,000	
Accumulated depreciation ($6,750 + 9,000)	15,750	
Loss (difference)...	5,250	
Machine (cost)...		48,000

Exercise 2

In 2009 the Suffolk Mining Company purchased a coal mine at a total cost of $5,000,000. The mine is expected to produce 4,000,000 tons of coal over a 10-year period. No residual value is expected. In 2009 the mine produced 400,000 tons of coal. During 2010 the company's geologists revised the estimate of the total tons expected from 4,000,000 to 3,400,000. 300,000 tons of coal were produced in 2010.

Required:

1. Determine the amount of depletion the company should record in 2009.

2. Determine the amount of depletion the company should record in 2010.

3. Describe the disclosure note the company should include in its 2010 financial statements related to the change in estimate.

Solution:
Requirement 1

$$\frac{\$5,000,000}{4,000,000 \text{ tons}} = \$1.25 \text{ per ton} \times 400,000 \text{ tons} = \mathbf{\$500,000} \text{ depletion}$$

Requirement 2

$$\frac{\$5,000,000 - \$500,000}{3,400,000 - 400,000 \text{ tons}} = \$1.50 \text{ per ton} \times 300,000 \text{ tons} = \mathbf{\$450,000} \text{ depletion}$$

Requirement 3
A disclosure note should describe the change and the effect of the change in estimate on income items for the current year. The change in before-tax income is a decrease in income of $75,000 [$450,000 less ($1.25 per ton × 300,000 tons)]

Exercise 3

On June 30, 2007, the Hollowell Corporation acquired a patent from Burke Company at a cost of $560,000. At that time, the patent had a remaining legal life of 14 years. However, Hollowell determined that the patent would be useful only for another 10 years. During 2007 and 2008, the patent was amortized over a 14-year period using the straight-line method.

Required:
1. What is the amount of annual patent amortization that the company should record?

2. Assume that in 2009 the company controller discovered the error in calculating patent amortization. Ignoring income tax considerations, prepare the journal entry to correct the error.

Solution:
Requirement 1

$$\frac{\$560,000}{10 \text{ years}} = \textbf{\$56,000} \text{ per year amortization}$$

Requirement 2

	Correct amortization		Incorrect amortization	
2007	$28,000	($56,000 × $^6/_{12}$)	$20,000	($40,000 × $^6/_{12}$)
2008	56,000		40,000	
Totals	$84,000 ↘		↙ $60,000	

difference
$24,000

Retained earnings...	24,000	
Patent..		24,000

MULTIPLE CHOICE

Enter the letter corresponding to the response that **best** completes each of the following statements or questions.

_____1. The method that does *not* necessarily produce a declining pattern of depreciation over an asset's service life is:
    a.   The double-declining-balance method.
    b.   The sum-of-the-years'-digits method.
    c.   The units-of-production method.
    d.   All of the above produce a declining pattern.

_____2. A delivery van that cost $40,000 has an expected service life of eight years and a residual value of $4,000. Depreciation for the *second* year of the asset's life using the sum-of-the-years'-digits method is:
    a. $4,500
    b. $7,000
    c. $8,000
    d.   None of the above.

_____3. In question 2, depreciation for the *second* year of the asset's life using the DDB method is:
    a. $7,500
    b. $6,750
    c. $4,500
    d.   None of the above.

Operational Assets: Utilization and Impairment

_____4. On January 1, 2009, the Holloran Corporation purchased a machine at a cost of $55,000. The machine was expected to have a service life of 10 years and no residual value. The straight-line depreciation method was used. In 2011 the estimate of residual value was revised from zero to $6,000. Depreciation for 2011 should be:
   a. $3,800
   b. $4,400
   c. $4,750
   d. $5,500

_____5. In question 4, assume that instead of revising residual value, in 2011 the company switched to the SYD depreciation method. Depreciation for 2011 should be:
   a. $ 5,500
   b. $ 9,778
   c. $ 8,444
   d. $11,000

_____6. Felix Mining acquired a copper mine at a total cost of $3,000,000. The mine is expected to produce 6,000,000 tons of copper over its five-year useful life. During the first year of operations, 750,000 tons of copper was extracted. Depletion for the first year should be:
   a. $ 600,000
   b. $ 375,000
   c. $1,500,000
   d. None of the above.

_____7. In 2010, the controller of the Green Company discovered that 2009 depreciation expense was overstated by $50,000, a material amount. Assuming an income tax rate of 40%, the prior period adjustment to 2010 beginnings retained would be:
   a. $0
   b. $30,000 debit.
   c. $30,000 credit.
   d. None of the above.

_____8. A machine is purchased on September 30, 2009, for $60,000. Useful life is estimated at four years and no residual value is anticipated. The SYD depreciation method is used. The acquiring company's fiscal year ends on December 31. Depreciation for 2010 should be:
   a. $26,250
   b. $24,000
   c. $18,000
   d. $22,500

_____9. In question 8, assume that the company instead used the DDB depreciation method. Depreciation for 2010 should be:
   a. $15,000
   b. $30,000
   c. $26,250
   d. None of the above.

_____10. Which of the following approaches *cannot* be used to determine the fair value of an impaired operational asset?
   a.   Prices of similar assets.
   b.   The market price of the asset.
   c.   The sum of the discounted expected cash flows.
   d.   The sum of the undiscounted expected cash flows.

_____11. Which of the following types of subsequent expenditures is *not* normally capitalized:
   a.   Additions.
   b.   Improvements.
   c.   Repairs and maintenance.
   d.   Rearrangements.

_____12. In January of 2009, the Phillips Company purchased a patent at a cost of $100,000. In addition, $10,000 in legal fees were paid to acquire the patent. The company estimated a 10-year useful life for the patent and uses the straight-line amortization method for intangibles. In 2011, Phillips spent $25,000 in legal fees for an unsuccessful defense of the patent. The amount charged to income (expense and loss) in 2011 related to the patent should be:
   a. $103,000
   b. $ 36,000
   c. $113,000
   d.   None of the above.

_____13. The Cromwell Company sold equipment for $35,000. The equipment, which originally cost $100,000 and had an estimated useful life of 10 years and no salvage value, was depreciated for five years using the straight-line method. Cromwell should report the following on its income statement in the year of sale:
   a.   A $15,000 loss.
   b.   A $15,000 gain.
   c.   A $35,000 gain.
   d.   None of the above.

Question 14 is based on Appendix11A.

_____14. MACRS depreciation is equivalent to:
   a.   The straight-line method with a switch to SYD.
   b.   The DDB method with a switch to straight line.
   c.   The straight-line method.
   d.   The DDB method.

Answers:

1.	c.	6.	b.	11.	c.
2.	b.	7.	c.	12.	c.
3.	a.	8.	d.	13.	a.
4.	c.	9.	c.	14.	b.
5.	b.	10.	d.		

Investments

LEARNING OBJECTIVES

After studying this chapter, you should be able to:

1. Demonstrate how to identify and account for investments classified for reporting purposes as held-to-maturity.
2. Demonstrate how to identify and account for investments classified for reporting purposes as trading securities.
3. Demonstrate how to identify and account for investments classified for reporting purposes as available-for-sale securities.
4. Explain what constitutes significant influence by the investor over the operating and financial policies of the investee.
5. Demonstrate how to identify and account for investments accounted for under the equity method.
6. Explain the adjustments made in the equity method when the fair value of the net assets underlying the investment exceeds their book value.
7. Explain how electing the fair value option affects accounting for investments.

CHAPTER HIGHLIGHTS

Many companies invest in securities, such as stocks and bonds, issued by other entities. The motivation for such an investment might be (a) to *earn a return* on temporarily idle cash or (b) to obtain a *favorable business relationship* with another firm (perhaps a major customer or supplier). Such investments may be *short-term* or *long-term.*

The investment *initially* should be recorded *at cost* (including incidental costs such as brokers' fees) in accordance with the *cost principle,* as in the acquisition of any asset. Following the acquisition, the appropriate accounting for an investment depends upon the nature of the investment as differentiated below:

Types of Securities	Characteristics	Method
Equity	The investor *controls* the investee	**Consolidation**
Equity	The investor can *"significantly influence"* the operating and financial policies of the investee	**Equity Method***

If neither consolidation nor the equity method is appropriate, the investor lacks significant influence, and the investment should be accounted for as follows:

Types of Securities	Characteristics	Method
Debt	Investor has the "positive intent and ability" to hold to maturity	**Held-to-Maturity*** Amortized cost
Debt or equity	Held in active trading account for immediate resale	**Trading Security** Fair value (with unrealized gains and losses included in earnings)
Debt or equity	Investments not classified in another category	**Available-for-Sale*** Fair value (with unrealized gains and losses excluded from earnings and reported as other comprehensive income)

* Investee also can elect the "fair value option" and choose to account for in a manner similar to trading securities, with unrealized gains and losses included in earnings. That choice is made when the security is purchased, and is irrevocable.

PART A: ACCOUNTING FOR INVESTMENTS WHEN THE INVESTOR LACKS SIGNIFICANT INFLUENCE

For reporting purposes, all investments in *debt* securities and investments in *equity* securities that have readily determinable fair values (except those for which the equity method or consolidation is appropriate) are classified in one of three categories and accounted for differently depending on the classification as shown in the graphic above. These are described below.

Securities Held-to-Maturity

A bond or other debt security, unlike a share of stock, matures on a specified date. If an investor has the "positive intent and ability" to hold debt securities to their scheduled maturity, those investments are classified as "held-to-maturity." These investments are initially recorded at cost, which may differ from the principal amount (or "face value") that eventually must be paid to the investor because the bonds pay interest at a rate that differs from the current rate demanded in the market. If the bonds pay interest at a rate that is lower than the market requires, they will trade at a discount; if the bonds pay interest at a rate that is higher than the market requires, they will trade at a premium. Discounts and premiums are amortized to interest revenue. The bonds are carried on the balance sheet at amortized cost, and not adjusted for changes in the fair value of the securities. Holding gains or losses from market price changes are ignored. This is the mirror image of the approach that debt issuers use to account for bond liabilities and other debt, covered in detail in chapter 14. Here's an example:

ILLUSTRATION: HELD-TO-MATURITY SECURITIES

Pederson Company occasionally buys bonds for which they have the ability and intent to hold to maturity. The company's fiscal year ends on December 31. Assume Pederson had no investments at the beginning of the year.

2009

To record the purchase on July 1 of $10 million face value of Thomas, Inc bonds. Pederson pays $9 million for the bonds at a time when the market rate of interest for similar bonds is 10% (5% every six months). The Thomas bonds pay interest at 8% (4% every six months).

	($ in millions)
Investment in Thomas bonds	$10
Discount on investment in Thomas bonds (contra account to the bond investment).................................	1
Cash..	9

Note that, because Thomas is paying interest at 8% when the market demands 10%, Thomas has to sell their bonds at a discount. The "Discount on investment" account is a contra account that reduces the carrying value of the Thomas investment to its cost.

Investments

To record receipt of interest on December 31.

	($ in millions)
Cash ($10 million × 4%)	$0.4
Discount on investment in Thomas bonds	0.05
Investment revenue ($9 million × 5%)	0.45

The discount is amortized to investment revenue.

Assume that, on December 31, the market price of the Thomas bonds has fallen to $8.5 million due to a temporary fluctuation in interest rates.

Pederson would not make any entry to adjust the fair value of the bonds.

2009 Income Statement

Investment revenue..$ 450,000

2009 Balance Sheet

Assets:
Investment in Thomas bonds ($10 million – [$1 million – $50,000])   9,050,000

Shareholders' equity:
Retained earnings is higher by $450,000   450,000

2010

To record the sale on January 1 of the Thomas bonds for $8.5 million.

	($ in millions)
Cash	$8.5
Discount on investment in Thomas bonds ($1 million - $50,000 amort.)	0.95
Loss on sale of investments (difference, to balance)	0.55
Investment in Thomas bonds	10

Of course, given that Pederson indicated the Thomas bonds were to be held to maturity, sale before maturity would be very unusual.

Trading Securities

Trading securities are actively managed in a trading account for the purpose of profiting from short-term price changes. Keep in mind that relatively few investments are classified this way because only banks and other financial operations invest in securities in the way necessary to be categorized as trading securities.

Like securities available-for-sale, they are reported at their *fair values*. Holding gains and losses for trading securities are *included in earnings*. This is appropriate because trading securities are actively managed for the purpose of profiting from short-term market price changes. Thus, gains and losses that result from holding trading securities during market price changes represent measures of success or lack of success in doing so.

Note that each of the transactions in the securities available-for-sale illustration shown later and the adjustments to *fair value* would be recorded in precisely the same way for trading securities. The only difference is the way the holding gains and losses would be reported. Here's an example:

ILLUSTRATION: TRADING SECURITIES

Blanchard Transport Company occasionally buys trading securities. The intent is to profit from short-term differences in price and *not* to hold debt securities to maturity. The company's fiscal year ends on December 31. Assume Blanchard had no investments at the beginning of the year.

2009

To record the purchase on March 12 of 2 million NXX common shares for $36 per share or $72 million.

	($ in millions)
Investment in NXX shares	72
Cash..	72

To record cash dividends of $3 million received on October 9 on the investment in NXX common shares.

Cash	3
Investment revenue	3

Investments

To record on December 31 the necessary adjusting entry when the market price of NXX stock was $37 per share.

Fair value adjustment	2	
Net unrealized holding gains and losses – I/S		
([$37 × 2 million shares] – $72 million)...................................		2

2009 Income Statement ($ in millions)

Investment revenue ($3 of dividends + $2 of unrealized holding gain).......	$5

2009 Balance Sheet ($ in millions)

Assets:

Investment in NXX shares	74

Shareholders' equity:

Retained earnings is higher by $3 + 2 = ...	5

2010

To record the sale on January 14 of 1 million of the NXX common shares for $38 per share.

Cash (1 million shares × $38)..	38	
Gain on sale of investments (difference)		2
Investment in NXX shares ($72 million cost × ¹/₂)...............................		36

To record on December 31, 2010 the necessary adjusting entry when the market price of NXX stock was $39 per share.

Fair value adjustment	1	
Net unrealized holding gains and losses – I/S		1

Cost	Fair Value	Fair Value Adjustment
$36 ($72 million × ¹/₂)	$39 ($39 × 1 million shares)	$3

Moving from a balance of $2 (2009 balance) to a balance of $3 requires an ***increase of $1***. Note that this adjustment is accomplishing two things: (a) it is recording new unrealized gains of ($39 – $37) × 1 million shares = $2 million for changes in the fair value of unsold shares during 2010, and (b) it is removing from the fair value adjustment (and reversing from net income) any unrealized gain recorded previously, now that the shares are sold (in this case, one half of the unrealized gain of $2 million recorded in 2009 = $1 million). As a result of (b), the total gain recognized in income over the life of the sold investment is $2, the difference between its sales price ($38) and its cost ($36), with $1 recognized in income in 2009 as an unrealized gain and another $1 recognized in income in 2010 ($2 realized gain – $1 backed out of income as part of fair value adjustment and recognition of net unrealized gains and losses). That makes sure that we don't have double accounting for gains and losses (once when unrealized because fair value changes, and once when realized because the investment was sold). Note: see discussion under available-for-sale securities for a more detailed explanation.

2010 Income Statement ($ in millions)

Investment revenue ($2 of realized gain + $1 of net unrealized gain)......... $3

> Note: Unlike for securities available-for-sale, <u>unrealized</u> holding gains and losses **are** included in income for trading securities.

2010 Balance Sheet ($ in millions)

Assets:

Investment in NXX shares 39

Shareholders' equity:

Retained earnings is higher by $2 + 1 = ... 3

Available-For-Sale Securities

For investments of unspecified length, market returns due to changes in fair values offer an indication of management's success in managing its investments. It's appropriate, then, to adjust those investments to fair value when market prices change.

Investments in debt and equity securities that won't be held to their scheduled maturity and don't meet the strict definition of trading securities are classified as "available-for-sale." These investments are reported at their *fair value*s. Holding gains and losses from holding on to securities during periods of price change are *not included in the determination of net income* for the period. Instead, they are reported as part of Other comprehensive income (OCI), and accumulated in a *separate component of shareholders' equity* called Accumulated other comprehensive income (AOCI). Here's the same example we used previously, modified to illustrate securities available-for-sale:

ILLUSTRATION: SECURITIES AVAILABLE-FOR-SALE

Blanchard Transport Company occasionally buys securities to be available for sale as circumstances warrant. The intent is *not* to profit from short-term differences in price and *not* necessarily to hold debt securities to maturity. The company's fiscal year ends on December 31. Assume Blanchard had no investments at the beginning of the year.

Investments

2009

To record the purchase on March 12 of 2 million NXX common shares for $36 per share or $72 million.

	($ in millions)	
Investment in NXX shares	72	
Cash..		72

To record cash dividends of $3 million received on October 9 on the investment in NXX common shares.

Cash	3	
Investment revenue		3

To record on December 31 the necessary adjusting entry when the market price of NXX stock was $37 per share.

Fair value adjustment	2	
Net unrealized holding gains and losses – OCI		
([$37 × 2 million shares] – $72 million).....................................		2

2009 Income Statement ($ in millions)

Investment revenue $3

2009 Statement of Other Comprehensive Income ($ in millions)

Unrealized holding gain on investments $2

> Note: Unlike for trading securities, for securities available-for-sale we report unrealized holding gains and losses as *other comprehensive income (OCI)* rather than part of net income.

2009 Balance Sheet ($ in millions)

Assets:

Investment in NXX shares 74

Shareholders' equity:

Accumulated other comprehensive income
Net unrealized holding gain on investments 2

2010

To record the sale on January 14 of 1 million of the NXX common shares for $38 per share.

Cash (1 million shares × $38)	38
Gain on sale of investments (difference)	2
Investment in NXX shares ($72 million cost × $^1/_2$).............................	36

To record on December 31 the necessary adjusting entry when the market price of NXX stock was $39 per share.

Fair value adjustment	1
Net unrealized holding gains and losses – OCI	1

Cost	Fair Value	Fair Value Adjustment
$36 ($72 million × $^1/_2$)	$39 ($39 × 1 million shares)	$3

Moving from a balance of $2 (2009 balance) to a balance of $3 requires an *increase of $1*.

Reclassification Adjustment. Let's look closer at the $1 million gain reported for 2010 as other comprehensive income. It actually is comprised of two amounts:

$ in millions

(1) An additional $2 million unrealized gain from the increase during 2010 in the value of the remaining 1 million shares (from the $37 million [$37 × 1 million] fair value last year to the $39 million [$39 × 1 million] value now). $2

(2) A **reclassification adjustment**: the "reversal" of the $1 million unrealized gain reported in 2009 on the 1 million shares sold ($2 million 2009 unrealized gain × $^1/_2$) reported again this year as part of the gain realized when half the shares were sold.   (1)

Other comprehensive income for 2010 $1

Component one is relatively intuitive. It represents a change in the fair value of Blanchard's investment portfolio while holding securities available-for-sale during 2010.

The second component, however, needs further examination. We saw earlier that a $2 million unrealized holding gain was reported in 2009 on the 2 million shares because the shares had risen in value from a $72 million ($36 × 2 million) cost to $74 million ($37 × 2 million) at the end of 2009. One million dollars of that was for the 1 million shares sold. When those shares were sold in 2010 for $38 million they had increased in value another $1 million and a gain was recorded for the entire $2 million increase in value because that was the amount realized through the sale of the shares. So the gain consisted of the $1 million increase in value in 2009 and the $1 million increase in value in 2010.

Recall, though, that comprehensive income includes both *net income* and *other comprehensive income*. Net income in 2010 includes the $2 million realized gain. However, $1 million of that gain already has been reported in comprehensive income – as an unrealized holding gain in 2009. Isn't that double-counting? Yes it is, unless we compensate by reducing comprehensive income by the $1 million portion of the 2010 realized gain that already has been reported. That's what the second component does; it reduces this year's comprehensive income by the amount that was reported last year to keep it from being reported twice.

The reclassification adjustment takes no additional action. It's automatically accomplished each period when we compare the cost of the investment portfolio with its fair value. Remember, we compared the $36 million cost with the $39 million fair value to see that balances in the fair value adjustment needed to be $3 million. Comparing that with the $2 million existing balance indicated that we needed the $1 million increase. As shown above, that $1 million increase already includes the $1 million reclassification adjustment.

In the last journal entry, we simply reported the total $1 million unrealized holding gain– other comprehensive income. It's common practice, though, to separately report the current period's net unrealized holding gains or losses and the adjustment for the reclassification of previously reported holding gains and losses.[1] Doing so would cause our statement of comprehensive income to appear as follows:

STATEMENT OF COMPREHENSIVE INCOME

Net income		$xxx *
Other comprehensive income:		
Unrealized holding gain on investments	$ 2	
Reclassification adjustment of 2009 unrealized gain included in 2010 net income	(1)	
Net unrealized holding gain		1
Comprehensive income		$xxx

* net income includes the $2 million realized gain from the sale of 1 million shares in 2010.

It usually is called a "reclassification adjustment" because we are reclassifying an amount ($1 million in this instance) from what otherwise would appear as a 2010 holding gain to a disclosure that a portion of the *2010 realized gain* was reported previously as a *2009 holding gain*.

---

[1] If not separately reported within the statement in which comprehensive income is reported, components must be separately reported in the disclosure note pertaining to comprehensive income per "Reporting Comprehensive Income," *Statement of Financial Accounting Standards No. 130*, (Norwalk, Conn.: FASB, 1997).

Other-than-Temporary Impairments

If a decrease in the fair value of a held-to-maturity or available-for-sale investment is viewed as "other than temporary", that loss is reported in net income, as if it had been realized on sale of the investment. The carrying value of the investment is reduced to its fair value by the amount of realized loss, and the new reduced value is treated as the investment's cost going forward.

Cost Method

The fair value of an equity investment is not viewed as "readily determinable" if the equity is not traded currently in a stock market like the NYSE or NASDAQ (all debt investments are viewed as having "readily determinable" fair values). If fair value of equity is not viewed as readily determinable (and the investor lacks significant influence over the investee), the cost method is used, whereby the investment is carried on the balance sheet at cost, any dividends received are recorded as investment revenue, and no temporary unrealized holding gains and losses are recognized in income. The investment still is vulnerable to other-than-temporary impairment charges, so if an impairment indicator is present, fair value still must be estimated, and if fair value is lower than cost, the investment must be written down to fair value.

Financial Statement Presentation and Disclosure

Trading securities, available-for-sale and held-to-maturity securities can be either current or noncurrent depending on when they are expected to be sold or mature. Trading securities usually are current assets.

A transfer of a security between reporting categories is accounted for at fair value and in accordance with *the new reporting classification.*

Inflows and outflows of cash from buying and selling trading securities are considered operating activities on the statement of cash flows. However, because available-for-sale and held-to-maturity securities are not purchased primarily to be sold in the near term, cash flows from their purchase, sale, and maturity are reported as investing activities.

Disclosure notes for each year presented should include:

- ❖ Aggregate fair value.
- ❖ Gross realized and unrealized holding gains.
- ❖ Gross realized and unrealized holding losses.
- ❖ The change in net unrealized holding gains and losses.
- ❖ Amortized cost basis by major security type.
- ❖ The level of the fair value hierarchy (1,2,3) in which inputs to determining fair value are classified.
- ❖ For level 3 inputs (unobservable, based on estimates), need to indicate:
  - Total gains and losses (realized and unrealized), and where those are included in income and equity.
  - Purchases and sales.
  - Transfers in and out of level 3.

For debt securities, information should be reported about maturities by disclosing the fair value and cost for at least 4 maturity groupings: (a) within 1 year, (b) after 1 year through 5 years, (c) after 5 years through 10 years, and (d) after 10 years.

PART B: EQUITY METHOD

As pointed out earlier, an investment of 51% or more of the voting stock (common or preferred) of another corporation, generally results in consolidation of the financial statements of the "parent" and "subsidiary."[1] When an investor does not have "control," but still is able to exercise *significant influence* over the operating and financial policies of the investee, the investment should be accounted for by the equity method. It should be presumed, in the absence of evidence to the contrary, that the investor exercises significant influence over the investee when an investor owns between 20% and 50% of the investee's voting shares.

By the equity method, the investor recognizes investment income in an amount equal to the investor's percentage share (based on share ownership) of the net income earned by the investee, instead of the amount of that net income it receives as cash dividends. The investor adjusts its investment account for the investor's percentage share of net income reported by the investee. When the investor actually receives dividends, the investment account is *reduced* accordingly. The rationale is that as the investee earns additional net assets, the investor's share of those net assets increases. As the investee's net assets decline due to paying dividends, the investor's share of those net assets decreases. The investor's share of net assets is reflected in the investment account. Let's look at an example:

ILLUSTRATION

EQUITY METHOD:

On January 1, 2009, Deuce Hardware paid $200 million for 12 million of the 48 million outstanding shares of Farrah Faucets, Inc. common stock. In December 2009, Deuce received dividends of $1.00 per share. For the year ended December 31, 2009, Farrah Faucets reported net income of $160 million. The market value of Farrah Faucets' common stock at December 31, 2009, was $19.25 per share.

.   The book value of Farrah Faucets' net assets was $600 million.

.   The *fair market value* of Farrah Faucets' depreciable assets exceeded their *book value* by $80 million. These assets had an average remaining useful life of 10 years.

.   The remainder of the difference between the cost of the investment over the book value of net assets purchased was attributable to goodwill.

---

[1] A detailed discussion of consolidated financial statements often is a major focus of the "Advanced Accounting" course or is taught as a separate "Consolidations" course. In this chapter, we'll briefly overview the subject only to provide perspective to aspects of the equity method that purposely mimic some effects of consolidation.

To record the purchase of the shares.

	($ in millions)	
Investment in Farrah Faucets shares..	200	
Cash		200

To record Deuce's share of Farrah Faucets' net income.

Investment in Farrah Faucets shares (25%* × $160 million)	40	
Investment revenue		40

* 12 million ÷ 48 million outstanding shares

To record Deuce's receipt of cash dividends.

Cash (12 million shares × $1)	12	
Investment in Farrah Faucets shares...		12

When the *fair value* of assets acquired in an investment exceeds their *book value*, both the investment account and investment revenue may need to be adjusted for differences between net income reported by the investee and what that amount would have been if consolidation procedures had been followed.

To adjust for depreciation.

Investment revenue ($20 million [calculation below‡] ÷ 10 years)................	2	
Investment in Farrah Faucets shares...		2

‡**Calculations:**

	Investee Net Assets ⇩	Net Assets Purchased ⇩	Difference Attributed to: ⇩
Cost		$200	
			} Goodwill: $30
Fair value:	$680* × 25% =	$170	
			} Undervaluation of assets: $20
Book value:	$600 × 25% =	$150	

*[$600 + 80] = $680

The adjustments for depreciation approximate the effects of consolidation, without actually consolidating financial statements. Both the investment account and investment revenue are adjusted for differences between net income reported by the investee and what that amount would have been if consolidation procedures had been followed. In consolidated financial statements, the acquired company's assets are included in the financial statements at their *fair values* rather than their book values.

To record on December 31 the necessary adjusting entry when the market price of Farrah Faucets stock was $19.25 per share.

> No entry; equity method investments are not adjusted to fair value.

The investment is reported as follows:

Investment in Farrah Faucets Shares

Cost	200		
Share of net income	40		
		12	Dividends
		2	Depreciation
	226		

When the Investment is Acquired in Mid-Year

When an investment is acquired sometime after the beginning of the year, the adjustments to cost are modified to include the appropriate fraction of each of those amounts. For instance, if in our illustration Deuce had purchased the Farrah Faucets shares on March 1, rather than January 1, we would simply record income, dividends, and amortization for 10 months, or $^{10}/_{12}$ of the amounts shown.

When the Nature of the Investment Changes

When a change *from* the equity method to another method is appropriate because the investor's level of influence changes, for instance, if a sale of shares causes the investor's ownership interest to fall from, say, 25% to 10%, we make *no adjustment* to the carrying amount of the investment. Instead, we would simply discontinue the equity method and apply the new method from then on.

When a change *to* the equity method is appropriate, we would retroactively adjust the investment account to the balance that would have existed if the equity method always had been used.

Decision-Makers' Perspective

The way we account for an investment is dictated by the nature of the investment itself. It has little effect on a company's cash flows. But, despite the lack of "real" impact on cash flows, the accounting method affects net income, including calculations of earnings per share and any rate of return ratios. So, it's important for both company managers and external decision-makers to clearly understand those impacts and make decisions accordingly. Analysts should be particularly alert to changes in the method from one year to the next.

The equity method was designed in part to prevent the manipulation of income. That could occur if investing corporations who have significant influence over investees were permitted to recognize income only when received as dividends. The equity method limits that potential way of managing earnings. However, the discretion management has in classifying investments creates other potential abuses.

Appendix 12-A: Other Investments
(Special Purpose Funds, Investments in Life Insurance Policies)

A company can establish a special purchase fund for virtually any purpose. Common examples are petty cash and funds for future expansion. Some special purchase funds – like petty cash – are current assets. Special purchase funds that are noncurrent are reported within the category "Investments and funds." Any *investment revenue* these funds produce is reported as investment revenue on the income statement.

Companies frequently take out life insurance policies on the life of key personnel. Some life insurance policies can be surrendered while the insured is still alive in exchange for its *cash surrender value*. A portion of each insurance premium the company pays represents an increase in the cash surrender value. This investment portion is recorded as an asset.

Appendix 12-B: Impairment of an Investment in a Receivable Due to a Troubled Debt Restructuring

If a receivable becomes impaired (worth less than before), it is remeasured. It is remeasured based on the discounted present value of currently expected cash flows at the loan's original effective rate (regardless of the extent to which expected cash receipts have been reduced). One way impairment can occur is when the terms of a debt agreement are changed as a result of financial difficulties experienced by the debtor (borrower). This new arrangement is referred to as a troubled debt restructuring.

If, instead, the receivable is *settled outright* at the time of the restructuring the creditor simply records a loss for the difference between the carrying amount of the receivable and the fair value of the asset(s) or equity securities received. But, if the receivable is *continued, but with modified terms*, the difference between the receivable's carrying amount and the discounted present value of the cash flows after the restructuring is reported as a loss.

SELF-STUDY QUESTIONS AND EXERCISES

Concept Review

1. For a security available-for-sale, the investor initially records the investment at the _____ and subsequently adjusts the investment account balance to fair market value.

2. Investment securities are classified as _____, _____, or _____.

3. Securities are classified as "held-to-maturity" if an investor has the positive _____ and ability to hold the securities to maturity.

4. Securities *available-for-sale* are reported at fair value, and resulting holding gains and losses are reported _____.

5. Unrealized holding gains or losses on _____ securities are reported on the income statement as if they actually had been realized.

6. If a drop in the market price of an investment security is an other-than-temporary impairment, when the investment is written down to its fair value, the amount of the write-down should be treated as if it were a _____ loss, meaning the loss is included in _____ for the period.

7. A company is not required to report individual amounts for the three categories of investments – held-to-maturity, available-for-sale, or trading – *on the face of the balance sheet*, that information should be presented in the _____ .

8. The equity method is used when an investor can't *control*, but can exercise _____ over the operating and financial policies of the investee. We presume, in the absence of evidence to the contrary, that this is so when the investor owns between ____ % and ____ % of the investee's voting shares.

9. By the _____ method, the investor reports its equity interest in the investee as a single investment account. That single investment account is periodically adjusted to reflect the effects of consolidation, without actually consolidating financial statements.

10. By the equity method, dividends from the investee should be accounted for by the investor as a reduction in the _____ account.

11. The equity method attempts to approximate the effects of accounting for the purchase of the investee. Consolidated financial statements report _____ for the excess of the acquisition price over the fair value of the acquired net assets.

12. By the equity method, both _____ and the investment would be reduced by the negative income effect of "extra depreciation" due to the fair value of depreciable assets exceeding book value.

13. The investment account was decreased. Cash increased by the same amount. There is no effect on the income statement. These sentences describe an adjustment to an equity method investment due to receiving _____ .

14. If it becomes necessary to change from the equity method to another method, _____ is made to the carrying amount of the investment.

15. Fair values that are estimated from unobservable inputs are categorized as Level _____ in the fair-value hierarchy specified by SFAS No. 157, and require extra disclosures to be included in the footnotes.

16. The "fair value option" can be elected for investments that would normally be accounted for as _____, _____ or _____ investments.

Answers:
1. price paid at acquisition **2.** a. held-to-maturity, b. available-for-sale c. trading securities.
3. intent **4.** as a separate component of shareholders' equity **5.** trading **6.** realized, income
7. disclosure notes **8.** significant influence, 20, 50 **9.** equity **10.** investment **11.** goodwill
12. investment revenue **13.** dividends **14.** no adjustment **15.** 3 **16.** a. held-to-maturity,
b. available-for-sale c. equity method.

Investments

REVIEW EXERCISES

Exercise 1

On January 3, 2009, Mercer Industries paid $48 million for 6 million shares of Sable House, Inc. common. The investment represents a 30% interest in the net assets of Sable House and gave Mercer the ability to exercise significant influence over Sable House's operating and financial policies. Mercer received dividends of $1.00 per share on December 15, 2009, and Sable House reported net income of $40 million for the year ended December 31, 2009. The market value of Sable House's common stock at December 31, 2009, was $9 per share.

Required:

Prepare the journal entries required by Mercer for 2009, assuming that:

a. The book value of Sable House's net assets was $90 million.

b. The *fair market value* of Sable House's depreciable assets, with an average remaining useful life of 6 years, exceeded their *book value* by $20 million.

c. The remainder of the excess of the *cost of the investment* over the *book value of net assets* purchased was attributable to goodwill.

Mercer purchases the Sable House shares.

($ in millions)

Sable House reports net income.

($ in millions)

Sable House pays cash dividends.

($ in millions)

Adjustments.

Depreciation:

($ in millions)

Increase in fair value of shares:

($ in millions)

Solution:

Mercer purchases the Sable House shares.

		($ in millions)
Investment in Sable House shares	48	
Cash		48

Sable House reports net income.

Investment in Sable House shares (30% × $40 million)	12	
Investment revenue..		12

Sable House pays cash dividends.

Cash (6 million shares × $1)..	6	
Investment in Sable House shares		6

Adjustment.

Depreciation:

Investment revenue ($6 million [calculation below‡] ÷ 6 years)	1	
Investment in Sable House shares		1

‡**Calculations:**

	Investee Net Assets ⇩	Net Assets Purchased ⇩	Difference Attributed to: ⇩
Cost		$48	
			Goodwill: $15
Fair value:	$110* × 30% =	$33	
			Undervaluation
Book value:	$90 × 30% =	$27	*of assets:* $6

*[$90 + 20] = $110

Increase in fair value of shares:
No entry; equity method investments are not adjusted to fair value.

Investments

Exercise 2

Prepare the appropriate journal entries for Mercer in Exercise 1 for 2009, assuming that the investment represents a 10% interest in the net assets of Sable House.

Mercer purchases the Sable House shares.

($ in millions)

Sable House reports net income.

($ in millions)

Sable House pays cash dividends.

($ in millions)

Adjustments

Depreciation:

($ in millions)

Increase in fair value of shares:

($ in millions)

Solution:

Mercer purchases the Sable House shares.

	($ in millions)	
Investment in Sable House shares	48	
Cash		48

Sable House reports net income.

No entry

Sable House pays cash dividends.

Cash (6 million shares × $1)..	6	
Investment revenue...		6

Adjustments.

Depreciation:

No entry

Increase in fair value of shares:

Fair value adjustment ([$9 × 6 million shares] – $48 million)	6	
Unrealized gain on investments–other comprehensive income.......................................		6

MULTIPLE CHOICE

Enter the letter corresponding to the response that **best** completes each of the following statements or questions.

_____1. On January 1, 2009, Normal Plastics bought 15% of Model, Inc.'s common stock for $900,000. Model's net income for the years ended December 31, 2009, and December 31, 2010, were $600,000 and $1,500,000, respectively. During 2010, Model declared a dividend of $420,000. No dividends were declared in 2009. How much should Normal show on its 2010 income statement from this investment?
   a. $0.
   b. $63,000.
   c. $288,000.
   d. $378,000.

_____2. Fair value is used as the basis for valuation of a firm's investment securities when:
   a. Management's intention is to dispose of the securities within one year.
   b. The market value is less than cost for each equity security in the portfolio.
   c. The investment security is not classified as held-to-maturity.
   d. The investment security is classified as held-to-maturity.

Investments

_____3. Unrecognized holding gains and losses are included in an investor's earnings for:

	Trading Securities	Securities Available-For-Sale
a.	Yes	No
b.	Yes	Yes
c.	No	Yes
d.	No	No

_____4. Investment securities are reported on a balance sheet at fair value for:

	Trading Securities	Securities Available-For-Sale
a.	Yes	No
b.	Yes	Yes
c.	No	Yes
d.	No	No

_____5. Which of the following statements is **untrue** regarding investments in equity securities?
   a. If the investor owns less than 20 percent of outstanding voting common stock, the equity method usually is not used.
   b. If the investor owns more than 50 percent of the outstanding voting common stock, the financial statements are consolidated
   c. If the investor owns 20-50 percent of the outstanding voting common stock, the equity method always is required.
   d. If the investor owns less than 20 percent of outstanding voting common stock, the securities generally are reported at their fair value.

_____6. Unrecognized holding gains and losses for securities to be held-to-maturity are:
   a. Reported as a separate component of the shareholders' equity section of the balance sheet.
   b. Included in the determination of income from operations in the period of the change.
   c. Reported as extraordinary items.
   d. Not reported in the income statement nor the balance sheet.

_____7. Unrecognized holding gains and losses for securities available-for-sale are:
   a. Reported as a separate component of the shareholders' equity section of the balance sheet.
   b. Included in the determination of income from operations in the period of the change.
   c. Reported as extraordinary items.
   d. Not reported in the income statement nor the balance sheet.

_____8. Unrecognized holding gains and losses for trading securities are:
    a. Reported as a separate component of the shareholders' equity section of the balance sheet.
    b. Included in the determination of income from operations in the period of the change.
    c. Reported as extraordinary items.
    d. Not reported in the income statement nor the balance sheet.

_____9. On January 12, Henderson Corporation purchased 4 million shares of Honeycutt Corporation common stock for $73 million and classified the securities as available-for-sale. At the close of the same year, the fair value of the securities is $81 million. Henderson Corporation should report:
    a. A gain of $8 million on the income statement.
    b. An increase in shareholders' equity of $8 million.
    c. An investment of $73 million.
    d. None of the above.

_____10. Evans Company owns 4.5 million shares of stock of Frazier Company classified as available-for-sale. During 2009, the fair value of those shares increased by $9 million. What effect did this increase have on Evans' 2009 financial statements?
    a. Net assets increased.
    b. Total assets decreased.
    c. Net income increased.
    d. Shareholders' equity decreased.

_____11. Level Company owns bonds of Leader Company classified as held-to-maturity. During 2009, the fair value of those bonds increased by $4 million. Interest was received of $3 million. What effect did the investment have on Level's 2009 financial statements?
    a. Total assets increased by $7 million.
    b. Total assets increased by $3 million.
    c. Net income increased by $7 million.
    d. Shareholders' equity increased by $4 million.

_____12. If the investment described in the previous question had been classified as available-for-sale, what effect would the investment have on Level's 2009 financial statements?
    a. Total assets increased by $7 million.
    b. Total assets increased by $3 million.
    c. Net income increased by $7 million.
    d. Shareholders' equity increased by $1 million.

Investments

_____13. On January 2, 2009, Garner, Inc. bought 10% of the outstanding common stock of Moody, Inc. for $60 million cash. At the date of acquisition of the stock, Moody's net assets had a book value and fair value of $180 million. Moody's net income for the year ended December 31, 2009, was $30 million. During 2009, Moody declared and paid cash dividends of $6 million. On December 31, 2009, Garner's investment should be reported at:
a. $60.0 million.
b. $66.9 million.
c. $69.0 million.
d. $71.1 million.

_____14. On January 2, 2009, Garner, Inc. bought 30% of the outstanding common stock of Moody, Inc. for $60 million cash. At the date of acquisition of the stock, Moody's net assets had a book value and fair value of $180 million. Moody's net income for the year ended December 31, 2009, was $30 million. During 2009, Moody declared and paid cash dividends of $6 million. On December 31, 2009, Garner's investment account should be reported at:
a. $60.0 million.
b. $67.2 million.
c. $69.0 million.
d. $71.1 million.

_____15. The equity method is used when an investor can't control, but can exercise significant influence over the operating and financial policies of the investee. We presume, in the absence of evidence to the contrary, that this is so if:
a. The investor classifies the investment as available-for-sale.
b. The investor classifies the investment as held-to-maturity.
c. The investor owns between 51% or more of the investee's voting shares.
d. The investor owns between 20% and 50% of the investee's voting shares.

_____16. On January 2, 2009, Germane, Inc. bought 30% of the outstanding common stock of Quality, Inc. for $56 million cash. At the date of acquisition of the stock, Quality's net assets had a book value and fair value of $120 million. Quality's net income for the year ended December 31, 2009, was $30 million. During 2009, Quality declared and paid cash dividends of $10 million. On December 31, 2009, Germane's should report investment revenue of:
a. $3 million.
b. $6 million.
c. $9 million.
d. $30 million.

_____17. When applying the equity method, an investor should report dividends from the investee as:
a. Dividend revenue.
b. An extraordinary item.
c. A reduction in the investment account.
d. An increase in the investment account.

_____18. Western Manufacturing Company owns 40% of the outstanding common stock of Eastern Supply Company. During 2009, Western received a $50 million cash dividend from Eastern. What effect did this dividend have on Western's 2009 financial statements?
    a. Total assets increased.
    b. Total assets decreased.
    c. Net income increased.
    d. The investment account decreased.

_____19. The accounting for unrealized holding gains and losses will be different if the fair value option is elected for all of the following types of investments except:
    a. Held-to-maturity.
    b. Trading security.
    c. Available-for-sale.
    d. Equity method.

_____20. The fair value option described by SFAS No. 159
    a. Must be elected when a security is purchased, and is irrevocable.
    b. Can be traded on exchanges, similar to other options.
    c. For debt is available only if anticipated to not be held to maturity.
    d. Is not available for equity investments.

Answers:

1.	b	6.	d	11.	b	16.	c
2.	c	7.	a	12.	a	17.	c
3.	a	8.	b	13.	a	18.	d
4.	b	9.	b	14.	b	19.	b
5.	c	10.	a	15.	d	20.	a